American Lithographers 1900–1960

Charles Sheeler (1882–1965), *Roses,* 1924. 280 x 234 mm., printed by George C. Miller. Collection, Tamarind Institute.

American Lithographers 1900-1960

The Artists and Their Printers

Clinton Adams

The University of New Mexico Press • Albuquerque

PHOTO CREDITS

Portions of this book have appeared in different form in the author's articles
on Grant Arnold, Lawrence Barrett, Bolton Brown, and Lynton R. Kistler
(see bibliography).

David McMullan, Albuquerque: 69, 109, 110; Midnight Media, Galisteo, N.M.:
108; Eric Mitchell, Philadelphia: 5, 24, 38, 45, 59, 72, 81, 120; Peter Morse,
Honolulu: 64; I. Serisawa, Los Angeles: 113; Stein-Mason Studio, Boston: 6, 7.

Cincinnati Art Museum: 112; Indianapolis Museum of Art: 111; Kansas City Art
Institute: 34; Library of Congress: 16, 17; Los Angeles County Museum of Art:
65; National Museum of American Art, Smithsonian Institution: 4, 14, 41, 54,
66, 77; New York Public Library: 80, 89, 117; Museum of Modern Art, New
York: 78, 116, 119, 121, 122; Philadelphia Museum of Art: 8, 13, 49, 84; Santa
Barbara Museum of Art: 106; Tyler Art Gallery, State University of New York,
Oswego: 30, 31, 32; University Art Collections, Syracuse University: 12;
University of Iowa Museum of Art: 25.

Photographer unknown: 40, 123, 124.

Except as noted above, all photographs are by Robert C. Reck, Albuquerque.

Contents

Preface

This book is a history not of American lithography but of the artists and their printers, their personal interrelationships, and their creative work in an obstinate but beautiful medium.

No single event marks its starting point. The development of American lithography during the first half of the twentieth century could be said to begin with the frustrated efforts of Montague Marks, who sought unsuccessfully in the late 1890s to form a Society of Painter-Lithographers in New York: it could equally be said to begin with the work of the American artists who made lithographs in Europe—James McNeill Whistler, Joseph Pennell, and Albert Sterner among them—both before and after the turn of the century.

The now flourishing state of American lithography makes it difficult to envision how greatly its circumstances have changed since the 1920s. Except among a small but dedicated group of supporters, lithography was then a rejected art form, generally thought to be fit only for crass, commercial purposes. Bolton Brown, who began to print for artists in New York in 1919, spoke of his endeavors as missionary work. George C. Miller, also in New York, was during the 1920s the only printer in the United States who worked full time as a professional printer for artists. Artists who sought to print for themselves were confronted by walls of technical secrecy erected by the members of the lithographer's unions. Even the most prominent artists who chose to work in lithography found little market for their work; Childe Hassam's lithographs, for example, remained largely unsold in his lifetime.

The lithography workshop organized by Joseph Pennell at the Art Students League of New York in 1922 appears to have been the first in an American art school. Not a single book on artists' lithography had been published in the United States; the first, by Bolton Brown, would not appear until 1930. Exhibitions of prints by American artists were limited principally to etchings, the accepted and fashionable medium among most collectors of fine prints. It was thus a daring step when in 1929 the Print Club of Philadelphia undertook to organize the first series of exhibitions devoted exclusively to artists' lithographs. The organization now known as the Society of American Graphic Artists was not to accept lithographs in its annual exhibitions until 1947.

It is a tribute to the fascinations of the medium that, against the currents of taste, so many of America's leading artists made fine lithographs during the 1920s. Some, notably George Bellows, explored lithography with an all-consuming passion, as a principal means of expression; others (Charles Sheeler comes to mind) made few lithographs, though often of high quality.

During the 1930s and 1940s, lithography came to enjoy its first period of relative prosperity and acceptance. Skilled printers were now available in cities other than New York. Subsequent to publication of Brown's book, a new generation of artist-lithographers was attracted to the medium during the 1930s. Many of these artists were painters of the American scene who found in lithography a medium well suited to their purpose. Additional stimulus came through the founding of the graphic arts workshops of the Federal Art Project during the years of the great depression, and through the use of lithography by social realist artists, strongly influenced by the Mexican painters Orozco and Siquieros.

The identification of lithography with these directions in American art was both a source of early strength and of later weakness. Although during and after World War II American artists made many lithographs that were modernist in spirit, the fact that the avant-garde painters of the School of New York perceived a relationship between lithography and social realist art caused them to reject it as a medium of expression, with the consequence that by the mid-1950s it reached an economic nadir.

This period in the history of American lithography comes to an end not with one but with a cluster of events: the organization of the Contemporaries Graphic Art Center—predecessor of the Pratt Graphics Center—in New York in 1955; the founding of Universal Limited Art Editions, which began work toward publication of artists' lithographs in 1957; and the opening of Tamarind Lithography Workshop in Los Angeles in 1960. After 1960, as a direct result of these events, American lithography took on a new spirit and direction.

Among the many American artists who made lithographs between 1900 and 1960, I have chosen to discuss the work of a relative few. With some exceptions, my selections (and omissions) differ from those that might have been made in the 1930s or 1940s. From the vantage point of the 1980s, some artists are seen to have increased in stature, others to have diminished. The names of modernist artists were conspicuously absent from the "ten best" lists published by *Prints* magazine in 1936 (see footnote, page 154); among those who were then acclaimed, some are now forgotten. Beyond doubt, other reappraisals will be made.

I have given emphasis to the work of artists who directly influenced the development of the medium—Albert Sterner, George Bellows, Jean Charlot, and Adolf Dehn as examples—and to others who produced fine lithographs, in New York and elsewhere. Inevitably, my account of history has been strongly conditioned by a personal involvement with lithography which began in 1948 when I made my first lithographs with the Los Angeles printer Lynton R. Kistler.

I have drawn heavily upon the personal recollections of artists and printers who directly participated in the events that are described, and who assisted me to understand the technical and aesthetic climate in which they worked. This book could not have been written without their cooperation. I am particularly indebted to Garo Antreasian, Grant Arnold, Will Barnet, Howard Cook, Constance Forsyth, Jules Heller, Jacob Kainen, Jerome Kaplan, Lynton R. Kistler, Burr Miller, Reginald Neal, Andrée Ruellan, Arnold Singer, Verna Jean Versa, Theodore "Ted" Wahl, June Wayne, and Emerson Woelffer, each of whom in conversations and interviews contributed indispensably to this history. I also express my appreciation for important help to Jack Bookbinder, Paul Brach, Eric Bransby, Ross Braught, Hans Burkhardt, Jean Charlot, Andrew Dasburg, Lorser Feitelson, Karl Fortess, Joe Funk, Robert Gardner, Larry Heller, Leonard Lehrer, William Libby, Helen Lundeberg, Martyl Landsdorf, Frank Lobdell, John McClellan, Loren Mozley, John Muench, Nathan Oliveira, Henry Pearson, S. Dale Phillips, Merlin Pollock, Michael Ponce de León, Raphael Sabatini, Raphael Soyer, Harry Sternberg, Raymond Steth, Jan Stussy, Maltby Sykes, John Taylor, Joseph Vogel, Roswell Weidner, and Ralph Wickiser.

I am similarly indebted to relatives of artists and printers who figure in this history: Mrs. Earl M. Booth (Jean Bellows), Mrs. Federico Castellón, Mrs. Francis Chapin, Mrs. Jean Charlot, Millicent Coleman (granddaughter of Bolton Brown), Constance Crown (formerly Mrs. Rico Lebrun), Mrs. Adolf Dehn, Mrs. William J. Dickerson, Mrs. Yasuo Kuniyoshi, Juliet Man Ray, and Mrs. Jack Rundell (Dorothy Barrett).

My appreciation is also extended to the many scholars, archivists, curators, museum directors, research librarians, and others who have generously shared with me their knowledge and experience. I express particular appreciation to my friend, the late Mitchell A. Wilder, whose encouragement led me to begin the writing of this book; to Sylvan Cole, Jr., Janet A. Flint, Sinclair H. Hitchings, Peter Morse, and Gustave von Groschwitz, whose suggestions have been of invaluable aid; to W. McNeil Lowry, formerly director of the Ford Foundation's Program in Humanities and the Arts; to Elizabeth Roth and Robert Rainwater of the New York Public Library, and to their predecessors who began compilation of the library's comprehensive clipping files; to Leo M. Dolenski, manuscripts librarian at the Bryn Mawr College Library, for his gracious assistance during my study of Bolton Brown's journals and manuscripts; as well as to Christine Armstrong, Fred S. Bartlett, Ben Bassham, Karen F. Beall, E. Maurice Bloch, Harry A. Broadd, James B. Byrnes, Peggy Coesfeld, Van Deren Coke, Sherry Cromwell-Lacy, Amy Doherty, Alf Evers, Ebria Feinblatt, Richard S. Field, Ruth E. Fine, August L. Freundlich, Ofelia Garcia, Ellen Jacobowitz, Elizabeth Jones, Bernard Karpel, Samuel S. Klein, June and Norman Kraeft, Lauris Mason, George L. McKenna, Joann Moser, Roxanne Nilan, Mindy Ostrow, William S. Pelletier, Bernard Reilly, Robert Schoelkopf, Jan-Marie Spanard, Kristin L. Spangenberg, David Tatham, Barbara Thompson, Barry Walker, and James Watrous.

Many members of the staff of Tamarind Institute have assisted me during the time I have been engaged in the writing of this book. I extend my gratitude to all of them, especially to Marjorie Devon and Susan von Glahn.

I wish above all to thank my wife Mary, who has read and made valuable comment upon the interminable preliminary drafts of this book, and who has been patiently supportive of the strains and disruptions that its writing has caused.

Finally, I wish to acknowledge that whatever errors of fact, emphasis, or omission may be found in this book are my responsibility alone.

Clinton Adams
Albuquerque, New Mexico, 1983

American Lithographers 1900–1960

Introduction

EUROPEAN LITHOGRAPHY DURING THE FIRST HALF OF THE NINETEENTH CENTURY

American lithography, like lithography in Europe, has long been caught in a tug-of-war between art and commerce, a struggle that has continued through most of two centuries. Alois Senefelder, who invented the process in 1798, was himself torn between the creative potential of "chemical printing," as he preferred to call it, and visions of the wealth that might come to him through its exploitation in industry.*

Although the principle of lithography is simple, depending upon the mutual repulsion of grease and water, in practice it is so complex and sensitive a process that throughout its history most fine lithographs have been produced by the combined effort of an artist and a highly skilled printer, working collaboratively together. The first original polyautographs, as they were then known, were printed in London by Philipp André, and among these the earliest dated work was drawn in 1801 by the American-born artist, Benjamin West, then President of the Royal Academy.[1]

Senefelder himself developed and explored virtually all of the "sundry manners of lithography," including the printing of images from metal plates as well as from stone, the use of transfer paper, and color lithography, and described them all in his book, *Vollständiges Lehrbuch der Steindruckerey,* first published in Munich in 1818 and the following year in London under the title, *A Complete Course in Lithography,* "containing clear and explicit instructions in all different branches and manners of that art: accompanied by illustrative specimens of drawings. To which is prefaced a history of lithography, from its origin to the present time, by Alois Senefelder, inventor of the art of lithography and chemical printing."[2] Lithography remains unique among the principal processes and techniques of the artist in the degree to which it originated in the inventions and discoveries of one man.

* For a brief description of the lithographic process see the Technical Appendix, p. 207. Further information will be found in Garo Antreasian and Clinton Adams, *The Tamarind Book of Lithography: Art and Techniques.*

3

Although it was in France that lithography enjoyed its first great creative period, it was slow to develop there. The turmoil that accompanied the Napoleonic wars frustrated all efforts, and it was not until after restoration of the monarchy in the summer of 1815 that the first successful workshops were established in Paris by Charles de Lasteyrie, late in 1815, and by Godefroy Engelmann, in the summer of 1816. So rapid then was the acceptance of lithography by leading French artists that within the next decade most of the prominent artists of the period had tried their hand at the medium. By 1820 Engelmann's workshop had become "probably the leading press in Europe, and certainly so for that branch of lithography in which France has ever since led the world, the production of artists' prints."[3]

It has been said that the importance of any new medium is proved when it is used by artists to create superb works of art. If this is so, then lithography's importance was conclusively proved by Eugène Delacroix, Richard Bonington, Eugène Isabey, and the other fine artists who collaborated with de Lasteyrie and Engelmann in Paris; by Theodore Géricault, who worked both in Paris and London, with the English printer Charles Hullmandel; and above all by Francisco Goya, whose late lithographs were drawn in Bordeaux in 1825 when the artist was seventy-nine. In no other works of the early nineteenth century were the directness and force of crayon lithography so fully explored as in Goya's portrait of his printer, Gaulon, and his series of four lithographs, collectively titled *The Bulls of Bordeaux*.

So numerous were the fine lithographs of the late 1820s and the 1830s that we have come to look upon those years as the first "golden age" of lithography. But by no means were the printers then concerned solely with artists' lithographs. By 1828 "there were, in the department of the Seine alone, twenty-four lithographic printing houses containing 180 presses and employing 420 workmen."[4] The work that was done at these presses was for the most part commercial printing, including sheet music and maps as well as illustrations for books and pamphlets. Quickly, lithography replaced in all such uses the laborious process of metal and wood engraving which had been until then the only way in which visual images could be reproduced.

Nowhere can the technical evolution of lithography be more clearly traced than in one monumental work, *Voyages pittoresques et romantiques dans l'ancienne France,* published in Paris by Baron Isadore Taylor over a period of fifty-eight years (1820–78). In the first ten volumes, all printed by Engelmann, we see the progression of lithography from its early, tentative beginnings to its rich and full maturity; in the later volumes we see its slow decline. More than any other, the single factor that most contributed to that decline was the invention of photography.

The invention both of lithography and of photography arose from the need, strongly felt in the late eighteenth century, to achieve a more direct and less costly means for the multiplication and dissemination of visual images. Although Senefelder's process did much to advance this goal, it was not alone the final answer. By no coincidence, the invention of photography resulted from the researches of two lithographers, Joseph Nicéphore Niépce and Louis Jacques Daguerre. Later, at mid-century, it was the lithographic printer, Rose-Joseph Lemercier, who found a way to fix a photographic image on a sensitized stone so that prints could be taken from it, thus creating photolithography.

The decline of hand-drawn lithography in the 1840s and 1850s came about as lithographic craftsmen attempted unsuccessfully to equal the verisimilitude of photography. It was an impossible task, and it soon became apparent that "as far as the masses were concerned, lithography had shot its bolt in competition with photography. From the mid-nineteenth century on, photography and not lithography was the darling of the public."[5]

PRINTMAKERS TO THE AMERICAN PEOPLE

The first lithographic press established in the United States was in Philadelphia and it was there in 1819 that the painter, Bass Otis, drew what is generally thought to be the first artist's lithograph printed in this country. As in Europe, the early American lithographs were little more than tentative and hesitant beginnings which in no way realized the full potential of the medium.[6] Although during the nineteenth century lithography was occasionally employed by American artists for creative purposes, notably by Thomas Cole, William Rimmer, William Morris Hunt, and Thomas Moran, the social and economic climate of the United States was such that here, even more than in Europe, the tug-of-war between art and commerce was a very one-sided battle.

Much more typical of American lithography than the work of the country's few painter-lithographers were the popular prints published in great number by commercial lithographers, best known among them the firm of Currier and Ives. The immense popularity of these hand-colored prints and of the chromolithographs that followed them gives testimony to the fact that in terms of social, if not of artistic, values, they met a genuine need.* There was in America no established tradition of the print as a work of art, nor was any great stock placed in originality. What mattered most to nineteenth-century Americans was the subject matter of a print and the degree of competence and detail with which it was rendered. The publishers of popular lithographs and the artist-craftsmen in their employ thus became, in Harry Peters's phrase, "printmakers to the American people."

> Artists were on hand at battles, funerals, boat-races, parades, fires, shipwrecks, camp meetings and circuses. People came to [lithography] shops with all kinds of queer things to be drawn on stone, from church pew plans and clerical portraits to phrenological charts and ribald comics, from maps of the Oregon Trail to a map of Woman's Heart. Great packages of prints were being rushed out to agents all over the East, and the latest available political cartoons, news print, and others, were being thrown from racing stages into the hands of lonely men at stations on the trails to the Pacific.[7]

It was inevitable, given the vast quantity of these lithographs, that most were done strictly by formula, in a manner chosen to satisfy but not to extend or excite the taste of the audience for which they were manufactured. By 1890 more than 700 lithographic printing establishments existed in the United States; they employed 8,000 people and had a yearly production valued at twenty million dollars. Lithography had become, in short, a major American industry.[8]

In the process of becoming an industry, it lost much of its attraction to creative artists, who increasingly perceived it as a me-

* By dictionary definition, *chromolithograph* means simply "a picture printed in colors from a series of stones prepared in the lithographic process." Over the years, however, the word has acquired a pejorative connotation, so that it is now applied only to the popular, commercial, and largely reproductive prints published in the nineteenth century. Original lithographs printed in colors and drawn by artist-lithographers are referred to as *color lithographs*. The term *colored lithographs* is used to describe lithographs to which color has been applied by hand.

5

dium fit only for commercial uses. Late in the century, when Joseph and Elizabeth Robins Pennell surveyed the history of lithography in America, they were forced to conclude that "the country was flooded with poor designs, wretchedly carried out. . . . Gradually Senefelder's invention was monopolised by the cigar-box maker, the printer of theatrical posters, or the publishers of chromos and comic prints."[9]

THE REVITALIZATION OF LITHOGRAPHY IN EUROPE

If the earlier decline of lithography in Europe had come about as craftsmen strove hopelessly to compete with photographic processes, its revival began when artists chose not to imitate the photograph but rather to challenge it in entirely different terms. The political and satirical cartoons of Honoré Daumier and Paul Gavarni clearly set the medium upon this new and productive path. Precisely because in the art of caricature there were no expectations of representational accuracy, they were free to put conventions and recipes aside and to draw their images boldly with a blunt and vigorous line. But great as was their strength, the fact that these lithographs appeared in popular journals served to reinforce the widely accepted view that lithography was illsuited to high art.

In the later nineteenth century it is not surprising that most of the artists who chose to work creatively in lithography were identified with the avant-garde movements of the time, first the Barbizon painters, then the Impressionists and Symbolists. Throughout the 1860s, 1870s, and 1880s the very unpopularity of the styles within which they worked made it possible for Edouard Manet, Edgar Degas, Henri Fantin-Latour, and Odilon Redon, among others, to adopt a medium which was also unpopular. They had no need (or desire) to cater to established tastes and were thus free to use the stone as they chose. With but few exceptions the lithographs made by these painter-lithographers were in black and white. "Black," wrote Redon, "is the most essential of all colors. . . . One must admire black. Nothing can debauch it." For him, lithography was impoverished by the addition of color, "which produces a different result, destroying its specific qualities so that it comes to resemble a cheap colored print."[10]

Despite this sentiment, shared by many artists, color was to be a major force in the revitalization of lithography during the 1890s. So rapidly did attitudes change during that decade that it is now possible without exaggeration to speak of what transpired as "the color revolution." The groundwork for this change was first laid by the artist-printer Jules Chéret, who beginning in 1869 had created a striking series of bold and colorful posters that served greatly to expand the range of color lithography. In the 1880s and 1890s the walls and kiosks of Paris were filled with the posters of Chéret, Théophile Alexandre Steinlen, Henri de Toulouse-Lautrec, Pierre Bonnard, and other artists of the period.

The revival of printmaking and of lithography in particular went far beyond the work of the poster artists. Although it was not until 1899 that the Society of French Artists acted to permit admission of color prints to its annual salon, previously restricted to works in black and white, their conservative attitudes did nothing to retard the enthusiasm of the young avant-garde artists who were to establish color lithography as a principal innovative force in the art of the 1890s. By 1893, the printmaking renaissance had attracted the attention of several enterprising dealers and publishers, among them Edmond Sagot, Gustave Pellet, Ambroise Vollard, and André Marty, whose print folios and albums were soon to revolutionize the field.[11] Within the next few years a series of such albums followed quickly one upon another, containing among them many of the works that now stand as unquestioned masterpieces of the art. Some of these albums were devoted to the work of a single artist (as examples, Bonnard's *Quelques Aspects de la vie de Paris,* published by Vollard, and Toulouse-Lautrec's *Elles,* published by Pellet); others included prints in several media and by different artists. Among these, none was more important than *L'Estampe originale,* a series of albums published between 1893 and 1895 by André Marty. Sixty of the ninety-five prints included in these albums were lithographs and of these twenty-eight were in color. Included were lithographs by Bonnard, Chéret, Redon, and Toulouse-Lautrec, as well as by Camille Pissarro, Pierre Auguste Renoir, Maurice Denis, Paul Gauguin, Paul Signac, and Edouard Vuillard.

The creation of such an unparalleled group of works depended not only upon the genius of the artists and the conviction and talent of their publishers, but also upon the very high ability of the printers who were then available in Paris. Without these printers, lithography's renaissance could never have occurred.

During the nineteenth century, lithographic printing had evolved at a rapid rate.[12] Spurred on by the requirements of commercial printing, the work of the printer became increasingly mechanized. Systems were developed for efficient color registration. By mid-century it was possible both to ink and to moisten the stones or plates using mechanized rollers, and shortly thereafter came presses driven by steam power. Although during the nineteenth century flatbed presses remained in general use, the first steps were taken toward development of the rotary offset presses which would in the early twentieth century make the lithograph stone obsolete for all but artists' uses. An ever-increasing proportion of lithographic printing involved use of photographic processes, and even in France the number of original lithographs (including posters) that were hand-drawn on stone by artists came to represent but a tiny fraction of all the printing that was done.

One result of these changes was to bring about an increasing specialization on the part of the French lithographic firms. The larger firms, those that used the most advanced technology, came to be impatient with artists, whose many requirements made of their work a poor source of profits. Artists, too, became impatient. "My God," Redon wrote, "how I have suffered in the printing shops, what inner rages have seized me when I saw the bewildered incomprehension which printers have shown toward my endeavors."[13] The frustrations that Redon protests were inevitable in any workshop that concentrated upon commercial printing but which yet provided occasional services to artists.* When, as a result of increasing activity upon the part of artist-lithographers, it became possible for a few printers to work primarily or exclusively with artists, the collaborative relationship became more satisfactory. Gradually, a clear division developed between commercial printing establishments and lithographic ateliers designed to meet the needs of artists.

* Even so, artists who worked in France were more fortunate than those who worked in England or the United States. While in the Parisian workshops some printers had little understanding of or sympathy for the demands artists made upon them, others possessed great sensitivity and skill. Among the numerous printers who provided services to artists in the 1890s were Edward Ancourt, Alfred Lemercier (nephew of Rose-Joseph Lemercier), Eugène and Charles Verneau, Monrocq Frères, Harry Stern (who printed for Toulouse-Lautrec), and Auguste Clot, who printed many of the finest color lithographs of the 1890s, including works by Cézanne, Bonnard, and Vuillard.

JAMES McNEILL WHISTLER AND JOSEPH PENNELL

In October 1895, the centennial of lithography's invention was somewhat prematurely celebrated in Paris, where an impressive exhibition of lithographs by leading artists of the nineteenth century was presented in the Champ de Mars.* Not only the great French masters were well represented; the exhibition also included lithographs from Germany, Holland, Belgium, and England.

In her report for the *Nation* Elizabeth Robins Pennell expressed regret at the inadequate representation of American artists in the exhibition and went on to write:

> When all is said, England, in the Champ de Mars, now owes its great distinction to America. . . . Mr. Whistler here, as in any and every show to which he contributes, towers above most of his contemporaries. . . . Whatever his method, he is ever the master, knowing just exactly what effects and qualities may be obtained from the stone. He forgets the painter and the etcher to become the perfect lithographer.[14]

Although Whistler lived for most of his life in England, he remained persistently and even agressively American. He took delight in holding unpopular views on almost every subject, be it art, religion, or politics, with the the result that throughout his life he was embroiled in controversy. His work likewise attracted both acclaim and disparagement. He was credited by Arthur Jerome Eddy as the maker of "the greatest etchings the world has known since the days of Rembrandt."[15] He was condemned by John Ruskin as an impudent "coxcomb . . . for flinging a pot of paint in the public's face."[16] But disagree as one may with either or both of these judgments, it remains beyond question that Whistler more than any other artist outside France exerted a primary influence upon the subsequent development of lithography in England and the United States.

He quickly demonstrated his mastery of the medium in a series of lithotints completed in 1878, including *Nocturne: The River at Battersee* and *Early Morning,* in which he achieved a range of subtle delicacy that had not before been seen.† His printer, Thomas Way, did everything possible to encourage Whistler's work on stone, even to the point, as Joseph Pennell relates, of providing him with wheelbarrows and with men to wheel them about.‡

> He found right away that if he wanted to draw out of doors, as he always did, from nature, and did not have his men and his wheelbarrows around, it was impossible, so he began to use [transfer] paper. The paper that he had at that time was horrible stuff. . . . It was covered with a shiny grain, and it was a nasty sticky substance, and it was one of the most difficult things in the world to work on.[17]

But Whistler was not dissuaded. Transfer lithography at least provided him with the freedom to draw when and where he wished. In this preference Whistler reflected Senefelder's own enthusiasm for the transfer method and set the stage for a long and continuing battle among artists as to the merits of the transfer process.[18] Whistler did much to refine it, soon abandoning the standard transfer papers supplied by Way in favor of specially prepared papers which made

* The date now commonly accepted for the invention of lithography is 1798. Confusion has arisen as a result of Senefelder's references to earlier printing from stone, although before the discovery of "chemical printing" (i.e., lithography). See Senefelder, *Complete Course,* pp. 5–11. Other exhbitions celebrating the centennial of lithography were held in New York (1896), Philadelphia (1896), and London (1898).

† Arthur Staley in his essay, "Whistler as Printmaker" (in Levy, *Whistler Lithographs,* pp. 7–10), refers to these Whistler prints as "strictly speaking, lithotints rather than lithographs." This distinction would not be made by contemporary lithographers. Although lithotint is a special kind of drawing, it is essentially a lithographic technique, not a separate medium.

‡ Whistler's lithographs are catalogued by Thomas R. Way, *The Lithographs of Whistler* (New York: Kennedy & Co., 1914), and by Mervyn Levy, *Whistler Lithographs, an Illustrated Catalogue Raisonné* (London: Jupiter Books, 1975). Whistler's first lithographs were made while a student at West Point in 1852; after leaving West Point he drew a single lithograph in 1855 and then did not again touch stone until 1878, at which time he began his first series of lithographs in collaboration with Thomas Way (father of Thomas R. Way). "It is generally supposed," F. E. Jackson states, "that Way was the actual printer of Whistler's lithographs. Way was the name of the firm but the man who pulled those proofs was my old friend, that delicate and sensitive artist of the lithographic printing roller—H. P. Bray." F. E. Jackson, "Modern Lithography," p. 214.

1 James A. McNeill Whistler (1834–1903), *Early Morning,* 1878. 163 x 249
[Way 7], printed (by H. P. Bray) at the workshop of Thomas Way. Collection,
University of New Mexico Art Museum.

Except as noted, all works are lithographs printed in black. Dimensions are in
millimeters, height preceding width, and are those of the image measured at its
widest point in each dimension. Alternative titles under which a work has been
previously published or exhibited are given in parentheses. References in brackets
are to catalogues raisonnés or checklists included in the bibliography.

it possible for his printer to preserve the most fragile and delicate of tones.[19]

Joseph Pennell, who first met Whistler in England, joined him in France in 1893, assisted him in the printing of his etchings, and observed his methods in lithography:

> Many of his drawings were made in Paris, and when finished the sheet of paper was sent over to London to his printer, Way, and there put down on stone.
>
> But you must know at this time the secrecy in the art of lithography was so great that Whistler, during the whole of his lifetime, had no idea how drawings were put on stone, or how they were etched, or printed. . . . Sometimes half the work was lost, and Whistler had to go to London, get the stone, and draw on it again the work which the printer had lost, in order to get the effect that he had in the beginning on paper. Had he been allowed to go into the printing office and see the drawing transferred, etched, and printed, we should have had more lithographs and even better lithographs than we have today from him. These hindrances drove him and many other artists from lithography.[20]

But Pennell, like Whistler, valued above all the freedom and portability that the transfer method provided and, despite its limitations, he adopted it in his work. In 1896 he arranged in a London gallery an exhibition of the lithographs he had drawn in Spain. Whistler applauded the freshness of Pennell's new works and pronounced them "charming": "There is a crispness in their execution, and a lightness and gaiety in their arrangements as pictures that belong to the artist alone; and he only, could, with the restricted means of the lithographer—and restricted, indeed, I have found them—have completely put sunny Spain into your frames."[21]

It was then that the simmering controversy among artists with respect to the merits and propriety of transfer lithography erupted into the open. In an article published in the *Saturday Review*,[22] the highly regarded young English artist, Walter Sickert, formerly one of Whistler's most favored pupils, attacked the Pennell exhibition and argued that "to pass off drawings made on paper as lithographs was as misleading to 'the purchaser on the vital point of commercial value' as to sell photogravures for etchings."[23] Although Sickert's article was directed at Pennell, it was clearly an attack on Whistler as well, for both artists made use of the transfer method.

Pennell viewed Sickert's comments as an accusation of dishonesty and demanded an apology. When none was forthcoming, he took the matter to court. There, in April 1897, it was decided as a matter of law that transfer lithography was indeed lithography, and the jury awarded Pennell fifty pounds in damages.[24] But although as law it had been decided, the issue had not been laid to rest; in later years it would be a continuing cause of dispute between Whistler, Pennell, and their followers on the one hand, and the advocates of stone lithography on the other.

THE CONSTRAINTS OF COMMERCIALISM

The controversy surrounding the use of transfer methods did nothing to restore the reputation of lithography in England, where it was

2   James A. McNeill Whistler (1834–1903), *The Smith, Passage du Dragon,* 1884.
Transfer lithograph with additions on the stone, 272 x 174 [Way 73.ii], printed
(by H. P. Bray) at the workshop of Thomas Way. Collection, Tamarind
Institute.

already held in low esteem. By the late 1890s, even the Pennells were
despondent as to its condition:

> As a method of dissemination of popular prints, lithography
> has been killed by the Trades' Union and the Limited
> Company. This was more the less the fault of the
> professional lithographers, who trained a number of
> people simply to do work for them. . . . The creative
> artist for twenty-five years, from 1870 to 1890, had no
> place in the lithographic establishment. To understand the
> full degeneracy of the art one has but to consult the pages
> of *Lithographic Times and Printer* and note how, in the
> beginning, lithography was discussed as one of the Fine
> Arts; how, to-day, its pages are filled with reports of
> strikes and the pitiful whinings of the intelligent
> workman, who is not free to do as little as he wants to,

3 J. Alden Weir (1852–1919), *Profile Portrait of a Woman Sewing,* c. 1896.
311 x 228 [Zimmermann 2], printer unknown. Collection, National Museum
of American Art, Smithsonian Institution, gift of Brigham Young University.

and that as badly as possible. As an artistic profession
lithography will never again be revived; it was throttled
by commerce and Trades-Unionism. As an individual art,
we have no doubt it will flourish again, as in the past, in
the hands of a few artists capable of practicing it.[25]

There was, in fact, little interest in the medium. Whistler, who
made few lithographs after 1896, died in 1903. Not until the founding of the Senefelder Club in 1908 did a small circle of artists again
seek to advance lithography in England. Among them were F. Ernest Jackson, John Copley, Ethel Gabain (Mrs. Copley), A. S.
Hartrick, Edmund Blampied, and Frank Brangwyn. Beginning in
1910 the Senefelder Club regularly exhibited lithographs by its members in London, and after 1914, in the United States.* But even as
they sought through these exhibitions to provide a stimulus, the artists had few illusions. Jackson called lithography "practically dead

* The Senefelder Club's first American exhibitions were in San Francisco and Los Angeles
in 1914, then in Philadelphia, Pittsburgh, and
Chicago. Not until 1922 did they find it possible to arrange an exhibition in New York.

A Lithograph with a Verdict," *Print Collector's Newsletter* 12 (November–December 1981): 133–37.

20   Pennell, *Graphic Arts,* p. 254.

21   Whistler, in a letter quoted by Carl Zigrosser, *Lithographs* (1916).

22   Walter R. Sickert, "Transfer Lithography," *Saturday Review,* 26 December 1896.

23   The Pennells, quoting Sickert in part, *Life of Whistler,* Vol. 2, p. 186.

24   For an account of the trial from the Pennell and Whistler side of the argument, see the Pennells, *Life of Whistler,* Vol. 2, pp. 186–92.

25   Joseph and Elizabeth Robins Pennell, "The Centenary of Lithography," *Fortnightly Review* 70 (December 1898): 983.

26   Jackson, "Modern Lithography," p. 218.

27   John Copley, "Some Lithographers of the Past and Future," p. 41.

28   Ibid., p. 50.

29   *Catalogue of an Exhibition Illustrative of a Centenary of Artistic Lithography, 1796–1896* (New York: Grolier Club, 1896), p. 9. The exhibition included 244 lithographs by 160 artists. See also note, page 000, *.

30   Frank Weitenkampf, "Painter-lithography in the United States," p. 547. See also Janet A. Flint, *J. Alden Weir, An American Printmaker,* p. 6.

1 · The Early Years

ALBERT STERNER
AND THE PAINTER-GRAVERS OF AMERICA

Unfairly eclipsed by time, Albert Sterner's lithographs from the first decades of the twentieth century are characterized by a vigor and power remarkable among American prints of the period. Like his compatriots Whistler and Pennell, Sterner spent much of his time abroad, and it was in Europe that he first explored lithography, initially at Lemercier's Paris workshop, then at the studios of Klein and Volbert in Munich.[1]

Born and schooled in England, Sterner lived as a youth in Germany and studied drawing in Paris with Gérôme and Boulanger. After beginning a career as an illustrator in New York, he again set out for Paris in 1890 to establish himself as a painter. At the age of twenty-seven he found a studio on the Boulevard Arago where, quickly adapting himself to the life of a young artist in Paris, he met and talked with the artists at the Chat Noir, among them Steinlen, then already well known as a painter and lithographer. In 1891 Sterner "sent his first contribution to the Salon, a canvas called 'Le Célibataire,' which was not only to bring him an Honourable Mention but considerable publicity as well."[2] He made a number of portraits, including a drawing of Oscar Wilde, and throughout the 1890s continued to work both as illustrator and painter. In 1894 he had his first public exhibition in New York while at the same time working to complete a series of illustrations for a ten volume edition of the works of Edgar Allan Poe. Honors came to him in quick sequence at the major international expositions of the period: a bronze medal in Paris in 1900, a silver medal in Buffalo in 1901, and a gold medal in Munich in 1905. In their scale and richness of execution, Sterner's first series of lithographs, completed in Europe prior to 1906, are much closer to the works of *fin de siècle* French and European artists than to the delicate and often sketchy images of Whistler and Pennell. In their themes of love and death, they not only reflect Sterner's

4

4   Albert Sterner (1863–1946), *Dame am Wasser,* 1902. Color lithograph,
543 x 516, printed at the workshop of Klein and Volbert. Collection, National
Museum of American Art, Smithsonian Institution.

affection for Poe, but also suggest that he may have known the early works of the German Expressionists and of Edvard Munch.

When Sterner returned to New York, the spirit and quality of his lithographs attracted the attention of Martin Birnbaum, the adventurous art dealer who between 1910 and 1916 served as manager of the American branch of the Berlin Photographic Company. Birnbaum during those years was a strong advocate of the avant-garde artists of central Europe and was among the first to present their work in the United States.* In 1911 and again in 1915 he arranged exhibitions of Sterner's monotypes and lithographs in his gallery;[3] the 1915 exhibition had particular effect upon the subsequent history of American lithography, if for no other reason than that it served to stimulate Bolton Brown's interest in the medium.

Sterner was by this time thoroughly committed to the concept of the painter-printmaker, and he made a continuing effort to attract other artists to the field.

> On the evening of January 9 [1915] . . . an informal meeting
> was held in Sterner's studio to discuss ways and means
> for the formation of a society of artists working in the
> graphic arts.† Childe Hassam, George Bellows, Boardman
> Robinson, Ernest D. Roth, George Elmer Brown, and
> Leo Mielziner were among those present and the upshot
> of this session was the founding of the Painter-Gravers of
> America. Sterner had long had such an organization at
> heart to help raise the general quality of prints in
> America, and he threw himself into the new project with
> full enthusiasm.[4]

He and Bellows obtained a space in a building on Fifty-eighth Street, which they quickly transformed into a suite of well-lighted galleries, so that by March of that year the new society found it possible to present its first exhibition, comprising no less than 198 prints. Among the exhibitors (in addition to those who had attended the January meeting) were many of the artists who would later become prominent as distinguished artist-printmakers, including John Taylor Arms, Kerr Eby, Eugene Higgins, Edward Hopper, Troy Kinney, Jerome Myers, John Sloan, Maurice Sterne, and J. Alden Weir.‡ Most of the prints exhibited were etchings, not lithographs.

JOSEPH PENNELL, THE TRANSFER LITHOGRAPHS: PANAMA, AMERICA, AND GREECE

During the years before World War I, American artists continued to travel regularly to Europe; some made lithographs while there, as had Whistler, Pennell, and Sterner before them.§ After the outbreak of the war in the summer of 1914, such excursions became difficult, and artists who wished to make lithographs increasingly sought to do so on this side of the ocean.

Even before the war, Pennell, motivated by his enthusiasm for "the wonder of work," had left England in 1912 to make a series of lithographs of the Panama Canal, then under construction. For Pennell, "the supreme interest was in the building, while the colossal cranes and steam shovels were at work, the cyclopean walls and gates of the locks fully exposed, the stupendous arrangements and effects changing day by day, never to be seen again once the locks were filled."[5]

* Birnbaum was among the first to exhibit the work of Ensor, Feininger, Kandinsky, Klee, Kokoschka, Kollwitz, Munch, and Pascin in the United States. Among the American artists he exhibited were Eugene Higgins, Paul Manship, Maxfield Parrish, and John Sloan. He wrote extensively and published articles on Bakst, Beardsley, Flaxman, Sterne, and others.

† I am indebted to Richard S. Field for information that Ralph Flint's account of the formation of the Painter-Gravers of America, from which this quotation is taken, is in error. Field reports (in an exhibition catalogue received after this book had been set in type) that a "copy of the *First Annual Year Book of the Painter-Gravers of America* at Harvard, clearly establishes that the founding date was 9 January 1917 (not 1915)." Field lists in full the charter members of the organization and those who were added to its membership during its initial year; although mentioned by Flint, Edward Hopper is not included in this list. See Richard S. Field, and others, *American Prints 1900–1950* (New Haven: Yale University Art Gallery, 1983), pp. 21–22.

‡ The Painter-Gravers of America held a series of exhibitions, interrupted by World War I.

§ George Biddle's early lithographs, printed in Paris between 1911 and 1917, are particularly notable. A proper Philadelphian, a graduate of Groton (where he and Franklin D. Roosevelt were classmates) and of Harvard, Biddle formed a friendship with Mary Cassatt (then in her late sixties), met her favorite niece Ellen Mary Cassatt, fell in love with her, and drew her portrait on stone.

* Although Elizabeth Pennell here indicates that Pennell planned to print his lithographs in Philadelphia, she elsewhere quotes a letter from Robert G. Leinroth, art manager for the Ketterlinus Company, who states that Pennell first tried to have the Panama drawings transferred in New York "but found no one there sufficiently interested to do it." See Elizabeth Robins Pennell, *The Life and Letters of Joseph Pennell,* vol. 1, pp. 111–12.

† It is characteristic that over a period of time the identities of many individual printers have been lost or only fragmentarily preserved. We know that after Pennell took his Panama drawings to Leinroth at the Ketterlinus Company he worked in collaboration with Gregor (his first name is not provided in Leinroth's account), "a printer trained in the Berlin shop where [Adolf von] Menzel worked" (Ibid.). Gregor, with whom Sterner also collaborated, was but one of a number of fine craftsmen who worked in the commercial lithographic establishments during the first decades of the twentieth century. The names of such printers were recorded no more carefully than those of the skilled masons and carpenters who built the nation's buildings. Thus, in New York, Childe Hassam identified his expert collaborator at Oberly & Newell in 1917 only as "Herr Faust," who, like Gregor, had learned his trade in Germany.

Hassam's account of his work with Faust, who printed his lithographs, *The Lithographer, Lafayette Street,* and *La Gloire (The French Cruiser),* is contained in an unpublished, handwritten autobiography in the collection of the American Academy of Arts and Letters, a portion of which is included in the Archives of American Art, Smithsonian Institution, reel NAA-1, frames 752–753. I am indebted to Janet A. Flint for bringing this manuscript to my attention.

Fuller Griffith's statement (in *The Lithographs of Childe Hassam*) that all of Hassam's lithographs were printed by George Miller is thus seen to be incorrect. A question is raised as to whether Hassam's *Portrait of Joseph Pennell* was printed by Miller. It does not have the look of Miller's printing (see page 50).

Before leaving England, Pennell had considerably extended his knowledge of lithography through a collaboration with the printer Charles Goulding, who, unlike Thomas Way, opened his workshop to the artist, permitting him "to see the work done and stand by the press until it was done."[6] As a consequence, Pennell had found it possible to move far beyond the limited lithographic techniques of his earlier work. His interest in travel and in drawing directly from the subject made it essential that he continue to employ the transfer method:

> His joy in experiment was without limit. . . . Papers, chalks, inks, stumps, scrapers were put to the test. He gave up the heavily coated papers at one time supposed absolutely essential. He found them unpleasant to draw on, sensitive to dampness and climate, and therefore unreliable to carry in traveling. Eventually he used almost altogether a paper prepared by Cornelissen in London, with hardly any coating, while towards the last his preference was for a paper with no coating whatsoever, the great advantage being that the print could be pulled on the same sort of paper and so still better preserve the character of the original drawing. . . .
>
> The anxiety was whether the drawings would transfer when he got back to Philadelphia, where he planned to print them.* How lithographic paper and lithographic chalk would stand the hot moist climate of Panama and a long journey by sea he did not know; no one could say. No one had ever ventured upon so delicate and uncertain a problem.[7]

6

After completing his work in Panama, Pennell made his way by steamer to San Francisco and, after stops at Yosemite and the Grand Canyon, where other lithographs were drawn, to Philadelphia, where his drawings from Panama and the West were transferred and printed at the Ketterlinus Lithographic Company. The following year, in the spring of 1913, he was off again, this time to Greece,

> [filled] with the desire to learn whether he would find as overpowering an inspiration in the Parthenon and the Temple of Jupiter as in the Gatun Lock and the walls of Pedro Miguel. . . . His methods were the same as in Panama. He would find the finest point of view, sit down on his camp stool in front of his subject and, with no preliminary notes or sketches, draw the columns and pediments of the Greek architect as in the far West he had drawn the locks and cuts of the American engineer.[8]

7

Pennell was not alone in seeking out the services of professional printers in the United States. Sterner also worked with the Ketterlinus Company in Philadelphia, and Childe Hassam made several of his lithographs with the firm of Oberly & Newell in New York.† Often, however, the difficulty encountered in working at the large lithographic establishments was considerable, as the printing such businesses did for artists was peripheral to their commercial work.

5   George Biddle (1885–1973), *Ellen Mary Cassatt,* 1917. Printed in brown,
397 x 262, printed in France. Collection, Philadelphia Museum of Art. Purchase,
Harrison Fund.

6   Joseph Pennell (1857–1926), *The Gates of Pedro Miguel Lock,* 1912. Transfer lithograph, 559 x 429 [Weurth 231], printed (by Gregor) at Ketterlinus Company. Collection, Boston Public Library.

7   Joseph Pennell (1857–1926), *Temple of Jupiter, Evening,* 1913. Transfer
lithograph, 540 x 422 [Weurth 335], printed in the workshop of Thomas Way.
Collection, Boston Public Library.

8   John Sloan (1871–1951), *Amateur Lithographers,* 1908. 469 x 395 [Morse 144], printed by the artist and Carl Moellman. Collection, Philadelphia Museum of Art. Purchase, Lessing J. Rosenwald gift and Farrell Fund income.

JOHN SLOAN, GEORGE BELLOWS, AND GEORGE C. MILLER

In the absence of other alternatives, some artists tried to print for themselves, making use of information that could be found in Senefelder or Hullmandel, or in such later works as Richmond's *Grammar of Lithography* and Cumming's *Handbook of Lithography*.[9] Press equipment was readily available for purchase. At the time, an interest in lithography was most likely to develop among artists who, like Sterner, had worked as illustrators. John Sloan, who drew his first lithograph in 1905, was sufficiently intrigued by the process to purchase a copy of Richmond's book and to think of buying a press.[10] Thus, when several years later his friend and (at that time) fellow illustrator, Arthur G. Dove, offered the loan of equipment, he happily accepted, and in May and June 1908 made a series of five lithographs. Very likely, Sloan could not have managed this without the

assistance of another friend, a professional lithographer, Carl Moellmann, who volunteered to help in off-hours. Even with Moellmann's
knowledge of the process, the task of graining, etching, and printing the stones was more than Sloan had bargained for, and in one of
8 the five lithographs, *Amateur Lithographers,* he made a typically witty
comment upon his experience at the press. In his diary he wrote:

> Ground and grained a stone and cut down the table on
> which the litho press is fixed and got ready for
> Moellmann who came for dinner. I roughed in a drawing
> of himself and myself struggling with the proving. And
> after dinner we struggled to much better purpose as I had
> some decent ink to prove with. Moellmann and I worked
> with the litho press till about 1:30.[11]

Sloan was not alone in the struggle. After setting up a press in
his studio, Sterner also learned that it was one thing to observe skilled
printers at work, as he had done in Paris and Munich, and quite
another to etch and roll up a stone. So subtle is the chemistry of the
lithographic process that even the most experienced of printers suffers
no surprise when something goes wrong. For the professional printer
an occasional failure is a part of the game; for the amateur it is an
9 everyday occurrence and a source of constant frustration.

In 1914, in one such moment of frustration, when Sterner had
all but ruined a drawing, he sought the advice of a friend who was
co-owner of the American Lithographic Company. Where, Sterner
wanted to know, could he find a good printer to print his lithographs?
He was given the name of a young printer, George C. Miller, who
had served his apprenticeship at the firm. Miller came to Sterner's
studio and managed to recover the stone that had given the artist
problems. Subsequently, he continued to print for Sterner and soon
for Pennell as well.

Sterner's enthusiasm for lithography was contagious, and in 1916
George Bellows also decided to buy a press and try his hand at the
process. His first print was *Hungry Dogs,* a lithograph based on a
crayon and ink drawing he had made some years before. Although
the lithograph's lack of technical polish reveals the inexperience of
its artist-printer, its somewhat muddy tonalities are not inappropriate
to its subject: a pack of dogs rooting among the ashcans of a Manhattan back alley. Other technical experiments followed this first print,
but it did not take Bellows long to accept the fact that

> he was too impatient to master the complexities involved
> in printing from a lithographic stone. When George
> Miller agreed to stop by evenings after work to help him,
> the understanding was that the printer would prepare the
> stone one night and return to print it the next night.
> Bellows's enthusiasm made waiting difficult, if not
> impossible. Too often Miller returned to find, much to
> his dismay, that the artist had unsuccessfully worked with
> the stone himself. Miller had no choice but to spend most
> of the evening repairing the damage.[12]

Even so, Bellows completed a substantial body of lithographs
during 1916 and 1917. All but the earliest were printed by Miller in
Bellows's studio on the top floor of the family house at 146 East
Nineteenth Street. Bellows took pride in his workshop, "a corking
11 little place," installed on a balcony overlooking a larger room below.

25

9   Albert Sterner (1863–1946), *The Abduction*, 1913. Transfer lithograph,
272 x 375, printed by the artist. Collection, Tamarind Institute.

10   George Bellows (1882–1925), *Hungry Dogs,* 1916. 340 x 252 [Mason 1],
printed by the artist. Collection, Tamarind Institute.

11   George Bellows (1882–1925), *The Studio, Christmas,* 1916. 139 x 110 [Mason 35], printed by George C. Miller. Collection, Tamarind Institute.

Miller was soon overloaded; he was working day and night. Although he had been made foreman of the stone-proofing department at the lithographic company, he saw that as a result of the new interest in lithography among artists—Sterner, Pennell, Bellows, Hassam, and others—he might now be able to make a living printing for them. He decided to try, and in 1917 opened his own small shop in New York. It was the first lithographic workshop in America to exist, as did the ateliers of Europe, for the sole purpose of providing printing services to artists.[13]

BOLTON BROWN, ARTIST-LITHOGRAPHER

Sterner, in a different way, was also partially responsible for Bolton Brown's decision to explore lithography. Brown later wrote this account:

> It was in the winter of 1914–15 when, passing down Lexington Avenue in New York, I came upon an exhibition of lithographs by Albert Sterner in the gallery of the Berlin Photographic Company. As I now look back across the eighteen years, it seems to me very likely that seeing those prints furnished just the last push needed to send me, in the spring, off to study lithography in London. Etchings I had made and printed from youth, but to this other art I was as yet a stranger.[14]

During Brown's first weeks in London, he studied the print collection at the British Museum, read extensively on the subject, purchased a copy of Pennell's newly published book,[15] and then, with this "mental background" established, enrolled in a class taught by F. Ernest Jackson, a prominent member of the Senefelder Club, at the County Council School.

> In the fresh and pleased possession of [Pennell's] treatise I emerged into the lithographic class. It was a mistake. At sight of it, upon some remark of mine, Professor Jackson glowered, "Joe Pennell knows nothing whatever about it," he promptly stated, "all he knows he learned standing by my press." . . . I hastened to observe that I knew very little about the gentleman and nothing at all about lithography. But even then something in the atmosphere warned me that a man with Pennell's book under his arm was a dubious person.[16]

After a brief stay in Jackson's class, Brown determined to learn the process in his own way and by himself. He purchased a press, a supply of stones and other equipment, and installed them on the top floor of a private house in Doughty Street where he had found a furnished flat. There in wartime London he taught himself lithography.*

Brown remained in England for a full year, during which time he worked obsessively, day and night. In his meticulously kept technical journals he made almost daily entries describing his problems, false starts, successes, and failures as he sought largely by informed trial and error to master the intricacies of an obstinate, difficult process.[17] Later he told a reporter for the *New York Times* that in that "one year he lost twelve pounds in weight and gained two inches across the chest manipulating lithograph stones."[18] It was a formidable undertaking for a man who had by then passed his fiftieth birthday.

*   On the basis of statements made by Frederic N. Price in "The Etchings and Lithographs of Arthur B. Davies," p. 8, by Merrill C. Rueppel in *The Graphic Art of Arthur Bowen Davies, and John Sloan,* p. 114 (later repeated by other authors) it has been assumed that Brown studied lithography with Thomas Way. As is seen, he did not.

28

At the time Brown began his work in lithography, he had already had a long and illustrious career as teacher, painter, scholar, mountaineer, writer, art dealer, and social critic.[19] Born in upstate New York on 27 November 1864, he came from a family whose history reached solidly back into revolutionary times. His father was a minister; his mother, a lady born in the antebellum South, encouraged his interest in art. He drew constantly as a child and youth, and at the university studied painting and aesthetics, receiving both his undergraduate and graduate degrees from Syracuse University (in 1885 and 1888). He was a member of the faculties of Cornell and Stanford universities, and while head of the Art Department at Stanford during the 1890s advocated ideas and practices much in advance of the day.[20] While in California, he married, had three children, formed a fine collection of Japanese prints, and developed a passion for the mountains. He enjoyed the rigorous life (he had been an athlete at Syracuse) and soon after his arrival in California set out to explore and conquer the deep canyons and high peaks of the Sierra Nevada. Mt. Bolton Coit Brown, in the Sierra's main range (elevation 13,538 feet) is now named in his honor.*

Upon leaving Stanford in 1902, Brown joined Ralph Radcliffe Whitehead in the founding of Byrdcliffe,[21] the Utopian art colony in Woodstock, New York. Brown selected the site in the Catskills and, with Whitehead's money, supervised construction of the buildings. Briefly, until he and Whitehead parted ways, he was director of the art school. He then devoted himself to painting and writing in New York City and Woodstock; he wrote pages and pages of notes on the materials of the artist, on color, on the techniques of the etcher.[22] To everything he touched he brought a spirit of total commitment, of exacting intellectual analysis, and of ardent enthusiasm.

Brown brought such a spirit to lithography during his year in London. On 29 August 1915 he made this entry in his journal:

> I have been doing a good deal of thinking—in the silent watches of the wakeful night and at other times—about lithography, and I have come to see that I cannot think my way to a mastery of it unless I take it completely apart and get it reduced to its absolute elements. . . . For me, the ideal lithographic print is that which most absolutely reproduces what I draw. . . . This bars all juggling with the printing and playing with it childishly "to see what will happen" (as is declared, erroneously, to be the beloved method of "artists" by Pennell). . . . My business is simple—make what I want on the stone and then print it. Nothing more.[23]

But though the business of the printer, conceived in these terms, is simple in theory, it is far from simple in practice, and the nearly eighty stones that Brown drew, proofed, and printed during his stay in England give testimony to that fact. Some are superb, as the remarkable *Sifting Shadows*, in which a delicate veil of crayon tones creates a drift of tenuous light across the flesh of the seated model; some are comparative failures; some are technical experiments that attest to the range of his study.†

At the end of his year abroad, when Brown returned to the United States, somehow managing to ship his press and equipment as well—this in the midst of World War I—he had indeed mastered

12

*   During the 1890s, Brown published a series of articles on mountaineering in the *Sierra Club Bulletin*. Brown's wife, Lucy Fletcher Brown, also found her place on maps of the Sierra Nevada: "Lucy's Foot Pass" is a high pass across the Kings-Kern divide, west of Mt. Ericsson.

†   Brown assigned serial numbers to his lithographs. These numbers were usually written within the image on the stone and encircled. (A seperate series of numbers, not encircled and usually prefaced by the letter *C*, refers to crayon formulas given in his journal; these numbers should not be confused with the serial numbers.) Using the serial numbers, he then made detailed technical entries in his journal. The entries for *Sifting Shadows* (Brown 54) are typical:

"22 Feb [1916]. Yesterday and to-day I drew and finished 54 [encircled], 'Sifting Shadows,' size 16" x 12". The most of it was done with grease, though blue and red were freely used. A little white, about the face and where great care and definition were called for. The grain [of the stone] was perfectly suited to the subject and I liked the technical solution very much. I anticipate that it will be a good printer." (Brown used color names to identify crayons of differing hardness: blue identified a soft crayon, number 1; red, medium, number 3; and white, very hard, number 5.)

"23 Feb. Just pickled 54. Stone stood back of the stove last evening and for four or five hours to-day—at no time quite reaching blood heat. Applied with soft brush rapidly used: then rolled the last minute. . . ." (Brown uses the word "pickle" to describe application of phosphoric acid "which does not 'etch' as other acids do, but *petrifies* (or 'pickles'—i.e., holds without change) what it is applied to." Journal 12, p. 757.)

"25 Feb. Proofs of 53 and 54 have to-day been added to my group in the British Museum—making a total of some 23 which are now there. When Mr. Binyon saw 54 he said, 'That's a beauty.' And it is." (Journal 3, p. 179).

12   Bolton Brown (1864–1936), *Sifting Shadows,* 1916. 394 x 299 [Brown 54],
printed by the artist. University Art Collections, Syracuse University.

the printer's art. Following a period of "rustication" at a family farm on Seneca Lake, he set up his press in Woodstock and began to print again.* As in London, his aim was no less than total control over the medium.

It was apparently late in 1918 or early in 1919 that Brown first began to print for artists other than himself.† He tells of a visit to the galleries of the Brown Robertson Company, then his agents; there he saw a proof of George Bellows's lithograph, *Murder of Edith Cavell*.‡ As Brown relates the story, "the Brown Robertson people were dissatisfied with the printing of Bellows's lithographs . . . [and] said they wished I was printing for him."[24] Brown volunteered his willingness to do so, and arrangements were made for him to meet Bellows at the artist's studio:

> I was there: prints under my arm; George, of course, his usual frank and genial self. He was new to me then; I thought he had beautiful eyes. Having looked at my prints, he said, "I have the best proof puller in the American Lithographic Company and I can't get what you get right along." I asked, "What is the matter? Can't you get what you put on the stone?" "No, that's just what we can't." Then we examined some of his prints: they seemed pathetic; they also seemed puzzling; I couldn't make out how they "got that way." Textures of extraordinary coarseness and black marks quite without autographic quality, not even suggesting lithographic crayon, left me guessing. . . . George said he did not like them but what could he do? "Let me print for you," I answered.§

They went on to make arrangements. Brown expected to be paid one dollar an impression, much more than Miller was charging at that time, but Bellows agreed to it. Brown relates that he printed an edition of fifty impressions of "a very rich design, *Gramercy Park*,"‖ and went on after that to print all of Bellows's work, principally in New York at Bellows's studio, but occasionally in Woodstock.

At about the same time he began printing for Bellows, Brown also printed for Sterner, who, according to Brown, was likewise dissatisfied with Miller's work as a printer.# Then, in March, 1919, arrangements were made for Brown to give a public demonstration of the lithographic process in the main exhibition gallery at Pratt Institute in Brooklyn:

> I became an exhibit. The walls were covered with my prints. I arranged with John Sloan, George Bellows, Ernest Watson, Albert Sterner, and others,** to appear here in public on stated evenings and make a drawing on stone. . . . John Sloan's lithograph was an artistic success: I printed an edition for him. Sterner drew a nude, with a background intended for trees. Bellows evolved a memory of the "Men's Night Class," a chaotic scene—an old stove, easels, one youth consuming a sandwich, another guzzling something out of an upturned bottle,

13

* Brown returned from London to the United States in May 1916. During the summers of 1917 and 1918 he worked extensively in lithography in his studio at Zena and completed about seventy-five stones. The dating of his journal entries during this period is sometimes unclear.

† Brown seldom made note in his journal of printing done for other artists. The principal source of information as to the dates at which he first printed for Bellows, Sterner, and other artists is thus "My Ten Years in Lithography." In that account, however, Brown does not always put dates to events, nor does he always discuss them in the order in which they took place. In "My Ten Years" he describes the demonstration at Pratt Institute before mentioning his visit to Bellows's studio, although his wording suggests that the visit came first, either in the fall of 1918 or in January of February of 1919.

‡ Bellows's lithograph, *Edith Cavell,* was drawn prior to October 1918.

§ Bolton Brown, "My Ten Years in Lithography," p. 38. Brown's phrase, "the best proof puller in the American Lithographic Company," appears to refer to George Miller. Bellows also worked with the printer Edward Kraus (or Krause), presumably while Miller served in the navy, Which of Bellows's lithographs were printed by Kraus(e), about whom little is known, has not been established. See Lauris Mason, *The Lithographs of George Bellows: A Catalogue Raisonné,* p. 24.

‖ There is no lithograph in Bellows's oeuvre titled *Gramercy Park,* nor has it been possible thus far to identify with certainty any known lithograph as the one printed by Brown on this occasion.

Brown wrote in "My Ten Years," p. 38: "Sterner showed me prints made for him by a professional printer. He was dissatisfied with them and engaged me to come for a week and print. . . . My first move was to make him throw away his yellow stones, furnished crayons, and pulled prints. He spoke enthusiastically of the quality of the impressions I handed him. . . . Behind my back he told Bellows, who repeated it to me with a chuckle, 'It's all right to be fussy, but Brown is too damned fussy.' However, we had a good time. Sterner can draw."

** The announcement of the Pratt Institute exhibition and demonstration also mentions Abel Pann, a Russian artist who had recently exhibited there.

13 John Sloan (1871–1951), *Saturday Afternoon on the Roof,* 1919. 268 x 326 [Morse 192], printed by Bolton Brown. Collection, Philadelphia Museum of Art, gift of American Federation of Arts.

* Brown's description of Bellows's image corresponds in every detail to the lithograph which Mason titles, *The Life Class, First Stone* (Mason 8). She quotes a catalogue published by the Art Institute of Chicago, *George Bellows: Paintings, Drawings and Prints* (1946) which concludes that this print, known only in one impression, "is probably one of Bellows's earliest—if not his first—lithograph." Instead, it may now be identified as the lithograph printed at Pratt Institute in 1919.

† Louis Bechtold was president of the Senefelder Litho Stone Company. The Senefelder Company continued into the 1950s to be the principal supplier of lithographic materials and equipment used in lithographic hand-printing throughout the United States.

and as a centerpiece, the nude female model, standing.* When, as usual, I put this stone on view with the others, it so shocked the sensibilities of the Institute that someone took it from its place and turned it to the wall. "I don't see what George wanted to go and do a thing like that for," said one. I called George up; he was surprised, but let the matter pass.

That winter I maintained a press, for public printing, at Mr. Bechtold's place, at 32 Greene Street.† I called it The Artists' Press, and claimed that it was the smallest and best press in New York. The plant remained there, functioning at intervals, for several seasons.[25]

BROWN AND MILLER: A CONTRAST OF PRINTERS

It would be difficult to imagine two men more different in background, temperament, and experience than Bolton Brown and George Miller. Francis Chapin put it this way: "Brown and Miller

14   Ellison Hoover (1888–1955), *George C. Miller, Lithographer,* 1949. 283 x 224, printed by George C. Miller. Collection, National Museum of American Art, Smithsonian Institution.

have only one thing in common except the magic of using a skin [leather] lithograph roller with amazing delicacy or bruising force, the 'discovery' of George Bellows. Each one would admit that throughout the lithographic process if one did exactly the opposite of the practice of the other, one would be right."[26] Chapin may overstate it but, even so, Brown and Miller had little in common as *14*   printers: in style, attitude, and approach they were polar opposites.

Miller, born in New York City on 17 June 1894, was thirty years younger than Brown (he was thus but twenty years old when he first printed for Sterner). He had little formal education, having begun work as a printer's apprentice at the age of fifteen. He came from a family of printers and thought of himself as a craftsman, not as an artist. In contrast to Brown, who had opinions on all subjects and few inhibitions as to their expression,* Miller was quiet and retiring: "easy but terse," according to Prentiss Taylor, who began

*   Examples are to be found in Brown's frequent letters to the *New York Times.* He wrote on a variety of subjects, upon all of which he held strong views: suffragists, schoolboy ethics, art exhibition practices, the discovery of a new comet, the right of self-defense, etc.

work with Miller in 1933. Taylor was but one among many artists who welcomed "the general air of acceptance" and "agreeable impersonality" of Miller's studio:

> It did not take long to learn that one of the great blessings of the place was that George made no aesthetic judgments. He did not show stylistic prejudices. He had some resentment of the vagaries of the lithotint but the creative aspects were entirely the realm of the artist. He gave the neophyte, the hack, and the well-known the best printing that could be brought from the zinc plate or the stone. He had justified pride in what he could do.[27]

Even so, throughout his years as a printer for artists, Miller never chose to put a mark of any kind on the lithographs he printed;* rarely did he sign one, and then only as a favor for an artist or a friend; Brown, on the other hand, characteristically signed in pencil the impressions he printed: "Only perfect impressions will be allowed to leave the shop," he wrote in his announcement of the Artists' Press, "and upon all such I place my signature or seal—which, in time, may come to have a value."[28]

Although Miller provided technical information, and on occasion, "advice on creative experimentation," he did not feel it was his place to intrude upon the artist; Brown, by contrast, saw his role as a full collaborator in matters both technical and aesthetic. For Miller, the printing of artists' lithographs was his business and his trade; he saw a clear division of labor between the artist and the printer. Here, as elsewhere, Brown disagreed:

> I have learned that, ideally, every artist should print his own work, because the manipulations incident thereto affect the result. If, however, for any reason he cannot himself master this somewhat exacting craft, the next best thing is that some other artist who has mastered it should print for him.
>
> I am this other artist, and now establishing a press for the purpose of doing just this work. All my life I have been a draughtsman and painter. At present I am an artist-lithographer offering to print for other artist-lithographers. . . . You may discuss your preferences and intentions with me to any extent. You may be present when the work is etched and proofs pulled if you wish. I desire and invite you to do so. However, if you do not, you are always assured that your work is in the hands of a fellow artist.[29]

Thus it was in 1919. George Miller, who had closed his lithography shop soon after the United States entered World War I in April 1917, reopened it after his release from the navy during the winter of 1918–19, at about the same time Brown established the Artists' Press. Miller soon learned that in his absence Bellows, for whatever reasons, had decided to work with Brown. This, Miller could accept—there was room for two printers in New York—but he resented what he considered to be Brown's improper and unjustified disparagement of his work. He disagreed, as well, with Brown's claim that artists' lithographs are best printed by fellow artists.

* Because George Miller, Lawrence Barrett, and other printers during the first half of the twentieth century did not choose to use a printer's mark, it is difficult—and at times impossible—to determine by whom a lithograph was printed. Seldom did printers maintain full records with respect to their work. Even published catalogues of artists' works often fail to identify the artists' printers. A consequence of these omissions is to deprive us of information which would do much to illuminate the history of lithography during this period.

Fortunately, beginning in the 1930s, some printers adopted the convention of placing an embossed mark, or chop, upon most of the editions that they printed. The first to do so may have been Grant Arnold, who began use of such a chop in 1933 or 1934 (A. G. ARNOLD, IMP.). Jacob Friedland also used a chop in the 1930s, and the practice was later adopted by Robert Blackburn, Theodore Cuno, Lynton R. Kistler, and others.

ARTISTIC AND SOCIAL CHANGE: THE ARMORY SHOW AND THE FIRST WORLD WAR

The aesthetic, social, and economic conditions that existed after the war were still less than ideal for the development of American lithography. The decade that was now coming to an end had been one of tumultuous change in the United States. In 1913, even before the war, the Armory Show had shattered the established values and complacent, genteel perceptions that until then had dominated the American art world. In retrospect, Stuart Davis called it "a non-refillable event . . . an amazing spastic convulsion in American provincial art culture."[30]

> The exhibition was really two in one, with radical foreign works imbedded in a great, somewhat anomalous mass of American art. The intention had been to show the most advanced work in this country as well as abroad, but what was considered progressive here had little relation to the revolutionary art of Europe. As a result, although our critics "thanked the Lord" for "American sanity" and "honest craftsmanship," the Europeans stole the show.[31]

And, although lithographs by Gauguin, Munch, Redon, and Vuillard were included in the exhibition, they were lost in its staggering size—about thirteen hundred works of art—and overpowered by the attention given to the then startling and unfamiliar work of the Expressionists, Fauves, and Cubists and, above all, by the scorn that was heaped upon Matisse's paintings and upon that "explosion in a shingle factory," Duchamp's *Nude Descending a Staircase*.

Among the exhibitors in the quieter American section of the Armory Show were George Bellows, Glenn Coleman, Arthur B. Davies, Stuart Davis, Childe Hassam, Walt Kuhn, Boardman Robinson, Charles Sheeler, and John Sloan. Each of these artists made lithographs at one time or another, though none exhibited lithographs in the Armory Show. Davies and Kuhn played principal roles in organization of the exhibition. Albert Sterner, Joseph Pennell, and Bolton Brown were absent—already perceived as conservatives.

If America's aesthetic complacency was shattered by the Armory Show, its social complacency was demolished by the war. Prominent among the forces of social change was the *Masses,* which proclaimed from its masthead that it was a magazine with "no respect for the respectable; frank, arrogant, impertinent, searching for true causes . . . a magazine whose final policy is to do as it pleases and conciliate nobody, not even its readers." Sloan, Bellows, and Davis were among its owner-editors; Coleman, Davies, and Robinson were among its contributors, as were several younger artists later active as lithographers, among them Adolf Dehn, William Gropper, and Reginald Marsh.

Looking back upon the wartime years, Carl Zigrosser recalled the "ferment in the air—stirrings not only of political revolt but also of social and cultural revolt. All this was reflected in the pages of the magazine. It was iconoclastic, and set out to puncture the pious hypocrises and double standards of conventional morality."[32] But the ferment provoked by the Armory Show and the war did not extend into the marketplace for prints. The established print dealers were traditional in their outlook and conservative in their politics. Their taste and the taste of their clients ran to the etchings of the

15 Albert Sterner (1863–1946), *Earth,* c. 1919. 248 x 197, printed by George C. Miller. Published by Weyhe Gallery in *Twelve Prints by Contemporary Artists.* Collection, Tamarind Institute.

British school—above all to Whistler and Haden—and the French academicians. They looked with suspicion or hostility upon the artists who had participated in the Armory Show and with even greater suspicion upon those who had been identified during the war with the *Masses* or other "communist" causes.* Before 1920 the only dealers to show modernist prints with any regularity in New York were Martin Birnbaum and Alfred Stieglitz.

It was then that Zigrosser, who before the war had worked for the influential but conservative print dealers Frederick Keppel and Company, undertook to run a print gallery for the art-book dealer, Erhard Weyhe. At Keppel's, when Zigrosser had urged the firm to exhibit the prints of the French Impressionist masters, they were thought to be too extreme; now at Weyhe's new gallery on Lexington Avenue he was given a relatively free hand to show the work he believed in.

> I now had a chance to try out the theories about "modern" prints that had not been acceptable at Keppel's. The first major exhibition that I held was of lithographs by Daumier and Gavarni on the first of November 1919. This was followed by lithographs by Odilon Redon. They were pioneering exhibitions. It is hard to realize nowadays [1975] the paucity of such material in this country at the time.[33]

* As a result of its unswerving opposition to the United States' participation in the war, the *Masses* was supressed in the summer of 1917. See Carl Zigrosser, *A World of Art and Museums,* p. 264.

16 Boardman Robinson (1876–1952), *Russia,* 1915. Transfer lithograph, 456 x 341 (sheet), probably printed by George C. Miller. Published by Weyhe Gallery in *Twelve Prints by Contemporary Artists.* Collection, Library of Congress.

Zigrosser's first project in the field of American art was the publication of a portfolio, *Twelve Prints by Contemporary American Artists,* including lithographs by Sterner, Robinson, and Maurice Sterne. Within the first three years of his association with Weyhe, he organized numerous exhibitions of prints and drawings by American artists whose work, though conservative by avant-garde European standards, was too modern to be accepted easily in New York, among them not only Bellows, Davies, Dehn, Kuhn, and Sloan, but also George O. "Pop" Hart, Marsden Hartley, John Marin, Walter Pach, Joseph Stella, and Mahonri Young.

15
16
17

ARTHUR B. DAVIES

Arthur B. Davies by this time occupied a unique position in American art. He had been exhibiting for some years in prominent galler-

17   Maurice Sterne (1877–1957), *Dancer (Dancing Figure),* c. 1919. 453 x 333, printed by George C. Miller. Published by Weyhe Gallery in *Twelve Prints by Contemporary Artists.* Collection, Library of Congress.

ies and was accepted by the conservative establishment as one of the nation's leading painters. Simultaneously, as a result of his central role in organization of the Armory Show, he had gained the respect and admiration of many younger artists, although some worried, as did Jerome Myers, that "Davies had unlocked the door to foreign art and thrown the key away. Our land of opportunity was thrown wide open to foreign art, unrestricted and triumphant; more than ever before, our great country had become a colony; more than ever before, we had become provincials."[34]

But Davies saw no national boundaries in art. He was against all forms of prejudice, open in his tastes, and a passionate collector of a diversity of art that ranged from ancient and pre-Columbian sculpture to paintings by Matisse and Picasso.[35] "He was ever ready to help a fellow artist, regardless of difference in style or opinion, and especially eager to aid the young or unknown. Together with Alfred Stieglitz, he helped to raise money in 1912 to send Marsden Hartley to Europe for the first time; and he was one of the few purchasers of Max Weber's work in the early years. . . ."[36]

Some years before, in the mid-1890s, Davies had made a series of small lithographs, but then, as his painting developed, made no more prints until 1916, when at the instigation of his friend, Walt Kuhn, he undertook a number of drypoints, some with aquatint. His interest in printmaking thus revived, he went with Zigrosser

38

one day in 1919 to meet George Miller at his workshop. He made four lithographs with Miller, then a number with Bolton Brown at his press on Greene Street. Brown told of the encounter somewhat tersely:

> One day Arthur B. Davies came in. He was a pleasant man. The drawings he wanted me to print were on zinc. I declined, on the grounds of ignorance. He rather insisted, however, saying he would take all the risks and, no matter what happened, I should be paid just the same. As I was charging a dollar a print and he wanted some hundreds I set to work and for the first and last time printed from zinc plates. Mr. Davies was satisfied with the impressions.[37]

Satisfied, Davies may have been, but there was no warmth in the relationship between the two men. Brown was then fifty-five and Davies fifty-seven; Brown, a proud, even arrogant man, confident of his abilities and accomplishments, must have felt acutely the gap between his relative obscurity as an artist and Davies's great reputation. Merrill Rueppel speculates that Davies returned to work with Miller (who after that encounter printed all of Davies's lithographs except for nine made in France) because he "was dissatisfied with Brown's work."[38] More likely, Brown poorly concealed his disdain for Davies's drawings and for his wish to use zinc.* In any event, Davies clearly preferred the professional, nonjudgmental attitude that Miller brought to his printing.

In retrospect, few of Davies's lithographs stand up well to the test of time. Many show the "want of conviction" that caused critics to regard Davies's later work as "the last gasp of nineteenth century romanticism . . . grown precious and sickly."[39] Despite his active and extended work in the medium between 1919 and 1921, a period in which he completed more than fifty lithographs, including some in color, Davies failed to achieve the freshness and vitality of his earlier drypoints and aquatints. The color lithographs, tender and delicate, are at times reminiscent of those made by Whistler in Paris. In some cases, Davies would first print an image in black and white, hand-color a few impressions, and only later decide to print an edition in color (*Golden Girl,* for example, was first printed in black in 1920; the color edition was not completed until 1923).

BELLOWS AND BROWN

Just as Davies worked well with Miller, Bellows worked well with Brown. Bellows drew almost constantly on stone during January, February, and March of 1921 and Brown came regularly to the Nineteenth Street studio to proof and print the many editions that Bellows completed then.† Bellows's daughter Jean describes their collaboration:

> I clearly recall the huge printing press in the balcony over-looking the studio . . . and Mr. Brown working at printing the lithographs. The floor was always strewn with discarded prints—which Anne and I would grab to use for drawing paper! I also remember posing for several of the portraits—drawn on large white, thick stones—among the clutter of that upstairs balcony. . . .

18

* Miller printed regularly from zinc. Brown was a passionate advocate of "crayonstone" (he wrote it always as one word) and argued strongly against any substitute. That Brown held Davies's work in low regard is suggested by his omission of any mention of it in his article, "Prints and Their Makers." A caption to one of the illustrations published with that article speaks of the "five American lithographers and etchers whom Bolton Brown classes as important: John W. Winkler, Bellows, Sterner, Sloan, and himself."

† Mason states that Bellows completed fifty-nine lithographs during the first three months of 1921. Brown's journal provides disappointingly scant information about his collaboration with Bellows. On 2 May 1921 he made this entry: "I acted as stone-preparer, crayon-maker, etcher and printer for upwards of fifty lithographic drawings by George Bellows. For the first time, I kept no written records." (Journal 10, page 524.)

Although the collaboration between Bellows and Brown was most active during the winters Brown spent in New York, they also worked together in Woodstock. Brown's journal (p. 557) gives evidence that at least one lithograph, *Introducing Georges Carpentier* (Mason 98), was completed there. Others thought to have been done in 1921 may have been made in a previous working session in April 1920, to which Brown makes reference in his journal.

18   Arthur B. Davies (1862–1928), *Twelve Men,* 1921. 383 x 345 [Price 84], printed by George C. Miller. Collection, Tamarind Institute.

> Bolton Brown was almost like a member of the household—or, at least a part of the house—as he seemed to be always there—working the big press.[40]

To meet Bellows's requirements, Brown made up batches of specially formulated crayons that permitted the artist to achieve the greatest possible tonal range, from a delicate and silky fineness to a deep and velvety black. Bellows himself grained the stones. "By this time," Brown wrote, *19*

> we had worked so much together that each knew precisely what his part was and how to play it. We made a gorgeous team. George's prints are real lithographs, not mere variations from some other material. Not that they resemble the early sort of lithograph, done with the sticky commercial crayons and in the convention of 1830. What I mean is that he worked on stone with an instinctive

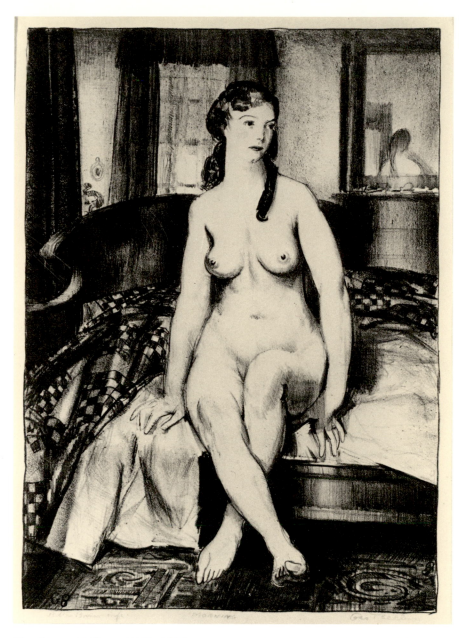

19   George Bellows (1882–1925), *Morning, Nude on Bed* (second stone), 1921.
280 x 200 [Mason 77], printed by Bolton Brown. Collection, Tamarind Institute.

appreciation of exactly its own nature and used the new
crayons with a joy that was an actual avidity. The literary
critics do not know it, naturally, but the work I printed
for George Bellows constitutes an entirely new chapter in
lithography; nothing like it was ever done before, nor
could have been, for none of his forerunners had the same
materials.[41]

Brown particularly applauded Bellows's lithographs when they were
at their most direct:

His best pieces are by no means those huge affairs, such as
prizefights, where he was largely the mere illustrator, but
certain simple and utterly charming rambles on stone,
more often than not with his wife or daughter . . . as
subject. It was in some of these that he touched his
high-water mark . . . and very high the highest was, too.[42]

Certainly it seems true that Bellows was at his best when he drew on the stone directly from nature, in portraits of his family and friends, or studies of the model in his studio, as in *Morning, Nude on Bed,* a fresh and radiant drawing which was one of the artist's favorites among the lithographs completed in 1921. By comparison, the illustrations which Bellows composed for *The Wind Bloweth* and *Men Like Gods* (novels by Donn Byrne and H. G. Wells, respectively) now seem dated and artificial, as do many of the more ambitious compositions of 1923–24, in which Bellows's fascination with Jay Hambidge's theories of dynamic symmetry is all too evident. But whatever the failings of the more calculated works, Bellows's lithographs of the early 1920s reveal a total mastery of the medium by both artist and printer.

BROWN IN WOODSTOCK

Brown kept busy during the winter months as a printer in New York. He printed for Sterner and again for Sloan; in 1920 he printed Rockwell Kent's first lithograph. But although Brown took satisfaction (and financial benefit) from such work, he looked forward each year to spring and to the opportunity to resume his work as an artist in Woodstock. He usually left the city in April or May and remained in Woodstock through late fall. "My housekeeper went away and got married. I became a hermit. It is not a good life, but it had in my case some advantages. It left me completely free of any household arrangements other than those related to my work."[43] And work, Brown did, completing more than fifty drawings on stone during an average summer. Occasionally, he was visited by other artists. Bellows regularly spent his summers in Woodstock beginning in 1920. Brown tried his best to interest Sterner in coming there as well, and at one point Sterner thought seriously that he might "come up to Woodstock and stay four months and 'wallow in lithography,' but he never did."[44]

Brown also printed for his close friend of many years, George William Eggers, a sensitive artist who had been a student at Byrdcliffe *21* long before. Though now diverted by his responsibilities at the Art Institute of Chicago, where he was director from 1916 to 1921, Eggers shared Brown's passion for lithography, and they often worked together. Eggers himself became a competent printer under Brown's tutelage, although many of his finest lithographs were printed by Brown in the early 1920s.

In the summer of 1921, John Taylor Arms, already well known *20* for his etchings of architectural subjects, spent two weeks with Brown "to study lithography in his Woodstock studio and in the lovely country that surrounds it. "It was an experience I shall never forget," Arms wrote:

> We arose early and went forth to draw in the fields, taking with us a wheelbarrow (which could be up-ended and converted into an excellent easel) those stones whose properties . . . Bolton Brown expounded so ardently. . . . We drew in sunshine and in pouring rain, the latter made possible by the fact that, among the literally hundreds of lithographic crayons which Bolton invented and made, were a number with which the artist might draw, with perfect facility, on a stone placed under

20   John Taylor Arms (1887–1953), *New York Skyline,* 1921. 171 x 127, printed by Bolton Brown. Collection, Tamarind Institute.

21   George William Eggers (1883–1958), *Daylight Savings,* 1924. 358 x 331, printed by Bolton Brown. Collection, University of New Mexico Art Museum, gift of Bernard Karpel.

water. We came home in the twilight . . . and always, before we went to bed, we sat and talked for a while about the great lithographers of the past, whom we knew and loved as if they were living today. . . . Those days and nights were perhaps the most strenuous, and certainly among the richest, of my professional life.[45]

In his journal, Brown recorded in great detail his experiments in the formulation of lithographic crayons. Inside the cover of the eleventh volume of the journal he inscribed a sentence from John Ruskin: "All art, working with given materials, must propose to itself the objects which, with those materials, are most perfectly attainable." Brown believed as Ruskin did that the materials were paramount: the stone itself and the crayon that drew on it—*crayonstone,* a total unity.

But perhaps, as one looks back at Brown's work as an artist, he was too much the prisoner of principle, too often confined by his knowledge, skills, and convictions. "Emotionally," Eggers observed, "Brown was the direct heir of the New England poets and the painters of the Hudson River School:

> The things he loved with an extraordinary love were the things all these men loved: the exquisite detail which fringes the big forms of the Highlands . . . the subtle variety of lights that hangs in the Catskills. . . . [But] constituted as he was, Brown's art was inevitably the result of a struggle between two forces: the beloved material of the scene and the stern, exacting science of the craft. He could not be blithe about it as many of his contemporaries were and ride the one and forget the other; he must break the two recalcitrants to the single yoke.[46]

Eggers perfectly characterizes the genuine dilemma of the artist who is also the printer, for all too often art and the craft of printing refuse to mix. This is clearly seen in Brown's work, particularly in the more "studied" pieces in which he set out to demonstrate his incredible control of silvery tonalities or the satin-smooth line of a newly invented crayon. Weakest among his works are those subjects to which he returned upon the basis of earlier drawings or sketches to reconstruct a fading memory: often the high ranges of the Sierra Nevada which he had left so long before.* Strongest are the works in which his experience of the subject is direct and immediate. Often these were lithographs made on days when he would draw directly on a stone that he had trundled out into the countryside near his studio at Zena on the outskirts of Woodstock. Such lithographs were made, in Brown's words, with "the incontrovertible and unescapable guidance of the materials themselves. A medium is like Mary's little lamb: if you love it, it will love you."[47]

This love of medium, of craft, of the simple pleasure of surfacing a fine stone, was combined in Brown's best work with his intense powers of close visual observation. His artistic influences derived from the plein-air and Luminist traditions of nineteenth-century landscape painting in Europe and America, from his strong interest in Japanese prints, from a softened version of the School of Pont-Aven, and, certainly not least, from the aesthetic attitudes of the Pre-Raphaelite painters. He drew sparkling, unassuming landscapes; stormy mountain vistas; and tender, nostalgic fantasies, as when in

*   It was Brown's customary practice, unusual among artists, to return again and again to earlier subjects. He restated some of his favorite subjects at intervals, sometimes with little change in composition, but only with the differences resulting from use of a newly developed crayon or technique of execution.

44

22 Bolton Brown (1864–1936), *Lake Ladies*, 1924. 215 x 305, printed by the
artist. Private collection.

22 1924, at the age of sixty, he drew the lovely *Lake Ladies,* seated beside
a forest stream, the light of the sun filtering through the trees onto
the soft young skin. It is in such works that one senses most clearly
Brown's essentially romantic temperament. His crayon caresses the
girls' bodies in a way that it is at once innocent and remote, yet full
of erotic longing.

> These lithographs are the result of these attitudes and ex-
> periences against a background of early disciplines and
> memories of landscape drawing—trees, leaves, clouds,
> earth, rocks, stones, water, air, light—in terms of human
> design—the whole natural world was mine. I love it all:
> I always shall. I still sit around outdoors trying to bring
> into terms of human design something of the fascination
> of the way a tree trunk grows, the land lies, the foliage
> hangs and shatters the glittering sunshine, the fall of
> shadows in fantastic patterns, the gleam of the white
> body of the bather among the dark rocks—these are my
> simple pleasures. In these I shall live and die.[48]

NOTES

1 See Ralph Flint, *Albert Sterner, His Life and His Art,* and Martin Birnbaum, "Albert Sterner's Lithographs."

2 Flint, *Albert Sterner,* p. 15.

3 Flint's discussion of the Sterner exhibitions at the Berlin Photographic Company is confused (pp. 26–27). The Cortissoz review, which mentions the 1913 Armory Show, necessarily refers to Sterner's exhibition of 1915, not to the exhibition of 1911.

4 Flint, *Albert Sterner,* p. 28.

5 Elizabeth Robins Pennell, "Introduction," in Louis A. Wuerth, *Catalogue of the Lithographs of Joseph Pennell,* p. xvii.

6 Joseph Pennell, quoted in ibid., p. xiii.

7 Ibid., p. xv, xviii.

8 Ibid., p. xix.

9 A new English translation of Senefelder was published in 1911 under the title, *The Invention of Lithography* (New York: Fuchs & Lang Manufacturing Co.), thus making it readily available to American readers; also available to artists and lithographers were Charles Hullmandel, *The Art of Drawing on Stone* (London: Hullmandel & Ackermann, 1824); W. D. Richmond, *The Grammar of Lithography* (London: Wyman & Sons, 1878); and David Cumming, *Handbook of Lithography* (London: Adam & Charles Black, 1904).

10 See Peter Morse, *John Sloan's Prints: A Catalogue Raisonné of the Etchings, Lithographs and Posters.*

11 John Sloan's diary, 27 May 1908, quoted by Morse, ibid, p. 160.

12 Lauris Mason, *The Lithographs of George Bellows: A Catalogue Raisonné,* p. 24.

13 For accounts of Miller's early career, see Janet Flint, *George Miller and American Lithography;* and Alfred P. Maurice, "George C. Miller and Son, Lithographic Printers to Artists since 1917."

14 Bolton Brown, "My Ten Years in Lithography," p. 9.

15 Brown could refer either to Joseph Pennell, *Lithography,* published in 1912, or, more likely, to the revised version of *Lithography and Lithographers,* written by Pennell in collaboration with his wife Elizabeth Robins Pennell, and published in 1915.

16 Brown, "My Ten Years," pp. 9–10.

17 The journal in which Brown recorded his lithographs and technical studies, together with occasional observations on other subjects is in twelve volumes, containing a total of 814 pages (hereafter cited as Journal).

After Brown's death in 1936, this journal and other papers were given by Lucy Fletcher Brown to John Taylor Arms, who later wrote that they remained in his library "awaiting a proper repository where they will do the most good." Subsequently, the Brown papers were acquired by Ward and Mariam Coffin Canaday (Bryn Mawr '06) and were then given to the Bryn Mawr College Library as a part of the John Taylor Arms Collection. The Brown papers were not separately catalogued, with the result that for many years their location has remained unknown. In addition to the journal describing his work in lithography, the Arms collection contains other Brown notebooks, miscellaneous papers, and the typescript of an unpublished book, "Lithography Since Whistler," which Brown completed in 1933. The autobiographical essay, "My Ten Years in Lithography," is one section of this book.

18 *New York Times,* 9 March 1922, p. 16.

19 For further information about Brown's early life, see Clinton Adams, "Bolton Brown, Artist-Lithographer."

20 See Bolton Brown, "What Should an Art School Be?" *Overland Monthly,* ser. 2, 19 (March 1892): 301–17.

21 For a description of the rise and fall of the Byrdcliffe art colony, see Karal Ann Marling, *Woodstock: An American Art Colony.* In her account

of the first meeting of Whitehead and Brown, Marling incorrectly assumed that Brown's "work in lithography was well known" at that time. Brown's own account of the Byrdcliffe days is given in his "Early Days at Woodstock." See also Clinton Adams, *The Woodstock Ambience, 1917–1939.*

22   These notes (18 September 1907 to 1 August 1910) are in a handwritten journal, designated "Book A" in the Arms collection at Bryn Mawr College. Brown published a book based on this research: *The Painter's Palette and How to Master It* (New York: Baker & Taylor, 1913).

23   Brown, Journal, p. 57 (entry dated 29 August 1915).

24   Brown, "My Ten Years," p. 38.

25   Brown, "My Ten Years," p. 17.

26   Francis Chapin, unpublished lecture notes, 1937. Chapin papers, Archives of American Art, Smithsonian Institution, reel 875, frame 750.

27   Prentiss Taylor, quoted in Janet Flint, *George Miller and American Lithography,* unpaged.

28   Bolton Brown, "Lithography: Advertisement of The Artists' Press" (New York: May 1919).

29   Ibid.

30   *Munson-Williams-Proctor Institute, 1913 Armory Show: 50th Anniversary Exhibition, 1963,* statement by Stuart Davis, p. 95.

31   Ibid. Essay by Milton Brown, p. 36.

32   Carl Zigrosser, *A World of Art and Museums,* p. 273.

33   Ibid., p. 37.

34   Jerome Myers, *Artist in Manhattan,* p. 36.

35   For information about the breadth of Davies's art collection, see Merrill C. Rueppel, *The Graphic Art of Arthur B. Davies and John Sloan,* pp. 21–23.

36   Ibid., p. 19.

37   Brown, "My Ten Years," p. 19. An entry in Brown's journal, p. 478, indicates that his work with Davies was in process during April 1920.

38   Rueppel, *Davies and Sloan,* p. 123.

39   Suzanne LaFollette, *Art in America, from Colonial Times to the Present Day,* p. 322.

40   Jean Bellows Booth to Clinton Adams, 8 August 1978.

41   Brown, "My Ten Years," p. 39.

42   Brown, "Prints and Their Makers," p. 2.

43   Brown, "My Ten Years," p. 47.

44   Ibid., p. 39.

45   John Taylor Arms, "Bolton Brown: The Artist and the Man," in Kleeman Galleries, *Catalogue of Lithographs by Bolton Brown,* unpaged.

46   George William Eggers, "A Brief Essay on Bolton Brown," in Woodstock Art Gallery, *Memorial Exhibition of the Works of Bolton Brown,* unpaged.

47   Bolton Brown. *Catalogue of an Exhibition of Lithographs by Bolton Brown, with an Introduction and Notes on the Prints Exhibited by the Artist,* p. 4.

48   Ibid.

2 · The 1920s: New York and Woodstock

JOSEPH PENNELL AT THE ART STUDENTS LEAGUE

23 Joseph Pennell was invited to teach etching at the Art Students League in 1921. Except among the small circle of artists and printers who practiced it, lithography had still not freed itself from the stigma of commercialism. Pennell, however, was its ardent advocate, and in 1922 he organized the league's first lithography workshop.[1] Unfortunately, Pennell's advocacy of lithography was far stronger than his knowledge of it; and although he had drawn many lithographs—principally on transfer paper—he had little knowledge of the finer points of the printer's craft.

As Pennell was then working with George Miller, he naturally sought Miller's help and asked many technical questions at the press. Burr Miller tells this story: "One day my father said to Pennell, 'Well, you wrote a book on lithography. What are you asking these questions for?' Pennell reached over and grabbed the handle of the press and put his nose right up in front of my father and said, 'You know damn well I don't know a thing about lithography!'"[2]

Despite this confession to Miller, Pennell enjoyed a popular (if undeserved) reputation as the principal American authority on artists' lithography, a reputation which greatly irritated Bolton Brown. Unwilling to recognize the quality of Pennell's work in transfer lithography—a method which Brown rejected as much inferior to his beloved *crayonstone*—Brown took pleasure in debunking what he considered to be the Pennell myth. He tells of a public "lithographic evening" at the Anderson Gallery in February 1923:

> Every seat in the hall was taken, at a dollar each, and many
> turned away. On the platform was Bellows, lecturing,
> and me at (not *by* but *at*) the press. Before the audience
> I etched and pulled perfect proofs of, first a stone by
> Bellows and then one by Sterner. Then Pennell's turn

49

23   Childe Hassam (1859–1935), *Portrait of Joseph Pennell,* 1917. Transfer lithograph, 405 x 305 [Griffith 3], printer unknown. Collection, University of New Mexico Art Museum.

came. As he does not draw on stone he handed me a drawing on paper. When I was getting ready to transfer it, he began to tell me how. I turned to him and said, "Mr. Pennell, I shall be very glad to have you do this transferring; will you not do it for yourself?" "Oh, no, no," he said, backing away. "Well, in that case, please allow me to do it," I said, and forthwith transferred, etched, and pulled a perfect proof.[3]

As a solution to his problems with the lithography class, Pennell first made arrangements with the league so that Miller might aid him in the transferring and "founting" of the students' work.* For this, Miller was to receive the sum of fifteen dollars for a three-hour morning session.[4] Ultimately, however, Pennell needed someone who could devote greater time to teaching than Miller was willing to do, and in 1923 he turned the lithography classes over to Charles W. Locke, a talented young artist-lithographer who had recently come

* Pennell wrote of "transferring and founting of the students' work" in a letter to Miller, 7 February 1923. *Founting* is not a term commonly used to describe the chemical processing of the stone or plate, although the term *fountain solution* is used to describe a mixture of slightly acidified gum and water. See Garo Antreasian and Clinton Adams, *The Tamarind Book of Lithography: Art and Techniques,* pp. 112 and 160–61.

50

24 Yasuo Kuniyoshi (1889–1953), *Milking the Cow,* 1923. 219 x 262 [Davis 1], printed by George C. Miller. Collection, Philadelphia Museum of Art, gift of Mrs. Alice Newton Osborn.

to New York after study of lithography at the Mechanics Ohio Institute in Cincinnati.* Pennell henceforward was content to teach the etching classes, a medium in which he had genuine expertise, and certainly the medium in which, as an artist, he had done his most effective work.

Miller's willingness to print for Pennell even briefly at the League reflected his need for money. Although his workshop was surviving, it was always on the brink of financial disaster. His prices were low—much lower than Brown's—but even so, many artists found it difficult to pay them, and there was still no broad interest in artists' lithography. Miller did his best to stimulate such interest in a variety of ways, sometimes, as Brown had earlier done at Pratt Institute, through public demonstrations of the process.

One such event, in 1922, was arranged by Juliana Force, then director of the Whitney Studio Club. Miller prepared zinc plates which "were given to Louis Bouché, Edmund Duffy, Niles Spencer, and Yasuo Kuniyoshi, and the drawings they made were then printed during the demonstration. Kuniyoshi produced his first lithograph that evening, *Milking the Cow,* and for years thereafter continued to

24

* Locke was first at the League as a student, and was monitor in Pennell's classes. He had, however, made a number of lithographs in Cincinnati before going to New York, and at the time he enrolled at the league he was more experienced than Pennell as a lithographic printer.

make lithographs, many of them printed by Miller."[5] But despite such efforts and an increasing number of artist-clients, Miller's financial problems persisted, and at the time of his marriage to Carrie Scharsmith in 1923 Miller was forced to think seriously about closing his business and returning to work as a commercial printer (he still had his union card). When Davies heard of this, he did his best to dissuade Miller from such thoughts: he would make the printer a gift of several hundred dollars in order that his business might go on.

> The gift was refused by Miller who would not take what he considered to be charity. Davies, however, persisted and convinced Miller that the money was not charity but an advance against the many prints he planned to do in the future. The money, which paid for the rent for a number of months, enabled Miller to keep the shop open. With an increasing amount of work coming in, the shop and Miller's printing services to artists was saved.[6]

GEORGE MILLER IN VERMONT

Though Brown and Miller differed in many ways, both were avid outdoorsmen. As an artist Brown loved nature for what it revealed to him; as a sportsman Miller loved it for the pleasures it provided. And as it was technically impossible to do fine printing in the heat and humidity of their workshops during the summer months, both men found good reason to leave the city. Brown took refuge in Woodstock, and Miller found his perfect place in Burlington, Vermont, on the shores of Lake Champlain.

An excellent carpenter and craftsman, Miller had built a substantial boat in his backyard—a thirty-three-foot cabin cruiser—and this he now moved to the lake. As his fortunes improved in the later 1920s, he joined the Lake Champlain Yacht Club and went up to Vermont as often as possible, living at first on his boat and then at a home he and Carrie had built at Apple Tree Point near Burlington. His son Burr was born in 1928.

Beginning in 1933, Miller taught summer classes in lithography at the art school Wayman Adams had established in Elizabethtown, New York.* Burr Miller recalls those wonderful summers when, still a young boy, he would accompany his father to the lake. They would live all summer on the boat:

> It was a fantastic boat. . . . We'd stay in Burlington . . . then every Monday morning we'd take the boat down to Westport, New York, which is the nearest port on the lake to Elizabethtown . . . and someone from the school would pick [my father] up on the boat. He would teach Mondays, Tuesdays, and Wednesdays in Elizabethtown, [then on] Thursday morning we'd go back to Burlington for the weekend.[7]

Miller soon found many friends among the members of the Yacht Club. "He fell in love with Burlington [and] finally bought some land up there. He got a nine-hundred dollar bonus from the government for being a World War I veteran, and he invested in some land—it was probably the best investment he ever made: about a half-an-acre of shorefront property."[8]

Miller did not form many close friendships with his artist-clients: his personal life and his work as a lithographer were for the most

*Maltby Sykes, who later became an influential teacher of lithography at Auburn University, was a student at Adams's school in 1934–35 and again in 1937. He describes Miller's classes there: "Adams liked to make lithographs himself, and he wanted his painting students to have an opportunity to try lithography. . . . An arrangement was made whereby Adams would furnish studio space at his school and Miller would provide lithographic printing services and instruction." Sykes became Miller's assistant: "Miller etched and printed all the stones himself, and my job was mainly to relieve him of menial tasks. . . . Printing was a team effort between printer and assistant. I usually dampened the stone, put down the tympan and cranked the press. Miller inked the image, put down the paper and lifted the print."

Sykes also tells of Miller's printing for artists to whom he shipped stones: "After putting an image on the stone, the artist shipped it back to Miller for etching and proving. Proofs were mailed to the artist, and when these were okayed, Miller went ahead with the edition. . . . Occasionally, [the stones] would come in with instructions for Miller to make additions to the image. I recall one prominent artist who returned a stone with the image completed except for the sky. Attached was a note reading "please wipe in a sky like the last one you did for me." George grumbled, but stretched silk over his finger, pressed it against a stick of rubbing ink, then wiped in a sky with two or three strokes. It looked just right! Occasionally, stones arrived which had been blacked in completely with a crayon, then scraped out from dark to light to form the image. Miller treated such techniques as special projects and the outcome was partly the result of his judgment and esthetic sensibility. I mention these incidents because there has been some controversy as to whether printers should have any part in creating or adjusting the artist's image. The fact is that, in many cases, the printer cannot avoid being part of the image!" (Maltby Sykes, "Recollections of a Lithographile," pp. 1–2, 4.)

25

25   Wayman Adams (1883–1959), *Clinging Vine,* c. 1930. 246 x 197, probably printed by George C. Miller. Collection, University of Iowa Museum of Art, gift of the artist.

part kept separate. But there were exceptions, foremost among them Rockwell Kent, who lived nearby at an impressive home on the other side of Lake Champlain. It became a common practice for George and Burr Miller to take the ferry across the lake to visit him. Burr remembers "swimming in Kent's pool while Kent and my father were playing tennis. . . . which was kind of odd, because they were probably at opposite ends on the political spectrum. [But] they had an admiration for one another as craftsmen."[9]

This admiration for fine craftsmanship was an essential attribute of the professional printer, yet for Miller—as for Brown—it was also a limitation. While both could respond to the demands of artists who—like Sterner, Bellows, Davies, or Sloan—brought traditional skills and training to their work, they found it difficult to accept the blunt directness of the early modernists. Brown even more than Miller was rigid in his attitudes and opinions. He would do things only in one way: his way; there were no alternatives; and while he was characteristically polite and civil in personal relationships, he was easily perceived to be arrogant and obstinate: a "prickly" man, as Alf Evers, the Woodstock historian, was to call him.

Given this temperament, it is not surprising that Brown's financial difficulties were even greater than Miller's. He was soon forced to accept the fact that while he "was having an interesting time and no doubt doing useful missionary work" at his workshop in the city, it was not a financial success. "Expenses, all along, were only with

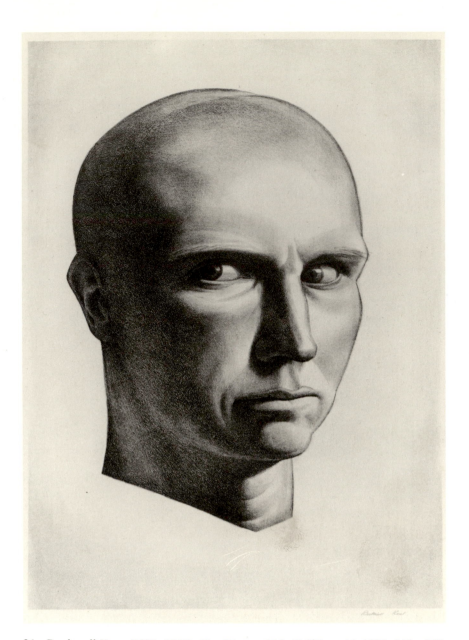

26 Rockwell Kent (1881–1971), *Das Ding an Sich (Self Portrait),* 1934. 340 x 247 [Jones 104], printed by George C. Miller. Collection, Tamarind Institute.

* Weber appears to have made six lithographs during this first encounter with the medium, all of them figure compositions and all drawn in a manner incorporating fauvist and cubist elements. See Daryl F. Rubenstein, *Max Weber: A Catalogue Raisonné of His Graphic Work.*

† Arthur Wesley Dow, who had worked in Pont-Aven in the late 1880s, had been influenced by the ideas of Gauguin and Fenollosa. More than other American artist-teachers of the early twentieth century, Dow emphasized formal, pictorial concerns in his teaching.

‡ Although Weber made no lithographs in Paris, it is possible that his interest in the medium may initially have been stimulated by the powerful series of lithographs which Matisse had completed a few years earlier—lithographs which Weber would almost certainly have seen either in the Matisse's studio or in exhibitions.

difficulty kept below the intake."[10] His prices appeared to be exorbitant and few artists found it easy to work with him.

AMERICAN MODERNISM: PARIS AND NEW YORK

Among the few modernist lithographs made in the United States before 1930, perhaps the first are those made by Max Weber between 1916 and 1925.* Weber's interest in modernist concepts had first been stimulated while a student of Arthur Wesley Dow at Pratt Institute between 1898 and 1900.† Then in 1905 he had gone to Paris and while there had formed friendships with other Americans abroad—Abraham Walkowitz, Marsden Hartley, Alfred Maurer, and Patrick Henry Bruce; through Gertrude and Sarah Stein he had met Matisse, and in 1909 he had organized a class that Matisse had taught.‡

Soon after returning to the United States in 1909, Weber met Arthur B. Davies, who became his strong supporter. Weber later said that it was Davies who led him to make his first lithographs.

27 Max Weber (1881–1961), *Mirror,* 1928. 206 x 327 [Rubenstein 80], probably printed by J. E. Rosenthal. Collection, Tamarind Institute.

Drawn on zinc plates and printed in small editions, these somewhat experimental prints have little technical polish. But while the raw vigor of Weber's lithographs would doubtless have appalled Bolton Brown, had he come across them, they nonetheless demonstrated a lithographic dimension not before seen in America.*

Though Weber exhibited regularly in New York after his return from Paris, there was little market for his work. "During the 1920s he was quoted as glad to receive $10 to $20 for a drawing. It is no wonder that he responded to the interest of his friend [William] Zorach and visited the newly formed Downtown Gallery of Edith Halpert and Berthe K. Goldsmith."[11]

Like Carl Zigrosser at the Weyhe Gallery, Edith Halpert actively encouraged her artists to make prints. In 1927 she became the sponsor of the annual exhibitions of the Society of American Print Makers,† and among the artists she represented were many of those who had been most active as printmakers during the 1920s, among them Davies, George Biddle, Ernest Fiene, Yasuo Kuniyoshi, and Louis Lozowick. During the summer of 1928, in response to Halpert's invitation to have a first one-man exhibition of his lithographs at her gallery that fall, Max Weber produced a new series of thirty-four black-and-white lithographs, diverse in style and subject matter, which served as a recapitulation of his work of earlier years. Most were transfer lithographs and all were printed from zinc plates.[12]

The critical attention given to Bellows's lithographs during the 1920s had assisted greatly in developing a market for lithographs by American artists, with the result that as more lithographs were made, other printers began to work for artists. Most were men who, like Miller, had backgrounds as lithographic proof printers in commercial establishments. Among them was J. E. Rosenthal, who printed at least some (and perhaps all) of the lithographs Weber made in

27

* We do not know who printed Weber's early lithographs. Although it is reasonable to assume that Davies might have led Weber to Miller's shop, there is no evidence that he did so, and the lithographs do not have the look of Miller's printing.

† "The Society of American Print Makers [was] a group of etchers and lithographers who broke away from the jury system to establish a society to exhibit prints chosen by artists. The society of twelve artists invited twenty-four artists yearly to submit four prints each for an exhibition . . . at Edith Halpert's Downtown Gallery. . . ." (Rubenstein, *Max Weber,* p. 75.)

Given the presence on the selection committees of such artists as Peggy Bacon, Ernest Fiene, "Pop" Hart, Stefan Hirsch, Walt Kuhn, Yasuo Kuniyoshi, Charles Locke, Reginald Marsh, and Kenneth Hayes Miller, it is surprising to look back at the reviews received by their exhibitions: "The organization was started by the radical wing of American print makers, and still remains radical." (*Art Digest,* 15 December 1931, p. 22.) The following year, under the headline, "Critics Both Praise and Scold 'Left Wing' Print Makers," the *Art Digest* reported that "Carlyle Burrows in the *Herald Tribune* spoke of the 'adventursome and progressive spirit' of the exhibition, 'extremely varied both as regards subject and means.' Margaret Breuning in the *Post* complained that the exhibition showed what "the standard of having no standards can effect in an art organization.'" (*Art Digest,* 15 December 1932, p. 20.)

1928.[13] Rosenthal is known also to have printed for George "Pop" Hart and Walt Kuhn, and as late as 1939 still operated a workshop on Broadway in New York.* Also active as a printer during the twenties and thirties was Jacob "Jack" Friedland, who printed for Nicolai Cikovsky, Adolf Dehn, Louis Lozowick, and Moses and Raphael Soyer, among others.†

BOLTON BROWN IN CHICAGO

In the winter of 1923–24, Bolton Brown worked actively with George Bellows and produced a large number of fine editions on the artist's press at his Nineteenth Street studio. These were to be Bellows's last lithographs. In January 1925, he suffered a severe attack of appendicitis and, following surgery, he died of peritonitis at the age of forty-two.‡ It is as though Bellow's death also signaled the end of Brown's work as a creative artist-lithographer, for while he continued to work during the summer of that year, it was not with his earlier intensity. The entries in his journal became sporadic, sketchy, and disorganized, then came abruptly to a stop.§

But if after 1925 Brown seldom again made lithographs, he remained much occupied with lithography. He set out to write a book in which he would summarize his experience in the medium. "Books telling how to make an etching have been published in considerable numbers," he wrote, "but of works intended to enable an artist to make a lithograph, with his own hands, there exists not one."[14] He determined to fill that gap, and in the process produced a detailed account of the lithographic process. In the writing of the book he drew heavily upon the technical notes he had entered in his journal over a period of more than ten years, and he wrote with the aim "to offer this book to my fellow-artists knowing that none can get out of lithography all there is in it unless he does his own printing—and does it fully understanding the resources of the craft."[15]

It is likely that Brown had substantially completed his book by 1926 or 1927. He then sought over a period of time to find a publisher either in England or in the United States. He was not successful in doing so, for even those who were interested in the manuscript, Erhard Weyhe among them, felt that the number of prospective purchasers of so technical a treatise (upon a still little-used art) was too small to justify its publication.[16] Time passed. Brown then received a letter from Robert B. Harshe, director of the Art Institute of Chicago, who wished to visit him in Woodstock:

> It was arranged and presently this gentleman and his son
> drove into my maple-shaded door yard. We sat on the
> front porch, talking and looking at prints and at the
> manuscript of the book. It was, he said, his wish to have
> one series of the Scammon lectures devoted to
> lithography and he wanted me to be the man that gave
> that series. I was reluctant, because, as I pointed out, I
> had not enough to say, to a general audience, to occupy
> the six hours of the Scammon lectures. He steadily
> overrode me on that point, and in the end a tentative
> agreement was reached that I was to give the lectures.[17]

It was agreed, furthermore, that Brown's book on lithography would be printed in place of the lectures he would actually deliver. This agreement was reached, however, only after an argument about

* The following description of Rosenthal's workshop appears in *Printmakers: New Techniques, Markets, History*, p. 11: "In addition to George Miller, J. E. Rosenthal, a proof printer, has offered to pull three or four proofs on a hand offset press for $2. For an additional $5 he will print an edition of 25. Mr. Rosenthal has done work for Max Weber, Pop Hart and others. The artist must furnish his own zinc plate and paper. The plate should be 16 x 22 inches. A two-inch margin must be left all around the impression. Mr. Rosenthal can be reached at 413 Broadway, New York, N.Y."

† Friedland operated a lithographic workshop into the 1930s and was for a time located at 55 East Ninth Street. Later he was active as a printer for the Federal Art Project. "Friedland was a strange man," Raphael Soyer says, "he could have had a lot of work printing for artists. . . . Later he started an art school. He had a letterhead, an office, a girl, all ready to go—then didn't go on." (Interview with Soyer, 4 May 1979.)

‡ A puzzling entry appears in the twelfth volume of Brown's journal, p. 746, at the top of a nearly empty page: "Was successful with Bellows stones when etched." The previous entry, p. 745, is dated 28 October 1925, more than eight months after Bellows's death. The entry on page 746 is not clear as to whether the stones to which Brown refers were stones that had not previously been etched (and hence stones not printed in Bellows's lifetime) or whether they were stones that had been stored after proofing. Brown gives too little information to permit a clear understanding of the posthumous printing of the Bellows stones.

§ Following the undated entry on p. 746 (made at some time after the entry of 28 October 1925), Brown made no further entries until 30 July 1932, p. 747. The last stone mentioned by serial number is *Woodstock Valley*, 1932 (Brown 608). Apparently he undertook no more than fourteen stones during the eight-year period, 1925–32, This contrasts sharply with his high productivity prior to 1925. The title Brown gave to his manuscript, "My Ten Years in Lithography," clearly indicates that he considered 1925 to have been the end to the work he had begun in London in 1915.

28 Walt Kuhn (1880–1949), *Hulda,* c. 1929. Transfer lithograph, 405 x 235, probably printed by J. E. Rosenthal. Collection, Tamarind Institute.

money and, more important to Brown, about his right to control the editing of the book. Harshe was concerned about what he felt to be an undue attack upon Joseph Pennell, a former Scammon lecturer.* Brown was equally concerned that his manuscript be published unchanged.

> What I had written was not an "attack" [on Pennell], but merely a correct statement of an important fact, namely the fact that, "When Mr. Pennell writes that 'you can do anything on paper that you can do on stone,' he writes what is not true." If this statement were true it would be a very important truth, but as it is not true it becomes simply an important lie. . . . Pennell had been playing the devil with lithography for years and I was the man that knew it, and it was not right that I should be choked off from saying so.[18]

Ultimately, in order to secure the book's publication, Brown was forced to give in. "Under clear and strong protest, I formally signed

* Harshe's sensitivity to Brown's criticism of Pennell may have been conditioned by Pennell's death on 23 April 1926.

over to the Institute the right to edit, that is, to change, my book in any way it pleased."[19] Much as Brown resented this, when he received the galley proofs he found that they were essentially unchanged from what he had written. "The words 'not true' were translated into 'mistakenly,' and that was all. The whole fuss had been about nothing."[20]

Brown delivered the Scammon lectures early in 1929 and agreed to return to Chicago in February 1930 to instruct a special course in lithography at the School of the Art Institute. While Brown was in Chicago for the class, the Albert Roullier Gallery arranged to hold an exhibition of his lithographs, an exhibition which proved to be financially the most successful of his career.*

Lithography was not then a part of the curriculum at the Art Institute, although etching had been taught there for some time. It was thus necessary to equip a small workshop to accommodate the class that Brown would instruct:†

> Brown conducted the class with great vigor and enthusiasm. He was very specific about the technical aspects of lithography. . . . Members of the class made their own crayons and tusche. . . . The mixture had to be cooked for an extended period and it let off a heavy, sweet smell which penetrated throughout the area. . . . Because of this, it had to be cooked on Saturdays when there was no school in session in that part of the building.‡

Among the members of the small class, Brown chose William J. Dickerson, a student from Wichita, Kansas, to fill the role of monitor, and when Brown's stay was over, Dickerson was offered a position on the school's staff to become the continuing instructor in lithography. Dickerson decided, however, to return to Kansas and to accept a position at the newly formed school of the Wichita Art Association, and Francis Chapin, also a student in Brown's class, was appointed to teach lithography in Chicago.§ Thus, as a direct result of Brown's brief workshop-class, lithographic instruction in the art of lithography—as distinct from the practice of lithography in the commercial trade—was begun in the Midwest.

Only slightly later, classes in lithography were established at Iowa State University in Ames through the efforts of S. Dale Phillips. While attempting to learn the process for himself, he read Brown's book soon after its publication:

> "I wrote to Brown asking if he could teach me. He answered saying if I could get two other students he would teach us for $100 each. It turned out that I couldn't find two others, so I appeared at his door one day in 1932 and he took me as his only student. . . . My impressions of Bolton Brown were not the same after working directly with him as they had been after merely reading his book. I had expected an egotistical, temperamental man whose self-esteem might shorten my stay. Just the opposite was true. During our collaboration he claimed that he had learned as much from his students as his students had learned from him."[21]

As they worked together, Phillips came to have a high regard for Brown both as a "supreme craftsman [and as] a friendly, creative person." When he went back to Iowa after three months of in-

---

*   Brown later wrote: "The newspapers wrote up the show most favorably, one even classing it as 'the most important that the gallery had given in half-a-dozen years.' I brought my students over from the institute and walked them about to see the application of the principles I was teaching them. And last, if not least, we sold prints. Of the *Moonlight,* priced at forty dollars, ten impressions were sold, and of *Sylvia,* at the same figure, six were sold, and of the others enough to bring the total receipts to nearly fifteen hundred dollars." (Brown, "My Ten Years," p. 53.)

†   In 1920, in the sixth of his Scammon lectures, Pennell had congratulated George William Eggers, then director of the Art Institute of Chicago, on his intention to establish a "School of Lithography" (Joseph Pennell, *The Graphic Arts: Modern Men and Modern Methods,* p. 276). Even so, when Brown went to Chicago, lithography was not taught at the School of the Art Institute.

‡   Merlin F. Pollock remembers the class as having had no more than eight students, among them Pollock, Francis Chapin, William Dickerson, Davenport Griffin, and Theodore Roszak (Pollock to Adams, 6 July 1981).

§   Chapin was far from secure in his knowledge of the lithographic process when in the fall of 1930 he became the Art Institute's instructor in lithography. He wrote to his friend Dickerson for help: "After leaving the science of Brown lithography in the lurch by not coming back, you at least owe the old technical and artistic alma mater the following dope (and damn quick): (1) How the devil do you etch a zinc? (kindly answer fully) . . . (2) Ditto aluminum (but not so important). I don't care much about the process personally but as the Art factory is paying me to explain it, I ought to know how. . . .

"Have you smutted up your part of Wichita making crayons? I have not the heart to make them indoors any more so I am having the hotplate moved into a court and may stir up some batches near room 210 tomorrow." (Chapin to Dickerson, 22 October 1930).

Subsequently, Chapin acquired a firm command of the medium and continued to teach lithography in Chicago, at the Ox Bow summer school, and at the John Herron School in Indianapolis. He acquired a press and printed his own lithographs, working increasingly in color during his later years. He introduced his friend Ivan Albright to lithography, but aside from this instance rarely printed for other artists (Interview, Vivian Chapin, 28 February 1980).

29

29 Francis Chapin (1899–1965), *Chicago Towers,* c. 1935. 396 x 284, printed by the artist. Collection, Tamarind Institute.

tensive work in Brown's studio, Phillips had confidence in his abilities: "I could print lithographs. I understood the process."[22]

For the next ten years Phillips continued to teach lithography at Iowa State University and to print for local and visiting artists—among them Jean Charlot—until 1943 when he left the art faculty and became an engineer.*

GRANT ARNOLD: NEW YORK AND WOODSTOCK

In New York, few students had been attracted to Charles Locke's lithography classes at the Art Students League.† In 1928, in an effort to stimulate enrollment, the league made an offer of reduced tuition: an offer which proved irresistible to Grant Arnold, who had come to New York that fall to study drawing and painting with Boardman Robinson and Max Weber. The league's tuition for a class was then twenty dollars a month. Lithography was now to be offered at one half that price, and the students who enrolled would also be given

* Phillips set up a lithography workshop in Ames, Iowa, in 1932 after his study with Brown. "Artists began coming and it soon developed with teaching and printing together [that] I had little time for my own work." He developed a number of special lithographic crayons, including a form of lithographic charcoal used by Charlot and other artists. (Dale Phillips, "Lithographic Charcoal"). While on leave of absence from Iowa State University in 1940, Phillips established a lithographic workshop at San Jose State University in California. In 1943, Phillips undertook a new occupation as an engineer: "I then sold or gave away all my litho equipment. What I couldn't give away was hauled to the city dump." (Letter, Phillips to Adams, 15 April 1978.)

† Notable among Locke's students was John Steuart Curry, who made his first lithographs at the Art Students League in 1927.

59

"the privilege of going into any of the painting and drawing studios any time they felt like it to work from the model."[23]

Arnold found such a cut-rate bargain impossible to refuse. Although he worked nights in the newspaper room at the public library, he was always hard up for money; a ten-dollar cut in tuition meant a lot to him, whatever the class might be. So when his month with Weber ended, he enrolled in lithography, and quickly found out that the lowered tuition had attracted no flood of students. On the first day he went to the studio, only two were to be found there, working on "slabs of stone." The studio, which was on an upper floor of the League's building, was equipped with two Fuchs & Lang presses and, at one end of the room, racks for many small stones, "stored like books, vertically, the larger ones below, the smaller ones above."[24]

When Charles Locke appeared the following day, Arnold was taught how to grain stones, one against the other, how to bevel their edges, and how to determine that they were level. That night he did a drawing and the next day he traced it onto a stone. In the following weeks, lithography became his obsession. He worked almost constantly in the studio, with the result that he soon became the person to whom other students turned for technical information or assistance. "I practically lived for lithography," Arnold recalls. "And as time went on, while I was still a student, the other students would ask me to etch and prove up their stones for them. By the time the end of the year came around, I was doing more work for the other students, just for the experience, than I was doing for myself."[25]

In the spring of 1929, Arnold Blanch came down from Woodstock to confer with Locke. The Woodstock Artists Association had acquired a lithograph press, and now sought someone who might serve as a printer for the local artists during the summer months.* Locke suggested Grant Arnold.

Together, Blanch and Arnold went up to Woodstock. They visited Hervey White at his house on Maverick Road, where White greeted Arnold warmly and offered use of one of his small cottages as a summer residence. Woodstock's fame as an art colony was then at its height, and it was for Arnold a wonderful opportunity to meet and print for well-known artists and to participate in a life he had never before encountered.

Blanch then took him to see the ill-equipped lithography workshop in the Artists Association building on the village green. "It was down in the basement, with a flagstone floor and unfinished walls. There was a Fuchs & Lang press, some tables, and a few stones. The improvised graining sink didn't even have running water. You got that out of the brook behind the building. It was all pretty primitive."[26] Even so, Arnold agreed to sign on for the summer. The arrangement that he made with the Artists Association permitted him to use the shop—such as it was—rent free. The association provided an initial stock of printing supplies, and the artists for whom he printed paid him for his work. His first artist-client was John Carroll, a friend of Dehn and Kuniyoshi:

> After Carroll was through, artists came in one right after another. My prices were modest, but the supplies were inexpensive, and I was able to finish the summer with $400.00, after all the expenses had been paid. I kept a signed print of each artist's work, and when the summer was over I had enough to show twenty-five matted prints in the League's gallery that fall.[27]

30

* Much earlier, in 1902 or 1903, it had been suggested that the Byrdcliffe art colony acquire a lithograph press to be used under the direction of John Duncan, a visiting Scottish artist, but Ralph Whitehead had turned the suggestion down. He considered lithography to be "too commercial." Sometime during the 1920s Hervey White brought a press to the Maverick, which—aside from Brown's—may have been the first in the community; late in that decade a press was also installed at the Woodstock Artists Association, perhaps at the initiative of Konrad Cramer, but as the artists who worked on these presses lacked knowledge of printing techniques, the result was more often frustration than satisfaction. See Clinton Adams, *The Woodstock Ambience, 1917–1939.*

John Carroll

John Carroll

30   John Carroll (1892–1959), *Head,* c. 1930. 250 x 195, printed by Grant
Arnold. The Grant Arnold Collection of Fine Prints, Tyler Art Gallery, State
University of New York, Oswego.

Arnold's exhibition of the lithographs he had printed in Woodstock
led directly to his appointment as the first staff printer at the Art
Students League. Now, for the first time, the lithography classes
began to attract students. Charles Locke taught them "how to draw
on the stones, and if some students wanted to learn how to print,
he'd teach them that too." Arnold printed at one press; students were
free to use the other. "Later on," Arnold says, "after I left the League,
the time came that students didn't do any printing at all. All the printing was done by the printer."[28]

   This collaborative approach to lithography served to make the
medium much more attractive to the league's students, most of whom
thought of themselves as painters, not as printmakers, and from that
time on, under a succession of printers, lithography classes were well
established. In addition to printing for the students, Arnold was able
as staff printer to provide printing services to the artists who taught
classes. While at the league, he printed editions for Thomas Hart

31 Thomas Hart Benton (1889–1975), *Coming 'Round the Mountain,* 1931.
284 x 216 [Fath 4], printed by Grant Arnold. The Grant Arnold Collection
of Fine Prints, Tyler Art Gallery, State University of New York, Oswego.

Benton, Aaron Bohrod, Adolf Dehn, Don Freeman, and many *31*
others.

Again in 1931, Arnold spent the summer in Woodstock, printing lithographs on the Artists Association press, this time accompanied by his young wife, Jenny, whom he had married earlier that
year. He made very little money, but he had a marvelous time:

> My wife and I, we had been New Yorkers all our lives. But
> that year we just got fed up with it—getting up early in
> the morning, riding the subway, going to
> mid-Manhattan, and changing to another line. I didn't
> mind it so much because I was working at the League,
> but Jenny . . . was cooped up in an office all day. . . .[29]

It was the depth of the depression and hardly a time for financial
gambles. Even so, attracted by the quality of life in Woodstock, they
decided to make the move. Arnold quit his job as printer at the league.

32 Grant Arnold (b. 1904), *Street Scene,* 1939. 227 x 351, printed by the artist.
The Grant Arnold Collection of Fine Prints, Tyler Art Gallery, State University
of New York, Oswego.

Woodstock, after all, was the home of many artists, and there was
the prospect that a number of these artists might be attracted to
lithography: a sufficient number, perhaps, to provide a printer with
a living.

A living it produced, although always precarious. Even so, it
was work that Arnold loved, and between work for the resident artists and the summer visitors, he had enough to do. Among those
for whom he printed in Woodstock were Wayman Adams, Arnold
and Lucile Blanch, Clarence Bolton, Ross Braught, Francis Chapin,
Konrad Cramer, Karl Fortess, Marion Greenwood, Rosella Hartman, Yasuo Kuniyoshi, John McClellan, Paul Meltsner, and Elizabeth Bush Woicescke.

ARNOLD AND BROWN

Bolton Brown was now back in Woodstock and his book was in
print. Arnold, who had read the book with interest and admiration,
had also been impressed by the quality of Brown's printing, particularly in the George Bellows lithographs which he had studied in New
York. He wanted to meet Brown, but he knew that he rarely left
his house to come into the village. Not once since Arnold had been
in Woodstock had Brown visited the lithography workshop at the
Artists Association.

> I mentioned to some of the Maverick artists that I would
> like to go and see him, [but] they discouraged me. They

told me he was a hard-bitten old crank, that he was a very jealous man and would be envious of a young printer. "He'll shut the door in your face," they said. Even Hervey White, who had known him so long, was a bit dubious about the reception I would get.[30]

Despite this discouragement, Grant and Jenny Arnold decided to seek Brown out. As Arnold recalls their meeting, Brown could not have been more gracious. "We walked over to his place in Zena. He opened the door and I introduced myself. Brown said, 'I know who you are. I've been wondering why you haven't come to see me before this.' "[31]

The two printers talked for some time, about lithography and about the methods Brown used in printing. Brown told Arnold about his experiments in making new kinds of crayons. His daughter Marian soon came from her house nearby to bring Brown his dinner of rice and milk.* She made some tea for the Arnolds. Then, after Brown had eaten, he opened portfolios and showed them his prints, explaining how they had been made. On subsequent visits, the Arnolds visited Brown's studio. In it, although now rarely used, were his two presses, the gearless press he had bought in England and a Fuchs & Lang press—his "American press," as he called it—upon which he had printed many editions for Bellows, Eggers, Albert Barker, and the other artists with whom he had collaborated. There were now no more than a dozen stones. The graining table did not have running water.

Brown told the Arnolds that although an occasional artist might yet come to him as a student,† he was no longer interested in making lithographs. With the publication of his book he had reached his high point in the medium. Now in his late sixties, Brown was no longer in good health and "the effort needed to lift, grain, set the stone on the press and print an edition was getting too much for his strength."[32] Even so, he felt quite able to express his views. When Arnold showed Brown some of his own lithographs, Brown admitted that they were well printed, allowing as how the stones had been drawn with those awful, sticky Korn's crayons. He gave Arnold samples of his own crayons, in which he took great pride, and admonished him to try them.

32

BROWN IN WOODSTOCK: THE LATER YEARS

After the 1930 exhibition in Chicago, Brown had little success in sale of his work. He gained a meager income through the sale of his ceramics, fired in the kiln he had installed in his studio in Zena, and augmented that during the summers by providing instruction in lithography to an occasional student. Brown worked with Dale Phillips during the summer of 1932 and also printed for Albert W. Barker, a professor of archeology, who had come to lithography late in his career. A fine and sensitive draftsman, Barker's luminous landscapes had much in common with Brown's; their work was based in a similar response to nature and a common love of crayonstone. Brown willingly shared his knowledge of the printer's art as he and Barker worked together at the press. They formed a strong—though curiously formal—friendship which they maintained throughout Brown's later years.[33]

33

* Following the Byrdcliffe years, strains developed between Brown and his wife Lucy, and they separated before he went to England. His daughter Marian, now married to Lloyd Woods, provided care for her father during his years of poverty and illness in the 1930s. See Clinton Adams, "Bolton Brown, Artist-Lithographer."

† There appear to have been few such students. Among those who later worked actively in lithography are Albert W. Barker, S. Dale Phillips, and Theodore "Ted" Wahl. Others mentioned by Brown in "My Ten Years" (p. 40) are Anna Frost and Mary Bonner.

33 Albert W. Barker (1874–1947), *The Stronghold,* c. 1932. 261 x 357, printed
by the artist. Collection, Tamarind Institute.

In the following summer, Brown played host to another young
artist-printer from the Midwest, Theodore "Ted" Wahl. Wahl had
begun his work in lithography while a student of Ross Braught at
the Kansas City Art Institute. A gifted but eccentric artist, Braught
had made his first lithographs with Grant Arnold in Woodstock before moving to Kansas City as a teacher of painting. Though Braught
had little technical knowledge of lithography, he stimulated interest
in the medium among the students at the Art Institute, and as a consequence of this interest a press was purchased and a course in lithography was begun. Necessarily, given his limited experience, Braught's
approach to printing was essentially that of trial and error, with heavy
reliance upon information to be found in books. It was not long be-
34 fore young Wahl came to serve as the printer of Braught's lithographs:
formalized landscape compositions and symbolic figures in an art
deco style.* Wahl's ability developed rapidly and in his senior year
at the Art Institute he received a gold medal for a lithograph entered
in a regional exhibition.

When Bolton Brown's book appeared in 1930, Braught and his
students were quick to seize upon it as a source of information. Later,
after Wahl had moved to the East, he made up his mind to study

* It is Braught's memory that his landscape
composition *Mako Sica* (an Indian name for the
Badlands of South Dakota) was printed in 1935
either by Ted Wahl or William McKim, who
later became instructor in lithography at the
Kansas City Art Institute (Braught to Adams,
22 November 1982). McKim was not yet in
Kansas City in 1935. Although Wahl was then
living in New York, he may have printed for
Braught during a visit to Kansas City.

* Braught and Brown did not meet during Braught's years in Woodstock. It is Wahl's best memory that he worked with Brown in the summer of 1933, but he considers it possible that it may have been in 1934.

† Further testimony to Brown's poverty is provided by his correspondence with Carl Zigrosser: "I am offering to sell my land up here, also *all* of my 'personal property'—including all my prints—to the end that, free from care, I may sail untroubled seas toward the declining sun." (Brown to Zigrosser, 10 August 1933, Carl Zigrosser papers, University of Pennsylvania Library.)

In his reply (17 August 1933, ibid.), Zigrosser expressed doubt that "Mr. Weyhe would be interested in your proposal. . . . It might be difficult to persuade him to make an investment of several thousand dollars in works of art." Such a price would certainly have been reasonable, however, as at that time Brown's 'personal property' included his printer's proofs of the many lithographs he had printed for George Bellows. (As *A Stag at Sharkey's* was printed by George Miller, it is possible that the print Brown offered to Wahl may have been another of the prizefight subjects, most of which Brown had printed.)

‡ Brown's unpublished book, "Lithography since Whistler," was written in five sections: "Senefelder Brings the Art into Existence," "The Old Lithography," "My Ten Years in Lithography," "Pennellism and the Pennells," and "Conclusion." Only one of these five sections, "My Ten Years in Lithography," has been published. (See also Chapter 1, note 17, above.)

with Brown. Braught offered Wahl use of the small house which he still maintained on the Zena road in Woodstock and early in the summer of 1933, Wahl sought Brown out.*

Brown greeted him with a proposal: If Wahl would spend half days clearing the weeds from Brown's property, they would spend the other half days in the studio. And it was on this basis that Wahl spent two months with Brown in Woodstock. "Brown was very hard up. He didn't have enough to eat. Once he gave me fifteen cents to go get a can of sardines for him."[34] Wahl also recalls that Brown tried to sell him for fifteen dollars an impression of George Bellows's *A Stag at Sharkey's,* which Wahl did not buy, as he did not have the money.†

Though he no longer cared to make lithographs, Brown completed work on another book in 1933, a history of lithography since Whistler, containing an account of his own ten years in lithography and a scathing chapter, "Pennellism and the Pennells," in which he set out once and for all to contest the notion that transfer lithography—as practiced by Pennell—could ever be more than a mere shadow of his beloved crayonstone. The book was not published in his lifetime.‡

Too proud to accept relief, Brown lived alone and in poverty. His health was failing; his work, he felt, was accomplished. To escape the often bitter Woodstock winters he drove each fall to South Carolina, staying en route with Albert Barker in New Jersey. In South Carolina he continued to draw, and wrote his sister Ellen that the drawings he had made there were "the best I have done in this medium."[35] He formed a friendship with a young South Carolina woman, Naomi McCracken, who accompanied him to Woodstock in the summer of 1934.

Brown's health grew steadily worse, and as it did, he prepared for death as he prepared for everything: methodically and carefully. He made final, explanatory entries in his journals and placed them in the care of John Taylor Arms.[36] He arranged for a large boulder to be taken from the Sawkill River to the artists' cemetery in Woodstock, where, despite his illness, he personally saw to its placement and carved his name and the dates into the rock. It would rest on his grave. He summoned Victor Lasher, the local undertaker, and instructed him. When he died, Brown insisted, there was to be no fuss; he was to be rolled in a blanket and taken to his grave. Grant Arnold remembers that "Victor agreed to do as [Brown] wished and then, like all of us in the Depression years, they dickered about the price. Bolton had very little money and he didn't want to saddle his wife and daughter with a large funeral bill. He didn't even want a hearse. 'Just put me in the back of your pick up truck, take me to the cemetery and put me in.' "[37]

Summer moved to its end, and on 15 September 1936 Bolton Brown died at the age of seventy-one. But if he truly wished to be carted off, unceremoniously and somewhat surreptitiously, that was not to be. True, a casket was not used. "He was buried at sundown yesterday," the *New York Times* reported, "on a pallet made of white birch by his son-in-law, Lloyd Woods of Zena."[38] The funeral was an echo and reminder of Woodstock's early days. Hervey White, with whom Brown had shared the Byrdcliffe adventure, was among the pallbearers; the others were his long-time artist friends, John Carlsen, Carl S. Linden, and Henry Lee McFee. A large gathering

34 Ross Braught (b. 1898), *Mako Sica,* c. 1935. 324 x 380, probably printed by
Ted Wahl. Study collection, Kansas City Art Institute.

was at the graveside and, though Lucy Brown knew that Bolton
would not have wanted it, a minister said a service.

At the time of Brown's death, Grant and Jenny Arnold had been
in New York City, trying to arrange for sale of some of Arnold's
lithographs. Shortly after their return to Woodstock, they received
an invitation from Lucy Brown. Would Arnold be interested, she
asked, in buying Brown's Fuchs & Lang press and his lithograph
stones? Arnold quickly agreed. He had never had a press of his own,
and as it was all but impossible to work in the basement shop at the
Artists Association during severe Woodstock winters, he had been
forced to abandon his work for months at a time. The Arnolds moved
Brown's press to their small house and set it up in the living room,
carefully reconditioning and painting it. It was for Arnold not only
a useful and handsome piece of equipment but one that had strong
meaning for him as a remembrance of Bolton Brown.*

EMIL GANSO

The presses owned by Brown, Arnold, and the Artists Association
were no longer the only presses in Woodstock. Several artists who
had established residence in Woodstock were by now able to do their
own printing, among them Emil Ganso, who had first visited the
Catskill village in 1926 as a student in the summer school of the Art
Students League.

* Grant Arnold printed on Brown's press until he went to Washington in 1940. Arnold did
not return to printing after World War II. He
completed a degree at Syracuse University and
became a teacher. "I dismantled the press and
stored it. I had the hope that I could set it up
again to do some lithographs, but the pressure
of teaching in a high school was too much."
Eventually, after moving several times, he sold
the press to a dealer in used equipment. See Clinton Adams, "Grant Arnold, Lithographer: New
York and Woodstock, 1928 to 1940," pp.
42–43.

35   Emil Ganso (1895–1941), *Model,* c. 1937. 432 x 192, printed by the artist. Collection, Tamarind Institute.

Ganso had come to the United States in 1912 at the age of seventeen and had worked as a baker—a trade he had learned in his native Germany—while attending classes at the National Academy in New York. Although for a while (around 1917) he shared a studio with Jan Matulka on Sixth Avenue, he appears to have had little interest in modernist art. He was still making his living as a baker when in 1924 he gathered together a large number of his drawings, prints, and paintings and took them to Carl Zigrosser at the Weyhe Gallery. As a consequence of that visit, he was given his first one-man exhibition in April 1925 and a continuing stipend from the gallery—a stipend which at last permitted him to devote himself entirely to his art. Shortly thereafter, possibly at Matulka's suggestion, he enrolled in Eugene Fitsch's night class at the Art Students League.

Ganso's dedication to craftsmanship was extreme, with the result, as Joann Moser observes, that he insisted on control of every aspect of his work:

68

In printmaking, he mixed his own inks, prepared his own grounds, and insisted on pulling his own proofs and printing the entire edition. This was no small feat, especially for lithography, in which the complexities of printing discouraged all but the most skillful craftsmen. . . .

He often printed for his friends as well as for himself. Leonard Bocour, a friend who helped Ganso with lithographic printing in the early 1930s, remembers an instance when he and Ganso were printing an edition of one hundred lithographs for Albert Heckman. . . . Toward midnight the hundredth proof was pulled, and both Ganso and Bocour agreed that it was the most beautiful. "Now we can begin the edition!" declared Ganso, as he threw away the first ninety-nine proofs.[39]

Ganso had by this time formed a close friendship with Jules Pascin, whom he had met in Woodstock in 1927. During the fall of 1927 Pascin for a while shared Ganso's New York studio, and in 1928 Ganso traveled to Paris to visit him.

35

For a while Ganso's art was strongly influenced by Pascin. His voluptuous, half-dressed models in languid, suggestive poses rendered with sure, quick lines and delicate shading, were at times almost indistinguishable from the work of Pascin . . . [although in contrast to the] enervated expressions of Pascin's nudes, Ganso's figures were robust, healthy, solid, and vital.[40]

Ganso continued to live and work in Woodstock, often printing lithographs for other artists—his friends Konrad Cramer and Yasuo Kuniyoshi among them—until 1939, when he accepted appointments to teach first as Carnegie Artist-in-Residence at Lawrence College in Wisconsin and then at the University of Iowa.

NOTES

1   For further information about Pennell's classes at the League, see *One Hundred Prints by 100 Artists of the Art Students League of New York, 1875–1975,* foreword by Judith Goldman.

2   Interview with Burr Miller, 4 May 1979.

3   Bolton Brown, "Pennellism and the Pennells," p. 28, in "Lithography Since Whistler."

4   Pennell to Miller, 7 February 1923. Miller files.

5   Janet Flint, *George Miller and American Lithography,* unpaged.

6   Alfred P. Maurice, "George C. Miller and Son, Lithographic Printers to Artists Since 1917," p. 136.

7   Burr Miller interview.

8   Ibid.

9   Ibid.

10 Bolton Brown, "My Ten Years in Lithography," p. 36.

11 Rubenstein, *Max Weber,* p. 75.

12 Ibid., p. 84.

13 Ibid., p. 90.

14 Bolton Brown, *Lithography for Artists,* p. 1.

15 Ibid., p. 2.

16 See Bolton Brown, "My Ten Years in Lithography," p. 46.

17 Ibid.

18 Brown, "My Ten Years," p. 51.

19 Ibid.

20 Ibid.

21 S. Dale Phillips, "Bolton Brown: A Reminiscence," p. 34.

22 Ibid., p. 35.

23 Arnold, quoted in Clinton Adams, "Grant Arnold, Lithographer: New York and Woodstock, 1928 to 1940," p. 38.

24 Ibid.

25 Ibid., p. 39.

26 Ibid.

27 Ibid.

28 Ibid., p. 40.

29 Ibid., p. 40–41.

30 Ibid., p. 41.

31 Ibid.

32 Ibid., p. 42.

33 The manuscript of an unpublished book by Albert W. Barker, "Print-Maker's Lithography," and a series of letters written by Barker and Brown between 1926 and 1935 have joined the Arms and Brown papers in the Bryn Mawr College Library, gift of Elizabeth Barker and Agnes Barker Davis.

34 Theodore Wahl, tape-recorded interview, 8 May 1979.

35 Brown, quoted by Ellen Coit Elliott in a letter to H. C. Reed, 26 September 1950 (Department of Manuscripts & University Archives, Cornell University Libraries, No. 1580).

36 Brown to Albert Barker, 3 June 1935, Barker papers, Bryn Mawr College Library.

37 Grant Arnold, "Woodstock: The Everlasting Hills," unpublished manuscript, p. 121.

38 *New York Times,* 17 September 1936, p. 23.

39 Joann Moser, *The Graphic Art of Emil Ganso,* p. 5–6. Heckman was himself an accomplished lithographer. See p. 124.

40 Ibid., p. 7.

3 · The 1920s: Europe and America

ADOLF DEHN

Many of the artists who made lithographs during the 1920s with the New York printers had come to the city from abroad: Max Weber; Nicolai Cikovsky; Louis Lozowick; Isaac, Moses, and Raphael Soyer; and Abraham Walkowitz had all been born in eastern Europe. Adolf Dehn, by contrast, had come to the city from the American Midwest.* Dehn was born in Waterville, Minnesota, in 1895; he had studied art at the Minneapolis Art Institute, had spent the wartime years as a conscientious objector, and then, in 1919, had received a scholarship for study at the Art Students League.

Dehn quickly made himself at home in the New York art world, where he met Boardman Robinson and saw his illustrations accepted by the *Masses*. Through Robinson he met George Miller and made his first lithographs with Miller in 1920. "[He] was praised by the [New York] *Herald* for his 'scenes of the city, the kaleidoscope of cabarets and night life, of war profiteers and beggars, presented with an unusual mastery of form and space, and the utmost economy of line.' "[1] He existed somehow by "tending furnaces, painting furniture, being night watchman for an electric burglar patrol. But starving in New York was not so different from starving in Minneapolis [where he had first attended art school]."[2] So like others before him— and with the thought that he might be able "to starve more elegantly" in Europe—Dehn went abroad. Soon, however, with the postwar inflation, he found himself not much better off than before:

> Often he did not know where his next meal would come from. He sold occasional drawings, and with them and a few commissions and sales to magazines he eked out a meager existence. . . . In 1922 he wrote from Vienna: "I expect to go to Berlin permanently around Xmas, for it is very alive. . . . Germany is cheaper than Austria, too. It is very costly here now. I have had to cut out one damn luxury after another so that I'm almost down to my

* He was born Adolph Dehn, but later changed the spelling to Adolf.

American basis. Disgusting isn't it? My expenditures are limited to $30.00 per month."[3]

But however limited were Dehn's funds, he still managed somehow to make lithographs and to pay the printers' bills. First in Vienna and Berlin, then in Paris, he drew incessantly. He spent the winter of 1927–28 in a studio on the rue Vercingetorix, borrowed from his artist-friend, Andrée Ruellan, from whence he wrote to her:

> I have done over the first two lithos for my folio and they look good to me. Also I have several others done—one of which was a fluke and it has come out. It has a texture of Chinese silk paintings and I think I am on the road to something important—and sellable! Soon you will be able to see some of these for I shall send them to Weyhe. —I am more excited than ever about it all.[4]

Carl Zigrosser's response, however, was less than enthusiastic when he received the prints at Weyhe's:

> You are right in sensing a certain lack of sympathy with your recent work, an attitude that is shared by such old friends as Wanda [Gág] and John Flanagan.* I was hoping to have a heart-to-heart with you in Paris, but the fates decreed otherwise. When I speak of sympathy I do not mean that I have lost faith in you as an artist—not by a long shot† . . . but there are certain superficial manifestations that are not to my taste. I think for the time being you are on the wrong road or track. As you probably suspect, this track in my estimation is Paris and the atmosphere of cafés and boulevards in general.[5]

It is likely, however, that Zigrosser was disturbed not only by the European flavor of Dehn's lithographs but also by their subject matter. Included in the Parisian series were many satiric subjects which—though usually jovial in spirit—were at times as sharply barbed as the prints of Dehn's German friend, George Grosz. *Madame and the Girls,* one of the more than seventy-five lithographs drawn by Dehn and printed by Edmond Desjobert during 1928, is typical; and although Zigrosser was impressed by the evident virtuosity of such prints, he much preferred Dehn's landscapes to the scenes in Parisian brothels.

When an exhibition of the 1928 lithographs opened at the Weyhe Gallery in February 1929, Dehn took comfort in praise from other quarters. "Show opens today," he wrote to Andrée Ruellan. "I can't say how it will go. Bolton Brown just complimented me saying I *had carried lithography further than anyone else.*"[6]

36

AMERICANS ABROAD: THE ATELIER DESJOBERT

Throughout the 1920s large numbers of American writers and artists went to Europe—as Weber and Dehn had done—not only to enjoy "the easy life of the cafés and boulevards, the bohemian's paradise," but also to seek out an intellectual and aesthetic stimulation that they could not find at home. Characteristically, they got to Europe by stages, first having come to New York—as Dehn had come from Minnesota—in the hope that in the city they could escape the constraints of the provinces, meet other artists, and, at the very

*   Dehn, Wanda Gág, John Flanagan, Arnold and Lucile Blanch, Henry Gottlieb, and Elizabeth Olds were all students together at the Minneapolis Art Institute.

†   Despite the misgivings stated to Dehn in this letter, Zigrosser continued publicly to support Dehn's work. He later referred to Dehn as "the Debussy of the lithograph. . . . He works on stone as if it were a sheet of paper. He has no one approach. He works with pen or crayon, with point or flat edge, with wash and splatter and rubbed tones, he rubs and picks and scratches and scrapes . . . whatever is at hand. He caresses or attacks the stone according to his mood." (Carl Zigrosser, *The Artist in America, Twenty-four Close-ups of Contemporary Printmakers,* pp. 18, 22.)

36   Adolf Dehn (1895–1968), *Madam and the Girls,* 1928. 228 x 268 [Lumsdaine
L.72], printed at the Atelier Desjobert. Collection, Tamarind Institute.

least, enjoy a cultural ambience which (they thought) New York
alone could provide.

But artists who moved from smaller towns and cities to New
York during the 1920s and 1930s were frequently disappointed, for
New York was in many ways no more than a larger and more complex version of rural America. Richard McKinzie notes that in its
response to modernist art "New York City, despite its cosmopoli-
tan posturing, was in fact as provincial as Dodge City or Kokomo."[7]
McKinzie overstates the point for effect but, even so, the stimulus
that the Armory Show had provided was now far distant, and there
was little interest in contemporary art. Modernism was supported by
a few art dealers—notable among them Stephan Bourgeois, Charles
Daniel, Edith Halpert, J. B. Neumann, and Alfred Stieglitz—but
the market for American art of an even mildly progressive or adventurous character remained small. Nor was it easy, as Dore Ashton
observes, to experience in New York the stimulating contacts with
other artists which the new arrival sought:

> Many of the artists who gravitated to Europe during the
> nineteen-twenties and early thirties have remarked upon

the complete absence of an artistic milieu in the United States, and above all, on the absence of verbal exchange and camaraderie among the painters. Paul Burlin once tartly commented that there was a total lack of discourse among artists in the first quarter of the century; and Carl Holty confirmed this observation, recalling that he went all the way to Germany in 1925 to study with Hans Hofmann in order to satisfy his need for contact.[8]

The ready availability of lithographic printers in France and Germany attracted many of the American expatriate artists to lithography, although the work that they did in Europe characteristically received little attention at home. Marsden Hartley, for example, made two fine series of lithographs in Europe, a series of still life subjects in 1923 and a group of mountain landscapes in 1933–34, but they were little known at the time. Few of the artists who exhibited at Alfred Stieglitz's New York gallery made prints, and among the Stieglitz group, only John Marin's etchings received significant attention. Arthur Dove, Charles Demuth, and Georgia O'Keeffe appear never to have been attracted to lithography:* "Long ago," O'Keeffe says, "when I might have made lithographs, there was no place to do it.† Once someone tried to interest me in it. I was given some metal plates—shiny metal plates—but I didn't do anything with them. By the time I could really work at it, it had gone out of my head."[9]

Throughout the 1920s, however, American artists continued to make lithographs in Europe, many of them working in collaboration with the printers of Paris, among them Edmond Desjobert. More than other printers, Desjobert made the Americans welcome, and as a consequence his workshop became a central point at which they might meet and work together.

It was at Desjobert's in 1928 that Yasuo Kuniyoshi made his first lithographs on stone. As a matter of convenience, his earlier work—all with George Miller—had been done on zinc plates, but now, as he drew for the first time on stone, he found the surface to be "much more sympathetic" than that of the metal plates. Kuniyoshi developed his compositions directly on the stone:

> I prefer not to trace [my sketch] on the stone. Instead I outline my conception . . . with a red conté crayon. Then I go over it with a lithographic pencil using a very light line. I use a #5 lithograph pencil sharpened to a very fine point. Darks are built up gradually by working over and over again. . . . There is very little scratching, no rubbing and no tricks. I believe in straight lithography.[10]

Although Kuniyoshi employed the purest of classical crayon-stone techniques to achieve an immensely sensuous range of "colors" in his black-and-white lithographs, other artists—including Adolf Dehn—delighted in Desjobert's willingness to undertake complex manipulations of the stone, including methods that George Miller most likely would have discouraged. There was an attractive, silky richness to Desjobert's printing, which reflected in part his style as a printer, in part the character of the French inks with which he printed, and in part his use of *chine collé:* a technique which makes possible the greatest of subtleties.‡ For Kuniyoshi as for Dehn such subtleties were critical, and the twenty-four lithographs he made that year with Desjobert remain among his finest works in the medium. Later,

* Although Dove at one time in his early career as an illustrator had sufficient interest in lithography to purchase a press (the press he later lent to John Sloan) he appears to have made no lithographs.

† Many years later, in November 1963, when there was "a place to do it," O'Keeffe was invited to make lithographs at the Tamarind Lithography Workshop in Los Angeles. She was in the workshop, exploring the medium, when President Kennedy was assassinated. She interrupted her stay and returned to her home in Abiquiu. After Tamarind relocated in Albuquerque in 1970, I again talked with O'Keeffe and tried to interest her in lithography, but it was too late.

‡ The use of "china" paper, a thin, smooth paper imported from the orient—but often from India or Japan as well as from China—permits the printer to retain every subtlety of the drawing. In the printing process, the thin, china paper is placed against the stone and is then covered with a sheet of heavier paper, to which the thin paper is adhered as it passes through the press; hence the term *chine collé.*

37 Marsden Hartley (1877–1943), *Alspitz,* 1934. 290 x 345 [Eldredge 16],
printer unknown. Collection, Tamarind Institute.

after his return to the United States, he worked again with Miller,
and with other printers as well—Grant Arnold and Emil Ganso
among them—but always thereafter on stone.[11]

It was also in Paris in 1928 and 1929 that Stuart Davis made his
first important series of lithographs: scenes of Parisian boulevards
and buildings, drawn in a Cubist shorthand. In these lithographs,
Davis evoked with characteristic clarity the spirit and appearance of
Paris as seen through the modernist, jazz-conscious eyes of an American visitor.

Davis, Dehn, Kuniyoshi, Lozowick, John Carroll, Howard
Cook, Mabel Dwight, Reginald Marsh, Andrée Ruellan, Benton
Spruance, John Storrs, and John Taylor are but a few of the Americans who made lithographs in Paris during the late twenties and early
thirties, working either with Desjobert or with other French printers.

Many of the American artists who were first attracted to lithography in Paris continued to make lithographs in the United States
after their return, and in so doing often brought new technical information to the American printers with whom they worked. Dehn,
in particular, explored a variety of highly inventive techniques and

38   Yasuo Kuniyoshi (1889–1953), *Nude at Door,* 1928. 333 x 188 [Davis 31], printed at the Atelier Desjobert. Collection, Philadelphia Museum of Art. Purchase, The Lola Downin Peck Fund from the Carl and Laura Zigrosser Collection.

* Whether Davis's lithographs of 1931 and 1932 were printed by George Miller has not been determined. In order to raise funds at a time of financial hardship during the depression, Miller sold a number of his printer's proofs in an auction sale at the Plaza Book Auction Corporation on 23 March 1934. Two of Davis's lithographs were included in this sale: *Place Pasdeloupe No. 1* (AAA 8) and *Sixth Avenue El* (AAA 16, listed in the auction catalogue as *Sixth Avenue*). While it is probable that Miller printed *Sixth Avenue El,* drawn by Davis in 1931, *Place Pasdeloupe* was printed in Paris in 1929. How, then, did Miller acquire this print? If he printed a number of Davis's New York lithographs, in addition to *Sixth Avenue El,* why is it that others were not included in the auction sale? A mystery remains.

processes which were at the time surely unknown on this side of the ocean, and which—from the evidence of his prints—he passed along to his printers. Ruellan and Taylor made brilliant use of tusche washes in their lithographs printed by Desjobert, with the result that they (like other artists) felt somewhat constrained during a later collaboration with Miller.[12] Davis's lithographs of 1930 and 1931 were more abstract than those he had made in Paris. He avoided all intricacies of technique, using black, white, and bluntly drawn crayon textures to create a sparkling interplay of patterns in such superlative prints as his *Barber Shop Chord* of 1931.*

It is reasonable to assume that Davis communicated his enthusiasm for lithography to his then close friend, Arshile Gorky, who in 1931 exhibited three lithographs in the fifth annual exhibition of the Society of American Print Makers at Edith Halpert's Downtown Gallery. *Mannikin* and *Painter and Model,* both of which were published in editions of twenty-five impressions, resemble Davis's litho-

76

39 Andrée Ruellan (b. 1905), *Circus,* 1931–32. 248 x 349, printed at the Atelier Desjobert. Collection, Tamarind Institute.

graphs in their simple, direct, but effective use of the medium.* In them, Gorky, like Davis, forthrightly acknowledges a stylistic debt to European modernism. Why, Davis asks, should it be otherwise?

> Why should an American artist today be expected to be oblivious to European thought when Europe is a hundred times closer to us than it ever was before? . . . [Picasso] has been incomparably the dominant painter of the world for the last twenty years and there are very few of the young painters of any country who have not been influenced by him. . . . I admit the study and the influence and regard it as all to the good. . . . Even so, I insist that I am as American as any other American painter.[13]

AMERICAN MODERNISM: CUBISM AND SURREALISM ASSIMILATED THE PRECISIONIST SPIRIT

For Louis Lozowick, as for Davis and Gorky, the Cubist vocabulary of forms was neither European nor American. It was an international vocabulary which by its formal character was well suited to statements about the essential spirit of America and its industrial civilization.

* The printer of Gorky's lithographs is not known. Jo Miller's suggestion (in "The Prints of Arshile Gorky") that Gorky might have printed them himself is difficult to accept, as Gorky did not have the technical experience requisite to production of well-printed editions of twenty-five impressions. It is more reasonable to assume that either Stuart Davis or Edith Halpert might have introduced him to a professional printer—most likely either J. E. Rosenthal or George Miller (although Miller did not include Gorky's name in a long list of artists with whom he had worked as of 1954).

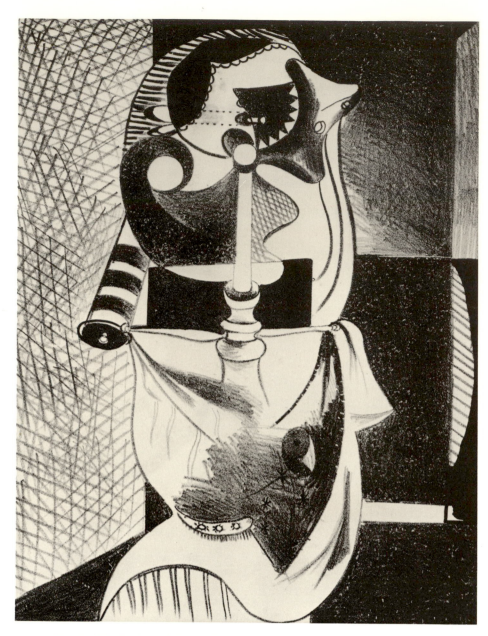

40   Arshile Gorky (1905–1948), *Mannikin,* c. 1931. 376 x 289, printer unknown.
Collection, Mr. & Mrs. Hans Burkhardt.

Lozowick had come to the United States as a child from Russia, had returned to Europe in 1919 after study in New York and Ohio, and had met El Lissitzky, Laszlo Moholy-Nagy, Theo van Doesburg, and other painters in Berlin. There he had joined the Association of Russian Artists and Writers, had exhibited with the Russian Constructivists in Düsseldorf in 1922, and had sought to develop a style that would be simultaneously modernist *and* American:

> The dominant trend in America of today, beneath all the apparent chaos and confusion, is towards order and organization which find their outward sign and symbol in the rigid geometry of the American city: in the verticals of its smoke stacks, in the parallels of its car tracks, and the squares of its streets, the cubes of its factories, the arc of its bridges, the cylinders of its gas tanks.[14]

Lozowick sought to express in his work not only the geometry of

41 Stuart Davis (1894–1964), *Barber Shop Chord,* 1931. 335 x 481, printer
unknown. Collection, National Museum of American Art, Smithsonian
Institution.

42   John Taylor (1897–1983), *St. Tropez,* 1931–32. 301 x 436, printed at the Atelier Desjobert. Collection, Tamarind Institute.

*   Most of the modernist artists who made lithographs during the 1920s and early thirties did so with Miller, Friedland, or Rosenthal. Some, however, were stimulated by the steadily increasing interest in lithography to study the medium at the Art Students League, working either with Charles Locke in the daytime sessions or with Eugene Fitsch at night. Although the lithographs thus produced were characteristically less well printed than those made in collaboration with professional printers, they frequently had a raw force that was entirely appropriate to the artist's intention. The cubist lithographs of Jan Matulka and Konrad Cramer, for example, are among the finest of the period, this in spite of—in some degree because of—their rough and often awkward printing.

See also Janet A. Flint, "Matulka as Printmaker: A Checklist of Known Prints."

the city but its spirit as well. "The American grain elevators and factories," Le Corbusier said, are "the magnificent first-fruits of the new age. The American engineers overwhelm with their calculations our expiring architecture."[15] For Davis, Lozowick, Walkowitz, Konrad Cramer, Jolan Gross-Bettelheim, Jan Matulka, Niles Spencer, *43* and other modernist artist-lithographers it was paradoxically evident that the forms of the European modernists provided an ideal means through which to evoke the "urban optimism" of the new America.* The spirit of the new age could not be captured within the limitations of the essentially nineteenth-century aesthetic of Joseph Pennell and John Taylor Arms.

In a series of brilliant, early lithographs, including *Coney Island,*   *44* Lozowick employed Futurist devices to depict the energy and move- ment of typical American places; Walkowitz, in a style related to   *45* that of the German Expressionists, caught the air of jumbled excitement that characterized the New York of the twenties; and Matulka demonstrated his command of the Cubist idiom in a series of cityscapes and still lifes, of which *New York* and *Still Life with Phono-* *46* *graph* are two of the finest. Storrs, who worked both in Paris and   *47* Chicago, made occasional lithographs in New York, including his *Grays and Black,* a spiraling composition which reflects both his art   *48* deco spirit and his early study with Rodin; Spencer converted the flattened planes of *White Factory* into a sharply patterned vista of the   *49* American city; while in Woodstock, Cramer moved from the Fauvist style of *Country Road* (1921) to a series of well-structured Cubist still   *52* lifes in 1922 and 1923.

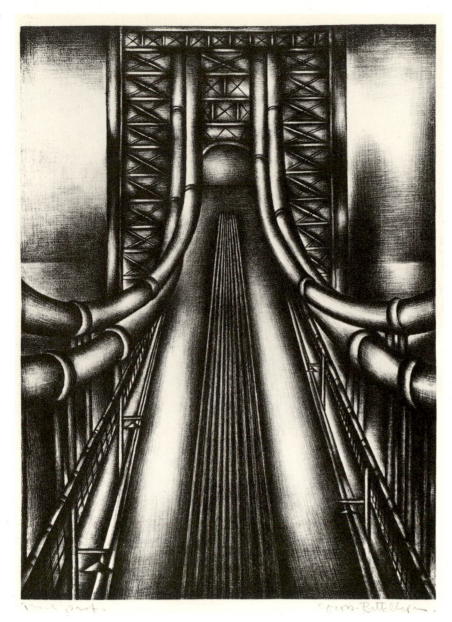

43 Jolan Gross-Bettelheim (b. 1900), *Bridge,* n. d. 353 x 256, printer unknown.
Collection, Tamarind Institute.

It was typical of the American response to modernism that many
artists sought, in Martin Friedman's phrase, "to harmonize [an] earlier American visual tradition with random elements from the ex-
ploding nebulae of modern European art." Alternatively called the
Precisionists or the Immaculates, they "were not so much innova-
tors or theorists as they were synthesizers. Unlike their contemporaries in Holland, Germany, and Russia . . . the Precisionists had
less interest in Cubism's abstruse ideology than in the pragmatic use
of its forms and formulae."[16] Friedman characterizes the Precisionist method as one of continual editing—a method in which neither
impulse nor spontaneity is permitted to play a part in development
of "an icily defined and flawless finish."[17]

Characteristically, the formal devices of the Precisionists revealed
their Cubist roots: the intensification of light and shadow and a sup-
pression of local value; the strong contrast of black and white; the
simplification of masses and volumes and elimination of extraneous
detail; and the frequent use of "Futurist force lines" that originated

81

44 Louis Lozowick (1892–1973), *Coney Island (Luna Park)*, c. 1925. 328 x 216
[Flint L.4], printed by George C. Miller. Collection, University of New Mexico
Art Museum.

45 Abraham Walkowitz (1880–1965), *New York,* 1927. 405 x 255, printed by George C. Miller. Collection, Philadelphia Museum of Art, gift of the artist.

in objects but extended into the surrounding space to activate and control it. Not surprisingly, many Precisionist artists found lithography to be an ideal medium, for on the perfect surface of the stone they could achieve the flawless finish they sought; and through use of the crayon in the classic manner they could erase all evidence of the physical processes through which their work had been created.*
In their range of tone and deep, crisp blacks, in their power and
50   vitality, such lithographs as Lozowick's *Tanks,* Howard Cook's *Edison*
51   *Plant,* Victoria Hutson Huntley's *Kopper's Coke,* and Ralston Craw-
53   ford's *Overseas Highway* demonstrate the artists' conviction that the
59   forms of American industry possess a grandeur in every way commensurate with that of the classical past.

More than any other artist Charles Sheeler perfectly typifies the Precisionist spirit. After study in Philadelphia, he made several trips to Europe between 1904 and 1908 and there encountered modernist art. He formed an early interest in architecture and set himself up in business as an architectural photographer. In 1913, at the invitation of Arthur B. Davies, he exhibited six paintings in the Armory Show. He found important sources for his work in the quintessentially American spirit of early Shaker furniture and crafts, and in 1920 he

* Martin L. Friedman quotes Charles Sheeler as having said in 1959: "I just don't want to see any more than is absolutely necessary of the physical materials that go into a picture." (*The Precisionist View in American Art,* p. 13.)

83

46   Jan Matulka (1890–1972), *Still Life with Phonograph,* 1925. 359 x 229 [Flint 36], printed by the artist. Collection, Tamarind Institute.

Roses, frontispiece, p. ii

*   George Miller was the printer of Sheeler's lithographs. At the time Sheeler worked with him, Miller's workshop was in a building at 6 East Fourteenth Street, across the street from the Delmonico Building. Later, Miller relocated his shop in the Delmonico Building at 3 East Fourteenth Street.

collaborated with Paul Strand in the making of *Manhatta,* a superbly photographed film in which he and Strand sang the praise of the rising city. Although so far as is known, Sheeler made only five lithographs, each is a definitive statement. His silvery *Delmonico Building* continues his homage to New York,* while his *Roses* stand elegant and pristine, sharply focused in space.   54

Akin to the lithographs of the Precisionist artists in their technical polish—although utterly different in their subjective content—are the small number of lithographs created by artists who had found their inspiration in Surrealism rather than Cubism. In the 1930s, this meant the veristic surrealism of Giorgio de Chirico and Salvador Dali, rather than the abstract surrealism (and automatism) which were so sharply to affect American art in the 1940s. Most remarkable among the Surrealist and Fantasist lithographs of the thirties are those of Federico Castellón, Helen Lundeberg, and Kyra Markham, each of whom created a personal universe of magic and mystery.

47   Jan Matulka (1890–1972), *New York,* c. 1925. 311 x 449 [Flint 33], printed by
the artist. Collection, Tamarind Institute.

48   John Storrs (1885–1956), *Grays and Black,* c. 1930. 505 x 330, printed by George C. Miller. Collection, Robert Schoelkopf Gallery, New York.

49   Niles Spencer (1893–1952), *White Factory,* 1928. 269 x 344, probably printed
by George C. Miller. Collection, Carl Zigrosser. Courtesy, Philadelphia
Museum of Art.

50   Louis Lozowick (1892–1973), *Tanks #1,* 1929. 353 x 213 [Flint L.39], printed by George C. Miller. Collection, University of New Mexico Art Museum.

51   Howard Cook (1901–1980), *Edison Plant,* 1930. 339 x 248, printed
by George C. Miller. Collection, Tamarind Institute.

52   Konrad Cramer (1888–1963), *Country Road,* 1921. 202 x 266, printed by the artist. Collection, Tamarind Institute.

53 Victoria Hutson (Huntley) (1900–1971), *Kopper's Coke,* 1932. 244 x 340,
printed by George C. Miller. Collection, Tamarind Institute.

54 Charles Sheeler (1882–1965), *Delmonico Building,* 1926. 248 x 183, printed by George C. Miller. Collection, National Museum of American Art, Smithsonian Institution, gift of Mr. & Mrs. Harry Baum in memory of Edith Gregor Halpert.

For Castellón, a trip to Spain in 1934 served as the catalyst to creation of a remarkable series of enigmatic Surrealist landscape and figure compositions, among them *The New Robe, #2* and *Memories.* *55*
Markham's lithographs, like those of Paul Cadmus, are obscurely *56*
ominous: none more so than the evocative and disturbing *Elin and* *57*
Maria, a beautifully drawn stone which was winner of the prestigious Mary S. Collins prize at the Print Club of Philadelphia in 1935. Across the country in Los Angeles, Lundeberg made few lithographs, but among those few, *Enigma (The Mirror)* is unsurpassed in its *58*
haunting authority.

For the Precisionist artists, as for all who sought a precise control of the medium, George Miller was an ideal printer. Miller's "miraculous technical perfection," as Howard Cook was to call it, was perfectly suited not only to the urban images of Cook, Gross-Bettelheim, Hutson-Huntley, and Lozowick; but also to the "magic realism" of Castellón and Markham, and to the more traditional state-

55   Federico Castellón (1914–1971), *The New Robe #2,* c. 1939. Color
lithograph, 315 x 253 [Freundlich 6], printed by George C. Miller. Collection,
University of New Mexico Art Museum.

56 Federico Castellón (1914–1971), *Memories,* c. 1940. 321 x 239 [Freundlich 10a], printed by George C. Miller. Published by Associated American Artists. Collection, Tamarind Institute.

ments of a number of romantic realists with whom Miller so effectively collaborated, among them Ellison Hoover, Martin Lewis, Luigi Lucioni, Robert Riggs, and Stow Wengenroth. Riggs, called a new master of lithography and a worthy successor to George Bellows at the time of his 1933 exhibition in New York, combined superb drawing, technical virtuosity, and a compelling psychological tension in such fine works as *Tumblers* and *Psychopathic Ward;* Wengenroth, in such early lithographs as *Black Cape* and *Summer Dusk,* with their range of smoky, deep tones, similarly demonstrated a total command of the medium by both the artist and his printer.

14

61
62

60

JEAN CHARLOT AND LYNTON KISTLER

In February of 1928, José Clemente Orozco, who was then in New York, wrote to his friend Jean Charlot, still in Mexico, about his interest in lithography:

Elin and Maria

Kyra Markham 1934

57   Kyra Markham (1891–1967), *Elin and Maria,* 1934. 308 x 274, probably
printed by George C. Miller. Collection, Tamarind Institute.

58 Helen Lundeberg (b. 1908), *Enigma (The Mirror),* 1937. 301 x 229, printed
by Carl Winter. Collection, Tamarind Institute.

59   Ralston Crawford (1906–1978), *Overseas Highway,* 1940. Color lithograph,
252 x 402 [Freeman L.40.1], printed by George C. Miller. Collection,
Philadelphia Museum of Art. Purchase, Harrison Fund.

60   Stow Wengenroth (1906–1978), *Summer Dusk,* 1932. 180 x 323 [Stuckey 27],
printed by George C. Miller. Collection, Tamarind Institute.

61 Robert Riggs (1896–1970), *Tumblers,* 1934. 361 x 480, printed by George C. Miller. Collection, Tamarind Institute.

I am going to do it, it's easy, it doesn't have to be done on stone, there are some special plates, I already have two of them. There is a Mr. Miller who has a lithography studio here and he is the one who makes prints for the art galleries. The plates I bought (26 by 43 centimeters) cost fifty cents each, and the printing of the first twelve proofs costs ten dollars, and each additional one is twenty-five cents, plus the paper. It's expensive for me, but I'll see if I can manage it.*

Charlot received Orozco's letter in Yucatán, where he was working as an artist on the staff of an archeological expedition that was excavating the ruins at Chichén Itzá. In the fall of 1928 he came to the United States to participate in the making of a field report upon the excavations.

Born in Paris in 1898, Charlot had made his first lithographs in France before emigrating to Mexico after World War I; he had worked again on stone with printers in Mexico, and now, in New York, it was natural that he would wish to work with Miller. Orozco introduced him to the printer, and in May 1929 he drew the first of a series of lithographs on zinc plates. He continued to work with Miller throughout the year that followed, usually on zinc rather than stone, presumably for the convenience that work on metal allowed him.[18]

62   Robert Riggs (1896–1970), *Psychopathic Ward,* c. 1940. 363 x 479, printed
by George C. Miller. Collection, Tamarind Institute.

Charlot's work with Miller ultimately proved to be but a prelude to the remarkable series of color lithographs made in Los Angeles in 1933. The prints that he made with Miller were entirely in black and white, which was fine, but which did not entirely satisfy Charlot's intention to create an art for the people. He meant in his work "to react against the 'art' lithographs, such as those done by the Nabis: Bonnard, Vuillard, and Maurice Denis. Granted that they are beautiful, they are such obvious works of art."[19] This attitude led Charlot to the concept of a "picture book," a *liber studiorum* in the tradition of the Middle Ages and the Renaissance, in which he would do "a repertory of the motifs" he had used in his work up to then: a series of small lithographs to be printed in large editions on an offset press, preferably in full, bright, not "artistic" colors. His attitude toward printmaking was that of a populist: he objected to the precious practices of conservative printmakers—particularly those of etchers in the Whistler-Pennell tradition—as "collectors' bait . . . a kind of fungus . . . of which modern works are relatively free,"[20] and except for small editions that were pulled primarily for his own pleasure, his preference was for "a large, unlimited printing, to give a work as wide a circulation as possible."[21]

Although the original purpose of Charlot's trip to Los Angeles in 1933 was purely personal—a visit to Zohmah Day, later to be Zohmah Charlot—the idea of the picture book was in his mind, and when he was introduced to the Los Angeles printers Will A. Kistler and his son Lynton R. Kistler, he was soon led to the thought that such a book might be produced at their printing plant.

Will Kistler had run a commercial printing business in Los Angeles for some years. Although in the 1920s letterpress printing and lithography were still thought of as completely separate crafts, he believed that the new photographic processes available to lithography would soon revolutionize the printing industry. In 1928 he bought a large Potter offset press. They were, Lynton Kistler recalls, among the first letterpress printers in the city to make use of lithography:

> Lithography became printing in our eyes. This was a viewpoint not generally accepted at that time. Knowledge of the processes of lithography was not accessible to the rest of the printing craft . . . [and] our workmen were unwilling to regard lithography as a commercial printing process. . . . But along with the Potter press, we acquired the services of a well-trained German lithographer. His name was Ludwig Melzner. . . . He had a background that included printing from stone.[22]

It was part of young Kistler's job to call upon the advertising agencies in Los Angeles and solicit work for the shop. In this way he met a number of artists and illustrators who worked for the agencies. Then, through a mutual friend, Kistler met Merle Armitage, a man of wide interests who was impresario and manager of the Los Angeles Grand Opera Company, an active collector of art—principally of fine prints—and a distinguished book designer.[23] It was Armitage who interested Kistler in the process of stone lithography.

Kistler read books on the subject—Senefelder and Hullmandel, among others. He persuaded some of the artist-illustrators he had met in the agencies to make drawings on zinc plates and he began to print these plates at his father's shop, on a Fuchs & Lang press still used for transfer work.

> Of course I got in the way of the commercial printing that was going on, so I sent to New York and bought [my own press] . . . and set it up in my garage. I got some stones, one place and another, including some from Melzner. They were a drug on the market at that time. Finally, I ordered a whole ton of stones from the Senefelder Company in New York.[24]

It was at this point that Kistler met Charlot. Undaunted by the artist's already considerable reputation, Kistler began in July 1933 to work with Charlot on a lithograph which was to be not only the first edition that Kistler had printed from stone, but also the first lithograph in color for both artist and printer, *Woman with Child on Back*. It is not surprising in these circumstances that technical problems prevented the printing of a full edition. "I remember the image spread fast on this print, and we only got about thirteen good proofs."[25] But the personal relationship between Charlot and Kistler was a good one from the beginning, and throughout a long career during which Charlot worked with many fine printers, Kistler remained his printer of choice.

At the time Charlot and Kistler began their collaboration, Merle Armitage was preparing a small book on the work of the California painter, Henrietta Shore. Charlot and Shore had met in Mexico when she had asked his permission to do his portrait. At Armitage's suggestion, Charlot now returned the compliment and made a small two-color lithograph as a frontispiece for the Armitage book. It was drawn on zinc plates and printed on the offset press at Will Kistler's shop.

Charlot's success in the making of this portrait, together with Lynton Kistler's encouragement, led directly to the decision to attempt production of the picture book. As a first step, Charlot drew 63 the plates for a single lithograph, *Malinche,* for use in a prospectus.

> The prospectus picture was really done to reassure Lynton's father, who owned the litho shop, because he was most skeptical. . . . Lynton was working with his father, but was tending toward doing art work, which Will Kistler wasn't. . . . So the little prospectus was really done to show Will that it could be done. . . . Anyhow, as the copies of the little *Malinche* came off the press, Will Kistler was delighted. He gathered together his fellow printers of Los Angeles—they were a pretty crusty group—and he showed them that print. They wanted to know how it had been done. "It's very simple," Will Kistler said. "He's French."[26]

But the making of the *Picture Book* was by no means simple, despite Charlot's almost incredible virtuosity in the drawing of the complex color separations. The thirty-two lithographs, all multicolor, were drawn on four sets of large zinc plates, eight subjects on each plate. Charlot first drew a linear key plate (not used in the printing of the lithographs) from which red-chalk transfers were put on the other plates.[27] "Jean drew into the red-chalk offsets," Kistler recalls. "There was no proofing except on the first set of eight. That was to

101

see whether we would be able to accomplish what we had in mind and maintain our register and get work of the quality we expected. After the printing of the first set of plates, there was no proofing at all; they were simply run from the plates as Charlot had drawn them. It was a remarkable feat."[28]

Charlot later inscribed one copy to Kistler: "Dear L. R. This book is as much your achievement as it is mine. So this is just as a testimony of friendship and to repeat to you how much working in common on zinc and stone has brought me some of the most pleasurable moments of my career."[29]

Throughout the months in which they collaborated on the *Picture Book,* Kistler and Charlot also continued to work on stones in Kistler's garage "as a change of pace" from work on the book. Many fine prints came from this collaboration, and by October 1933, Kistler was ready to present his first exhibition—"Impressions printed by hand from stone and zinc by Lynton R. Kistler"—at the Stendahl Galleries. The catalogue included an introduction by Armitage and one of a series of small "vignettes" by Charlot. In February 1934, Charlot worked with Kistler on the most ambitious color lithograph they had thus far printed from stone, *Woman with Child in Front,* **64** and in March, after a festive farewell dinner, he returned to New York. So complete was the understanding that had been achieved between artist and printer that it proved possible for them to continue to work together despite the intervening distance. Between 1934 and 1937, while in New York and Chicago, Charlot frequently made drawings on stones and zinc plates and sent them to Kistler to be printed in Los Angeles.

LITHOGRAPHY IN LOS ANGELES

Los Angeles was not then the art center it later became, and California remained in the arts an isolated province. Not until 1920 did the Los Angeles County Museum hold "its first exhibition of avant-garde art organized by . . . Stanton Macdonald-Wright [who] recalled many years later that the show 'was the cause of near riots.' "[30] Following this beginning, as a means to break the iron grip of the California Art Club, a group obdurately opposed to "modernism" in any form, the Los Angeles Group of Independent Artists was formed in 1922. It held its exhibitions in a downtown building and showed the works of Macdonald-Wright; his fellow-Synchromist pioneer, Morgan Russell; Wright's close friend, Thomas Hart Benton; Peter Krasnow, a Russian émigré modernist; Nick Brigante, an Italian-born artist; and the sculptor William Zorach.

As in the east, printmaking was a stronghold of conservative artists, and during the 1920s and early 1930s the exhibitions sponsored by the Print Makers Society of California—like those of the California Art Club—were composed principally of unadventurous landscapes rooted in popular, romantic traditions. The favored medium was etching, and in technique and execution the works of the Los Angeles etchers derived directly from routine English prints of the nineteenth century. Why, one society spokesman asked, should we "displace good conservative work to make place for something we do not like? . . . The only difference is that [conservative prints] are more carefully composed and drawn and are submitted in clean mats while the more radical a print the dirtier the mat."[31]

Lithography was a rarely used medium. The first Los Angeles

63   Jean Charlot (1898–1979), *Malinche,* 1933. Offset color lithograph, 154 x 203
[Morse 116], printed by Will Kistler and Lynton R. Kistler. Private collection.

64   Jean Charlot (1898–1979), *Woman with Child in Front,* 1934. Color lithograph, 665 x 445 [Morse 230], printed by Lynton R. Kistler. Collection, Lynton R. Kistler.

artists to make lithographs were those who, like Charlot, had experienced the medium elsewhere. Also like Charlot, they were artists sympathetic to modernist directions in art: Douglas Parshall, who had studied at the Art Students League; Henrietta Shore, who had worked in Mexico; Millard Sheets, who made his first lithograph in Paris; Richard Day, whose strongly drawn black-and-white prints   65
had a structural clarity akin to Sheeler's; and Peter Krasnow, whose   68
expressionistic lithographs, drawn in 1928, may well be the most important series of works printed in Los Angeles before the Charlot-Kistler collaboration of 1933.

Following Charlot's departure for the East, Kistler in 1937 moved his press from the garage at his home to a larger space in Earl Stendahl's candy factory, above his gallery on Wilshire Boulevard. He continued to print there, for Charlot, Lorser Feitelson,* and other   69
artists, until 1940, when he left for the East.

* Although Lorser Feitelson made few prints, having "found the discipline of the lithographic medium too inflexible for [his] way of working," he remained one of Kistler's strongest supporters. Together with his friend S. Macdonald-Wright, Feitelson was a principal force for modernist art in Los Angeles from the 1930s until his death in 1977. See San Francisco Museum of Modern Art, *Lorser Feitelson and Helen Lundeberg: A Retrospective Exhibition.*

104

65   Richard Day (1896–1972), *Boats in the Ways,* c. 1931. 250 x 200, printed
by Lynton R. Kistler. Collection, Los Angeles County Museum of Art, gift of
Merle Armitage.

BOARDMAN ROBINSON AND THE
COLORADO SPRINGS FINE ARTS CENTER

Although lithography was slow to develop in Los Angeles, it is no
surprise that so large and active a city should soon have joined New
York, Philadelphia, and Chicago as a place for work in the medium.
Less obvious are the circumstances that brought artists' lithography
to Colorado Springs. The "carrier" in this case was Boardman Robinson, whose interest in lithography had begun long before. He had
been there in Sterner's studio on that January night when the Painter-
Gravers of America had been founded; he had made a number of
lithographs with George Miller during the 1920s; and as an instructor at the league he had come to know both Joseph Pennell and
Charles Locke.

Then, in 1930, "Mike" Robinson moved west to join the faculty of the Fountain Valley School in Colorado Springs. It was a

105

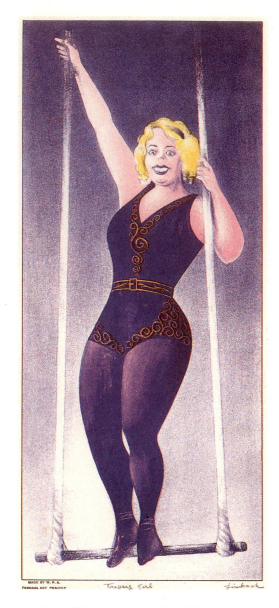

66   Russell T. Limbach (1904–1971), *Trapeze Girl,* 1935. Color lithograph,
368 x 159, printed by the artist. Collection, National Museum of American Art,
Smithsonian Institution, gift of the artist.

68-54   Lebrun 1945

67   Rico Lebrun (1900–1964), *Villon's Ballad #2 (Man and Armor),* 1945. Color
lithograph, 345 x 448, printed by Lawrence Barrett. Collection, Tamarind
Institute.

68 Peter Krasnow (1887–1980), *The Stallion,* 1927. 420 x 308, printer unknown. Collection, Tamarind Institute.

startling juxtaposition: Boardman Robinson and Colorado Springs. Robinson, a New York "Red" who had been an illustrator for the *Masses* and John Reed's companion on a mission to Moscow; and Colorado Springs, a staunchly conservative citadel, "the Newport of the Rockies."

> [It] should have been enough to bring conservatives out with fiery crosses on Cheyenne Mountain. . . . [Instead] Socialist Robinson was taken to the local Republican bosom like a prodigal son and was even made an instructor at the Broadmoor Art Academy. Soon after, the Art Academy found itself without a head . . . [and] Robinson was named director.[32]

Before coming to Colorado, Robinson had been for some years both popular and effective as an instructor at the league. "One of the reasons," Thomas Hart Benton said, "was that he had a rare

69   Lorser Feitelson (1898–1978), *Reading (Reclining Figure),* c. 1938. 250 x 300, printed by Lynton R. Kistler. Private collection.

kind of ability to keep his students enthusiastic, and he could help them strengthen their will to use this enthusiasm."[33] The Art Academy, now renamed the Fine Arts Center School, became in many ways an image of its new director. "In this school," Arnold Blanch wrote, after teaching there, "the students seemed to reflect the abundance and vigor of Mike's personality.

> In the classrooms there were violent discussions about art, science, music, marriage or anything that might come to mind. Often there were school picnics, where we would play baseball. Mike was umpire, and always the game would end in a loud but genial scrap. There were costume parties too. . . . We would drink beer and dance noisily.[34]

For the socialites of Colorado Springs, as for many student dilettantes, the Fine Arts Center, and before it the old Broadmoor Art Academy, were ornaments in a Gatsby world: places for parties and grand balls. For Robinson, despite his camaraderie, such fun and games remained always subordinate to the difficult but good business of making art.*

In 1931, the year of Robinson's appointment as director, the

*   Robinson adopted a quotation from Goethe as his motto and had it inscribed on the portico of the art school: "The business of art is with the difficult and the good."

70   Ralston Crawford (1906–1978), *Etoile de l'occident,* 1955. Color lithograph,
270 x 423 [Freeman L.55.21], printed at the Atelier Mourlot. Collection,
University of New Mexico Art Museum, gift of Garo Antreasian.

board also decided to construct an ambitious new building for the Fine Arts Center. Without waiting for its completion, Robinson set out to develop an art school of national stature: a school in which lithography would be developed as a major area of instruction.

A press was acquired, together with other equipment, and in the summer of 1932 a first class in lithography was offered, with the painter Ward Lockwood as its teacher. Constance Forsyth, who was among the students in that class, recalls that

> Lockwood with his rare charm and honest, unabashed humility made no claim to knowing a great deal about it. He said he had drawn on stones and seen them printed. . . . The location was a spacious garage. It fortunately had a drain in the middle of the concrete floor over which was a good sized sink with water connections. . . . The class was supposed to meet two afternoons a week, but the interest and enthusiasm of the instructor and a few students kept the garage well populated most afternoons and many mornings. Problems were many, but with persistence and "elbow grease" we finally achieved some success. . . . Our only reference book was Bolton Brown's.[35]

These limitations notwithstanding, Lockwood's summer class was a beginning. The equipment was used from time to time after that by other students, with varying results. Then, in 1936, Robinson invited Charles Locke to come to Colorado Springs as visiting instructor during the summer term. The new Art Center building had been dedicated in April of that year and a proper lithography studio was thus for the first time available.

Archie Musick, Colorado Springs' resident artist-critic and professional gadfly, later described Locke as "the most thorough-going Manhattanite I had ever seen. His world was New York. All else was savage jungle, ox carts, Indian scalpings and the like. He was a semi-animated bundle of boredom who had brought along Ted Wahl as his printer and technician, thus relieving him of all but a minimal token of communication with the students."[36] It was Locke's plan— following the pattern of his classes at the Art Students League—that Wahl would do all the printing; the students would do no printing, nor would they be taught how to do so. But this arrangement in no way suited Lawrence Barrett, one of the students in the class; it was his intention to learn how to print, and Musick tells of his "white-faced anger" when Locke attempted to brush him off.

Locke gave in; he and Wahl taught Barrett how to print. Barrett achieved a grasp of lithography with phenomenal speed during the brief summer class, and in the fall, when Locke and Wahl returned to New York, Barrett became the lithographic technician and instructor at the Fine Arts Center school.

LAWRENCE BARRETT

Born in Oklahoma and raised in Kansas, Lawrence Barrett had come with his family to Colorado Springs in 1919. The following year he had enrolled as a student at the Broadmoor Art Academy, only to have his studies interrupted by a lengthy illness. He contracted tuberculosis, and during much of the time between 1920 and 1934—

between the ages of twenty-two and thirty-six, the years of his youth—he was confined to bed.

His long-time associate, Fred Bartlett, later to be director of the Fine Arts Center, spoke of him as an "inward person whose work was the only thing of consequence to him. You felt that he was not about to get close to anyone. There was something very private about Lawrence."[37] Others commented in similar terms, if in different words: "He felt great compassion for animals, which is often true of people who aren't close to other people. He was very reserved even with his students. He seldom said a word, but when he did, it was always much to the point."[38] Taciturn though he was (thus resembling George Miller), Barrett nonetheless exhibited a dry and whimsical sense of humor, often when least expected. He genuinely empathized with his students. Intolerant of pretension in any form, he could be strongly and subjectively opinionated at times. His sister Dorothy called him "strong-minded."

Barrett's long illness had made him something of a hypochondriac; he was conditioned always to worry about germs and uncleanliness. He kept an ultraviolet lamp in his studio, and students with colds were not welcome in his classes. Once, when staying with Stanley William Hayter in New York, he left from his own fear that the Hayter children might catch an illness he had contracted. He never married. "Lawrence was straitlaced and terribly moral," Dorothy recalled. "He didn't drink and he didn't smoke. He thought Archie Musick's book [a rambling account of life and art in Colorado Springs] was terribly vulgar."[39]

Musick would not have been fazed by Barrett's response. He was used to words much stronger than *vulgar;* his good friend, Thomas Hart Benton, in characteristic style, had called him a "flea-bitten red rock coyote."[40] Musick, Benton, and their hard-drinking friends reflected more accurately the bohemian ambience of Colorado Springs than did Barrett's ascetic ways; even so, they came to respect the printer's skills and met him on his own terms.*

Barrett had no tolerance for careless work. He was serious about his shop and lithography, and he felt that discipline and quality came from slow, careful work. Emerson Woelffer, the painter who later became director of the school, remembers Barrett's words: "He said, it takes a long time. The longer you work, the better your lithograph will be."[41] As a printer, however, Barrett was quick and sure. He was "patient and swift in his movements. He worked fast and consistently. . . . With rare exceptions, the students in Barrett's classes did no printing. He etched all the stones and rolled them up. He printed the students' editions, usually about ten impressions, and sometimes printed as many as ten editions in a single day."[42]

Reginald Neal, who was Barrett's technical assistant during the summer of 1941, confirms these memories:

> We kept busy from eight in the morning until five in the afternoon printing the work of everyone who was in the class, including prints by resident artists. Unless you were there as a technical assistant, as I was, you learned nothing about printing; all you did was make the drawing. Adolf Dehn told the students how to use the crayons and what techniques would work.[43]

Neal recalls that in order to get information from Barrett he had to ask questions:

* Barrett also printed for local artists, including a project for Archie Musick, in whose somewhat unrealistic perception "the lithographic medium was riding the crest of an unprecedented wave in the East due largely to the promotional acumen of the Associated American Artists. . . . Five of us decided to make a killing with a limited edition folio of lithographs. The five were Guy Maccoy, Joseph Meert, Bernard Steffen, Jackson Pollock and Archie Musick. Except for Pollock all had studied or worked in Colorado Springs. All but one were fiercely loyal to Benton. . . . [But] the folio was a flop." (Musick, *Musick Medley: Intimate Memories of a Rocky Mountain Art Colony,* p. 85.) Barrett printed all of the lithographs in the folio except the Jackson Pollock, *Stacking Hay,* which was printed by Ted Wahl in New York.

71 Adolf Dehn (1895–1968), *Man from Orizaba,* 1941. 437 x 329 [Lumsdaine L.313], printed by Lawrence Barrett. Collection, Tamarind Institute.

He would answer them as minimally as he could. But I observed how he put the etch together, how many drops of acid he put in it and how he counteretched. He would never let anybody touch his roller or do any printing. I assisted him at the press, grained the stones, dampened paper, and occasionally printed my own work.[44]

In addition to his work with students, Robinson expected Barrett to provide lithographic services to the faculty and visiting artists. Soon he was hard at work printing for George Biddle, Arnold Blanch, *71* Randall Davey, Adolf Dehn, Doris Lee, Peppino Mangravite, and, of course, for Robinson himself. As most of these artists were experienced lithographers who had worked with professional printers elsewhere, Barrett had an opportunity to learn from them—particularly from Biddle and Dehn—a number of special techniques and procedures which they had either invented or observed in other workshops. Among the methods that came to be Barrett's favorites—

113

including a "rubbing method" and a procedure for working into a "middle tone" created by the inked roller—were some that he surely learned from Dehn, for among all of the artists with whom Barrett collaborated, Dehn's experience in lithography was by far the most extensive.[45] From the beginning of their work together, Dehn and Barrett enjoyed a special relationship, akin to that between Bellows and Brown, or between Charlot and Kistler.

Characteristically, the lithographs Barrett printed—like others of the period—were small in scale, at their largest about sixteen by twenty inches. Most of his editions for artists, and virtually all that he printed for students, were in black and white. His work in color, whether his own lithographs or those drawn by other artists, was simple in nature, usually limited to two or three colors. He did not encourage students to explore techniques other than traditional crayon drawing until he was certain that they had mastered that fundamental method.

In this respect, Barrett did not greatly differ from other American printers. For Bolton Brown, crayonstone had been a matter of ultimate conviction; for Miller and Kistler, as for Barrett, it was a matter of strong preference except in such cases as they were convinced that the experience of the artist was sufficient to justify use of other techniques. Many American artists have commented upon the resistance they felt from their printers when they attempted to use tusche washes or otherwise to depart from the straight and narrow path.*

Perhaps because of his background as an art student, Barrett was slightly more open to technical experimentation than were Miller and Kistler. For Adolf Dehn—as later for Rico Lebrun—Barrett's willingness to explore unconventional techniques was an important asset; although for some artists such technical freedom can become an enticing trap. An example is provided by George Biddle's work of the 1930s and 1940s which often suffers from an indulgence in technical complexities—including stone engraving, stipple and dry-brush techniques, and work in the manière noire—which overpower his images, becoming empty mannerisms. Few of Biddle's later works have the direct, expressive force of his early work in Paris. (See Biddle's portrait of *Ellen Mary Cassatt*.)

Barrett, Kistler, Miller, and other printers differed not only in their experience and attitudes but also in their technical methods—Kistler used weak etches, while Barrett used strong ones—and in artists' appraisals of their skills: Bellows preferred Brown to Miller; Davies, Miller to Brown. Soon after Barrett began to print, George Biddle spoke of him as at least equal to "if not better than" George Miller; Howard Cook, on the other hand, had little regard for Barrett but thought highly of Miller.†

In 1940 Barrett applied for and received a fellowship from the Guggenheim Foundation. While on leave from his position at the Fine Arts Center in Colorado Springs, he financed a trip to New York through the sale of timber from land that he owned. Unfortunately, as a consequence of the damp eastern climate, he soon suffered a recurrence of his earlier lung problems and was forced to return to Colorado before the year was over. There, however, he found that the Guggenheim Fellowship had done much to advance his prestige at the Fine Arts Center, with the result that his salary as a lithographic technician and instructor—which had remained un-

5

---

* Much has been made of the fact that Miller discouraged artists from use of techniques other than crayon, that he was reluctant to print stones drawn with tusche washes, or that he would not work in color. The evidence suggests that Miller's attitudes toward such work varied according to his feeling for the artist. He printed washes in color for Arthur B. Davies and Rockwell Kent: both were artists he knew and respected for their skill and craftsmanship. He permitted Adolf Dehn to use all manner of unorthodox techniques; what printer could do otherwise? But like Bolton Brown, Miller loved the purity and dependability of crayonstone, and many an artist came away from his workshop with the impression that no other manner of drawing was acceptable. That some artists found this inhibiting is undeniable.

† Though most of the artists who worked closely with Miller sang his praise as a man and as a printer (see the many tributes to his work in Janet Flint, *George Miller and American Lithography*), he could at times be difficult. He had a "sort of odd sense of humor," Burr Miller says. "He would laugh at things we wouldn't even crack a smile at," but if he did not like an artist with whom he worked "he'd just go through the motions. He'd do a good job for [him], but there wasn't any warmth or affection . . . [he was] just a person doing business." (Burr Miller, interview, 4 May 1979.)

changed at one hundred dollars a month since his initial appointment in the fall of 1936—was now increased to one hundred and twenty-five. And the center's director, Paul Parker, wrote that when Barrett went east "to pursue studies in the technique of lithographic printing, he must have been gratified and possibly embarrassed at the same time, to discover that he himself was considered to be no neophyte but the final authority, the Prophet of Stone."[46]

During the year away from the school, Barrett completed work on a brief, technical monograph describing drawing techniques on stone. Reproduced in mimeographed form by the Fine Arts Center, it was distributed in the fall of 1940 to several hundred museums, art schools, and universities throughout the country.* In revised and expanded form, Barrett's technical essay later became one of the two separate sections of a book which he and Adolf Dehn wrote as joint authors.[47] Their approaches to lithography are illuminated by their book and by a color film produced at the Fine Arts Center in the summer of 1940.† In the film, Dehn is first seen sketching, then drawing the stone for his lithograph, *Garden of the Gods;* Barrett then etches the stone and prints it on the hand press, which has been moved for the occasion from the inside studio to an outdoor portico, so that sunlight may be used for the filming. Quite aside from the insight that the film provides into Dehn's and Barrett's methods, it captures an aura of pleasant, golden days at a time when both art and life were far less complicated than they were later to become.

THEODORE CUNO

Except in New York, Woodstock, Los Angeles, and Colorado Springs, there were during the 1930s and 1940s few printers in America. Occasionally, an artist-teacher who did not regularly print for others would undertake to print an edition as a favor for a friend. That such favors were often uncertain in their result was demonstrated when around 1940 Francis Chapin undertook to print two stones for his friend Ivan Albright.‡ Both stones were broken in the press after the printing of small editions.

In some cities, a professional proof printer in a commercial workshop might print for artists, and occasionally one of these printers might run a "moonlight" business in a workshop at his home. One such printer, working in Philadelphia, was Theodore Cuno, "an old German craftsman who had printed for Joseph Pennell at the Ketterlinus Co. and was then working as a color prover for another firm."[48]

Philadelphia's place in the development of American lithography was curiously inconsistent. The city had long possessed an active commercial lithographic printing industry; many leading artists of the day—Pennell, among them—were Philadelphians; and the Print Club of Philadelphia, founded in 1914 (and thus the first organization of its kind in the United States) served to stimulate interest in prints among both artists and collectors, becoming increasingly active after the establishment of its galleries on Latimer Street in 1919.[49] By contrast, the Philadelphia Museum of Art had then shown little interest either in exhibiting or collecting fine prints, and classes in lithography had not been offered at the Pennsylvania Academy of Fine Arts.

When in 1928 Benton Spruance, a student at the academy, was given a Cresson Fellowship for study in Paris, lithography was for

* Barrett's paper must at this time have been received with little interest at most of the art schools and universities to which it was sent, as few offered courses in lithography.

† Two separate films were made, both in color. One, photographed by Mitchell A. Wilder in 16 mm. is approximately 900 feet in length, well-edited, with titles. The second film, shorter and in 8 mm., was apparently Barrett's own "home movie"; some of its sequences are similar to those in Wilder's film, while others are quite different.

‡ Published studies of Albright's early lithographs provide inconsistent and sometimes contradictory information with respect to their sequence and date. See Michael Croydon, *Ivan Albright;* Peter Pollack, "The Lithographs of Ivan Albright"; and Susan Pirpris Teller, "The Prints of Ivan Albright."

72   Benton Spruance (1904–1967), *The People Work—Night,* 1937. 376 x 480
[Fine 144], printed by Theodore Cuno. Collection, Philadelphia Museum of Art.

him a new discovery. As he began work at Desjobert's, he discovered that other American artists had difficulty in communicating with their printers because of the language barrier. Using this circumstance to his advantage, Spruance arranged with Desjobert that in return for his services as interpreter, he would be given the freedom of the workshop so that he might learn as much as possible about lithography before returning to Philadelphia. Once home, he was determined to go on with his work, and as he could not do so at the academy, he turned to Theodore Cuno instead.

Cuno, who was active as a printer for artists over a period of more than twenty years, lived with his married daughter in a modest row house in a northwest district of Philadelphia. William Libby, who worked with Cuno on Spruance's recommendation, recalls the printer as "a small, gentle, pale man, who shuffled about in soft bedroom slippers. His work-space was in the crowded (what else?) basement, where he had scarcely space for his comparatively large transfer press and himself. In that dark basement he worked under one light, which hung low over the press."[50]

Although few facts are available about the printer's life, it is possible to piece together a picture of his personality and technical methods from the accounts of artists who worked with him: "He

72

73

73 Benton Spruance (1904–1967), *Arrangement for Drums,* 1941. Color lithograph, 240 x 371 [Fine 191], printed by Theodore Cuno. Collection, Tamarind Institute.

was so enthusiastic, so warm, so friendly," Jack Bookbinder recalls. "In working with him, one felt it was a labor of love, he never made it feel like a business. . . . He never seemed to be concerned with how much he was charging." When he etched the stones he would use his fingers. "He knew exactly when to stimulate the etch. . . . If you wanted to add a tone, to counteretch, he would shake his head and say in his German accent, 'dots dangerous.' "[51] Jerome Kaplan remembers that "his etches were very 'hot' and light tones would drop out. . . . He didn't offer any technical information and as a matter of fact he was very close-mouthed about his technique."[52]

Cuno's presence in Philadelphia made work in lithography possible for a number of artists who lived there, among them Bookbinder, Libby, Spruance, Jean Francksen, Maxim Gottlieb, Peter Hurd, Martin Jackson, Jerome Kaplan, Joseph W. McDermott, Robert Riggs, and Raphael Sabatini. Cuno was a superior printer of the traditional crayon lithograph, with the result that artists who worked in this manner—as most did at the time—continued to seek out his 74 services. Long after he moved from Philadelphia to distant New Mexico, Hurd continued to pile his finished stones into a horse trailer and haul them across the country so that they might be printed by Cuno at his basement press.

Cuno continued to work with artists into the early 1950s, by which time he was by Bookbinder's estimate, "well into his seventies." Libby adds that "his vision was fading, and with it his skill." At some point—Bookbinder does not recall the date—Cuno came to see him with "some little litho prints that could pass for . . . greet-

74   Peter Hurd (b. 1904), *The Night Watchman,* 1935. 303 x 275, printed by Theodore Cuno. Collection, University of New Mexico Art Museum.

ing cards. It was somewhat touching and rather pathetic. He told me that he had fallen out of favor with his daughter or son-in-law, and that he had moved—but where he moved, I do not know."[53] Slightly later, when Libby called at the daughter's house to retrieve the last work Cuno had done for him, he was told that the old printer had died.

NOTES

1 Frank Weitenkampf, *American Graphic Arts,* pp. 177–78.

2 Zigrosser, *Artist in America,* p. 15.

3 Ibid., p. 16.

4 Dehn to Ruellan, 3 December 1927.

5 Zigrosser to Dehn, 13 January 1928. Dehn papers, Archives of American Art, Smithsonian Institution, reel 1048, frames 998–99.

6 Dehn to Ruellan, 25 February 1929.

7 Richard McKinzie, *New Deal for Artists,* p. 94.

8 Dore Ashton, *The New York School: A Cultural Reckoning,* p. 13.

9 O'Keeffe, in conversation with the author, Abiquiu, New Mexico, 29 September 1978.

10 Kuniyoshi, unpublished lecture notes, in the files of Sara Kuniyoshi.

11 Kuniyoshi's lithographs have been catalogued by Richard A. Davis, "The Graphic Work of Yasuo Kuniyoshi, 1893–1953." The following corrections should be made in Davis's catalogue: Davis 52 and 65 were printed by Grant Arnold, not by George Miller; Davis 54, 55, and 60 were printed by Arnold, not by Emil Ganso; and Davis 58, which is ascribed to Arnold, was not printed by him.

12 Ruellan and Taylor, in conversation, 7 May 1979.

13 Stuart Davis, "The Place of Abstract Painting in America (letter to Henry McBride)," *Creative Art* 6 (1930), reprinted in Diane Kelder, ed., *Stuart Davis,* pp. 109–10.

14 Louis Lozowick, "The Americanization of Art" (1927), quoted in Barbara Zabel, "Louis Lozowick and Urban Optimism of the 1920s."

15 Le Corbusier, *Towards a New Architecture,* p. 38.

16 Martin L. Friedman, *The Precisionist View in American Art,* p. 22.

17 Ibid., p. 13.

18 For further information on Charlot's work with Miller, 1929–31, see Peter Morse, *Jean Charlot's Prints, a Catalogue Raisonné,* pp. 50–75.

19 Charlot, quoted in ibid., p. 89.

20 Jean Charlot, *American Printmaking, 1913–1947,* p. 33.

21 Morse, *Charlot's Prints,* p. xiv.

22 Clinton Adams, "Lynton R. Kistler and the Development of Lithography in Los Angeles," pp. 100–01.

23 Among Armitage's books were *The Art of Edward Weston* (1932), *Igor Strawinsky* (1936), and *Martha Graham* (1937). Many of his books were printed by Lynton Kistler, who interpreted Armitage's designs in type; Kistler set the type by hand for *The Art of Edward Weston,* which was published by E. Weyhe, New York, and selected among the American Institute of Graphic Arts' "Fifty Books of the Year." See Norman Tanis, Dennis Bakewell, and Don Read, *Lynton R. Kistler, Printer-Lithographer.*

24 Kistler, quoted in Adams, "Kistler," p. 102.

25 Charlot, quoted in Morse, *Charlot's Prints,* p. 77.

26 Ibid., p. 89.

27 For a complete description of the technical processes used in the making of the *Picture Book,* see ibid., pp. 84–90.

28 Kistler, quoted in Adams, "Kistler," p. 102.

29 Morse, *Charlot's Prints,* p. 90.

30 Ebria Feinblatt and Bruce Davis, *Los Angeles Prints, 1883–1980,* pp. 8–9.

31 Ibid., p. 8. The spokesman was Howell Brown, the society's secretary and organizer.

32 Marshall Sprague, *Newport in the Rockies: The Life and Good Times of Colorado Springs,* p. 286–87.

33 Thomas Hart Benton, quoted by Albert Christ-Janer, *Boardman Robinson,* p. 56.

34 Arnold Blanch, "Boardman Robinson as a Teacher," ibid., p. 74.

35 Forsyth to Adams, 30 July 1979.

36 Archie Musick, *Musick Medley: Intimate Memories of a Rocky Mountain Art Colony,* p. 71.

37 Bartlett, interview, 15 April 1978.

38 Verna Jean Versa, tape-recorded interview, April 1978, later edited by Versa, who was a student in Barrett's class.

39 Dorothy Barrett Rundell, interview, 17 April 1978.

40 Musick, *Musick Medley,* p. 88.

41 Woelffer, tape-recorded interview, 1 June 1978.

42 Ibid.

43 Neal, tape-recorded interview, 17 November 1977, later edited by Neal.

44 Ibid.

45 For further information about Barrett's technical procedures as a printer, see Clinton Adams, "Rubbed Stones, Middle Tones and Hot Etches: Lawrence Barrett of Colorado."

46 Paul Parker, "Young Man Turns to Stone," Colorado Springs *Sunday Gazette and Telegraph,* 12 January 1941.

47 Adolf Dehn and Lawrence Barrett, *How to Draw and Print Lithographs.*

48 Carl Zigrosser, *Benton Spruance, Lithographs, 1932–67.*

49 For further information as to the history of the Print Club, see Dorothy Grafly, *A History of the Philadelphia Print Club,* and Ruth Fine Lehrer, "The Print Club of Philadelphia."

50 Libby to Adams, 22 June 1981.

51 Bookbinder, interview, 9 May 1979.

52 Kaplan to Adams, 21 May 1978.

53 Bookbinder interview.

4 · The 1930s:
The Great Depression

THE FEDERAL ART PROJECT

The end of America's great prosperity, signaled by the collapse of the stock market in 1929, had no immediate effect upon the country's artist-lithographers. Even in good times, there had been no substantial market for their work, so that now, during the first years of the depression, nothing was greatly changed. Throughout 1930 and 1931, George Miller was still busy with his printing, much the same as before the crash. "One way or another [artists] found the money to come in and do a lithograph.[1]

But if the artists managed somehow to continue their work, another important group of Miller's clients abruptly disappeared. In the mid-1920s he had developed a considerable business among the city's prospering architects, for whom he had printed elegant renderings of the many skyscrapers that were then on the drawing boards:

> He was getting a dollar a print, and he could print fifty,
> seventy-five, maybe a hundred . . . in a day. That was
> good money. That really carried him through until 1929,
> when the crash came. Ironically enough, some of those
> architects who [had been] making a tremendous amount
> of money came back to him looking for a job to grain
> stones, crank a press, whatever, a couple of years later in
> the early thirties.[2]

The cumulative effects of the Great Depression bore down on Miller as upon everyone else. In 1931, he had to give up his life insurance policy, and by 1934 his business was so much reduced that he was forced to sell many of the printer's proofs that he had retained over the years.* As in the early twenties, he again turned to teaching to supplement his income from printing, and together with Martin Lewis and Armin Landeck he announced the opening of

* Miller sold a good part of his collection of printer's proofs in an auction sale held at the Plaza Book Auction Corporation on 23 March 1934. See also footnote, page 76.

121

"The School for Print Makers," in Miller's shop on Fourteenth Street. But despite such efforts, he could barely get along.

By the time President Roosevelt took office in 1933, the market for art had greatly diminished, and the economic plight of American artists had become no less than desperate. They had survived the early effects of the stock-market crash, but now it had come to the point, as Dore Ashton relates, that

> [their] meager sources of desultory income—dishwashing, house-painting, carpentry, or occasional teaching—were no longer available. Poor as bohemia had been, it had always managed to survive on the left-overs from the affluence of the nineteen-twenties. . . . When the downtown New York artist stepped out of his door as the thirties dawned, his former exhilaration at just being in the center of whatever culture America had mustered was considerably diminished if he happened to live near one of the hastily improvised soup kitchens. The breadlines where silent, resentful, broken men filled the New York air with their dead quiet could not fail to depress him. . . . No artist, however deeply committed he was to art for its own sake, could have escaped entirely from the haunted eyes of his urban contemporaries.[3]

Within the first year of the new administration, the government began a series of programs to come to the artists' aid.[4] Olin Dows, who later became chief of the Treasury Relief Art Project (TRAP), observed that "human economic relief was the motive behind all the New Deal's art programs. . . . If it had not been for the great Depression, it is unlikely that our government would have sponsored more art than it had in the past.[5] The primary aim of these programs was thus to assist artists, not art, and only for this reason were they willingly accepted by the public and the Congress.

Although some original prints—etchings, lithographs, and woodcuts—were created by artists working on the treasury's several art projects, primary emphasis was placed on art for public buildings, and this, for the most part, meant sculptures and mural paintings. Not until the Federal Art Project (FAP) was created as a division of the Work Progress Administration (WPA), did the government establish an active program in printmaking. The FAP "was a part of a wider program called Federal Project No. 1, which included drama, music, and writing. It started in August 1935, was administered according to the rules of the WPA, lasted until June 1943, and cost about $35,000,000. Slightly over 5,000 persons were employed at its peak."[6]

Even earlier, before establishment of the Federal Art Project, efforts had been made to provide economic aid to artists in New York, principally by the privately financed Gibson Committee and by the College Art Association (CAA).[7]

> As unemployment continued, the Gibson Committee found that the demands exceeded those which a private organization could hope to meet, and its activities were absorbed by the Emergency Relief Administration (ERA). This was a state-based organization, which later became the Temporary Emergency Relief Administration (TERA) and received participating funds from the federal government. [The CAA] program was transferred to

these agencies and the employment of artists increased as more funds became available. In New York City, Mayor LaGuardia was the official sponsor, and employment quotas for artists, models, and allied personnel were allocated by his office to the CAA.[7]

Audrey McMahon, who had earlier been director of the CAA, "was placed in general charge, without stipend, [and her] services were donated by the CAA until inception of the WPA/FAP."[8]

> Although the Temporary Emergency Relief Administration's larger allocations for the employment of artists enabled the CAA to expand the program, it still failed to meet the need. . . . [Forbes Watson commented] bitterly on the fact that although the CAA, "the closest student of the relief problems of the artists of New York, and the most active worker on behalf of relief," was employing 300 artists through the FERA, there were "over 1400 artists in New York City . . . who were in need.[9]

When the WPA/FAP was established in August 1935, Audrey McMahon "became one of its five regional directors, with responsibility for New York City (administered as a separate state by the WPA), New York State, New Jersey, and, for a brief time, Philadelphia. [She] resigned from the CAA directorship."[10] It was shortly thereafter that plans were made to establish a graphic art division within the WPA/FAP. Jacob Kainen, who worked as an artist on the project, relates that

> Mrs. McMahon enlisted the aid of Russell T. Limbach, an artist and printer experienced in all forms of the graphic arts. His job was to plan the shop for maximum working efficiency, to procure the equipment and supplies, and to find skilled printers. . . .
> It was not easy to obtain the equipment. Although money had been allocated for paying artists and obtaining supplies, there were no funds for presses. Fortunately, the technical apparatus was donated by sympathetic individuals. Thus on February 6, 1936, the graphic division's first studio workshop, the first sponsored by the government, was officially opened on the twelfth floor of the building housing the WPA/FAP headquarters at 6 East 39th Street. . . . A special lithograph, *City Hall,* by Harry Taskey, was printed [by Ted Wahl] and presented [to the city.][11]

COLOR LITHOGRAPHY AND THE PROJECT

In the catalogue of the first in a series of five exhibitions of color lithography that Gustave von Groschwitz organized for the Cincinnati Art Museum during the 1950s, he took note of the fact that "no concentrated [American] activity in the medium [of color lithography] appears until 1936 when artists of the New York City Federal Art Project took it up during the few years of the project's existence and produced more fine color lithographs than had ever been made before in the United States."[12]

Von Groschwitz had himself been a primary force in the development of the graphic arts workshop in New York, where he served as its supervisor from the fall of 1935 until 1938. His interest in

75 Albert Heckman (1893–1971), *Old Locks at Eddyville,* c. 1928. 275 x 428, probably printed by the artist. Collection, Tamarind Institute.

lithography had first been stimulated through his association with Albert Heckman at Columbia University. Heckman, a painter and printmaker who then taught at Teachers College, had studied at the Leipzig Institute of Graphic Arts. He now lived in Woodstock where he had a press of his own upon which he printed his lithographs principally well-drawn landscape and still-life subjects that revealed a debt to Cézanne.

At the FAP workshop, von Groschwitz met others who shared his interest in lithography, among them Augustus Peck, Bernarda Bryson, and, above all, Russell Limbach. Limbach had himself worked extensively as an artist-lithographer in Cleveland throughout the late 1920s and had won a number of awards for his lithographs at the Cleveland Museum of Art and the Art Institute of Chicago. His lithograph, *Trapeze Girl,* had been in 1935 the first color lithograph drawn and printed by an artist employed by the project.

In the early days of the project, before the workshop was fully equipped, the printing was done elsewhere. Ted Wahl, Jacob Friedland, Will Barnet, and George Miller all printed for project artists, using their own press equipment. But by mid-1936 the Thirty-ninth Street workshop was in full swing, and Wahl had been joined as printer by Joseph Peroutka and Nathaniel Spreckley, both experienced lithographers. With the workshop's printing capabilities thus established, it was announced early in 1937 that artists were now free to make color lithographs, with Limbach's assistance as technical advisor.

Response was immediate, and by the following year it was possible to include twenty-three color lithographs by sixteen artists in

75

66

76   Jacob Kainen (b. 1909), *The Waitress*, 1940. 271 x 367 [Flint 42], printed by
Joseph Peroutka. Collection, University of New Mexico Art Museum.

an exhibition, "Printmaking: A New Tradition," at the Federal Art
Gallery on Fifty-seventh Street. The catalogue included a foreword
by Carl Zigrosser, an "explanation" by Gustave von Groschwitz,
and a description of color lithography by Russel Limbach.[13]

Ultimately, more than 130 color lithographs—many in four and
five colors—were made in the New York workshop by a long list of
project artists, including Friedland, Limbach, Wahl, Ida Abelman,
Arnold Blanch, Stuart Davis, Emil Ganso, Minnetta Good, Boris
Gorelick, Harry Gottlieb, Riva Helfond, Jacob Kainen, Margaret
Lowengrund, Louis Lozowick, Beatrice Mandelman, Jack Markow,
Elizabeth Olds, Leonard Pytlak, and Joseph Vogel. For most of these
artists—including Stuart Davis—the lithographs made on the project were their first in color. Without the facilities of the govern-
ment-supported workshop, the skills of the project printers, and the
encouragement of Limbach and von Groschwitz, it is most unlikely
that so extensive a development of color lithography would have
taken place in the 1930s, or even much later, for there was no way
in which the artists of the period could have afforded to pay the prices
which Friedland, Kistler, or Miller would necessarily have charged
for the printing of such complex works.[14]

In the later years of the project, however, a different kind of
price was to be paid. After von Groschwitz's departure as supervisor in 1938, the constraints imposed by the federal bureaucracy were
sometimes severely felt. Jacob Kainen relates that

> while work on the Project was exciting and stimulating, the
> hard facts of day-to-day relationships with the
> administration were generally unhappy. We realized that
> the Project administration was under pressure from its

76

77

125

own administrative superiors, but that didn't alter the fact that we had to fight not only for reasonable working conditions but also for our economic existence. . . .[15]

Artists were constantly irritated by unreasonable working rules, constant firings and rehirings, and restrictions which they felt—with good reason—hampered creativity. Kainen tells of an incident in 1940 when Werner Drewes, now supervisor, was overheard loudly arguing in an administrative meeting:

> [We could hear his voice] raised in vehement protest. When the meeting ended Drewes emerged, his face red with fury. When we asked what had happened, he said: "You now have another stupid regulation. You have to make finished drawings before making your prints. And by finished I mean that you must anticipate exactly what tones, lines, and textures you will use in your final print. In other words, you must copy your preliminary drawing exactly[16]

But in spite of these frustrations it was also possible for Kainen to observe that

> the experience of producing prints and having them professionally printed was a constant pleasure and made up for numerous indignities. It was in the shop that the printmakers felt most truly at home. There they could proof their blocks, plates, and stones in company with outstanding professionals such as Stuart Davis, Raphael Soyer, Yasuo Kuniyoshi, Adolf Dehn, Louis Lozowick, George Constant, and others. There was no "star" system—we were all in the same boat. We were stimulated by each other's presence and by the fact that productivity was a common requirement.[17]

Kainen's perception of the stimulation artists experienced while working together is strongly supported by others. Dore Ashton observes that when one examines "all of the statements made subsequently by the major artists of the forties and fifties, the obvious value the WPA had for them was that of artistic community. They often point out that the artist, like everyone else, was starving and the Project was a meal-ticket. . . . But the most compelling force that emerges is their sense of having found each other."[18]

TED WAHL AND JACKSON POLLOCK

Ted Wahl printed for the Federal Art Project in New York both before and after his sojourn in Colorado Springs during the summer of 1936. At first, before the project had been able fully to equip its workshop, Wahl had printed on his own press in his apartment-studio on Macdougal Street. Later, when the project workshop was in full operation, he continued to print for artists in his studio, not as a business but "just for the fun of it."

It was there that Wahl printed for Jackson Pollock, who had come from Los Angeles to New York in 1930 and had studied painting with Thomas Hart Benton at the Art Students League. Pollock did not enroll in the lithography class at the league, and apparently did not become interested in the medium until about 1934.* When in the summer of 1935 Pollock signed up with the Federal Art Project, he did so in the painting division, not in graphic arts, and all of

* Jackson Pollock's interest in lithography may have been stimulated by his older brother, Charles, who had made lithographs in collaboration with Grant Arnold while a student at the league.

126

77 Joseph Vogel (b. 1911), *Solicitations,* c. 1936–39. 379 x 292, printed by Jacob
Friedland at the FAP Graphics Workshop, New York. Collection, National
Museum of American Art, Smithsonian Institution, by transfer from the District
of Columbia Public Library.

his lithographs were printed privately by Ted Wahl. Though none
of Pollock's lithographs can be dated with precision, it is probably
that the first was done in 1934 and the last in 1937.[19]

Wahl vividly recalls the occasions when Pollock would climb
the stairs to his studio, seldom by prearrangement and often late at
night. "Ted," he would say, "I want to make a lithograph." Sometimes the only stone that Wahl had available on short notice was a
small stone he had been using for graining, but he would give it to
Pollock. Wahl would go on with his printing while Pollock made a
drawing, then at the end of the evening he would pull a few prints
from the young artist's stone: "I'd knock off two or three prints,
and he'd grab one of them. . . . And that was it."[20]

Pollock's lithographs serve well to reflect the evolution of his
style between 1934 and 1937, during which time he moved from a
series of strongly Bentonesque farm and ranch subjects,* to a later

* Among Pollock's Bentonesque subjects is the
lithograph, *Stacking Hay* (O'Connor IV 1059),
the print that was included (under the title
Harvest) in the portfolio published in Colorado
Springs by Archie Musick. Although Musick
gives this lithograph a date of 1937, it is more
likely that it was drawn in the fall of 1936 when
Wahl returned to New York after his summer
in Colorado Springs. See page 110.

127

group of prints that clearly reveal the influence of David Alfaro Siquieros, with whom he worked in New York in 1936. In Pollock's final lithograph with Wahl, *Figures in a Landscape,* he used an airbrush to chase pools of liquid tusche across the stone, creating "automatic" webs of line which strongly suggest his mature work of later years. Francis O'Connor suggests that it was at Siquieros's Experimental Workshop that Pollock was exposed to such "radical techniques as use of the airbrush,"* although by Wahl's account he was himself using an airbrush on one occasion when Pollock came to his studio. "Jack liked the idea, and he said, 'Hey, I want to do one.' And I said, okay. Then I got him a stone, and he did that [*Figures in a Landscape*.]"[12]

Soon after this print was done, Wahl learned that the building he occupied on Macdougal Street was to be torn down. Frustrated by the difficulties of life in the city, he decided to move out. For a time he worked as a printer at the FAP workshop in Newark, New Jersey; then moved across the state to Milford, built a modest home on a hill high above the Delaware River, and thereafter printed few lithographs other than his own work.†

THE FEDERAL ART PROJECT OUTSIDE NEW YORK CITY

Following the opening of the New York workshop in 1936, other printmaking workshops were soon established throughout the country by the graphic arts division of the WPA/FAP. Ted Wahl, as has been seen, became the lithographic printer in Newark. Grant Arnold, who continued to print in the basement workshop at the Woodstock Artists Association, now became the FAP printer there. In Philadelphia a graphic workshop was established in the old Johnson mansion on Broad Street near Lombard, where Dox Thrash and Ray Steth were hired as printers. In California, workshops were opened in San Francisco and Los Angeles, with Ray Bertrand and Karl Winter as the lithographic printers in the north and south, respectively. Other workshops were soon formed in cities throughout the country.‡

Such data as are available with respect to the operation of the FAP's graphic workshops suggest that the New York workshop may have accounted for almost half of the project's total national activity in the field of printmaking.§ Although Audrey McMahon relates that the lack of local authority was "often extremely trying (even a paint brush had to be requisitioned 'through channels')," it would appear that the local project directors were able to establish policy in some degree, and that many of the workshops enjoyed greater freedom from bureaucratic regulation than did the workshop in New York. In Woodstock, for example, artists were not required to submit preliminary drawings or sketches before beginning a print. "They would come in and pick up a stone," Grant Arnold recalls. "They would do their drawings and bring them back and I'd print them. It was just as simple as that."[22] He remembers no more than one occasion on which a print was questioned by the local administrator, and few of the firings and hirings that caused such trauma in New York.

In some cases the workshops responded to local conditions through varying technical methods. Not all of the workshops had facilities for work in all media. In some, lithography remained (as

* Pollock worked with Siquieros in the Mexican artist's experimental workshop on Fourteenth Street. "Siquieros was engaged in exploring new techniques and mediums . . . among [them] the use of spray guns and air brushes. . . . The spontaneous application of paint and problems of 'controlled accidents' occupied the members of the workshop. The floor was covered with spatter and drip. It is likely that this experience had an influence on Pollock's later development." (Francis V. O'Connor, *Jackson Pollock,* p. 21.)

† With terrible timing, Wahl undertook to open a private print shop in New Hope, Pennsylvania, on the first of December 1941, only a week before the Japanese attack on Pearl Harbor. He was unable to maintain it. Following the war, Wahl continued his own work as an artist and taught in Delaware Valley schools, but he did not again become active as a collaborative printer.

‡ By 1936 the graphic arts division had established sixteen print workshops in nine states: five in New York, four in California, and one each in Connecticut, Florida, Maryland, Michigan, Ohio, and Pennsylvania. These workshops have not yet been the subject of research sufficient to permit a full account of their activity.

For a summary of files, papers, problems in the conduct of research, etc., see "Notes on Sources" in Richard D. McKinzie, *The New Deal for Artists,* pp. 193–95.

§ Jacob Kainen writes: "The catalogue of the M. H. de Young Museum's exhibition *Frontiers of American Art* held in San Francisco in 1939, states 'Although only 250 artists are employed in the Graphic Arts Section of the Project [nationally], production in this field totals 84,350 prints of 4,000 original examples in lithography, wood engraving, color prints, and other media.' Recalling Mrs. McMahon's report that by November 30, 1938, in New York City alone, 36,571 prints had been made from 1,840 master designs, we can see that almost half the total production in the country came from New York." (Jacob Kainen, "The Graphic Arts Division of the WPA Federal Art Project in New York City and State," in Francis V. O'Connor, *The New Deal Art Projects: An Anthology of Memoirs,* p. 171.)

78 Jackson Pollock (1912–1956), *Untitled (Figures in a Landscape),* 1937.
260 x 388 [O'Connor T.IV:1088], printed by Theodore Wahl. Collection,
Museum of Modern Art, New York, John B. Turner Fund.

Limbach had described it) the "stepchild of the arts," and none of
the shops outside New York developed a capacity for extensive work
in color. Depending upon their personnel and equipment, some workshops gave emphasis to etching, others to relief prints, or to seri-
graphy, a medium which first received serious attention in the FAP's
workshops.

Geography was also a factor in the mode of operation. In a small
art colony such as Woodstock, artists could easily come to Arnold's
workshop to work on (or pick up) a stone, but in many parts of the
country, distance made this impossible. In such circumstances, transfer lithography assumed particular importance. In the San Francisco
workshop, which served artists throughout northern California, Joseph Danysh and Ray Bertrand developed a new kind of transfer
paper so that artists might draw on paper and send their drawings
to San Francisco to be transferred and printed.

Because eligibility for employment by the FAP was determined
by need, not by competence or talent, it was inevitable that many of
the prints made by project artists should be pedestrian or worse. This
fact does not, however, support Barbara Rose's judgment that
"outside of a few murals . . . the WPA program produced almost
no art of any consequence."[23] The success of the project should be
measured not by the many poor works it produced, but by its signifi-

cant accomplishments. In lithography it gave important stimulus to color printing, to the geographic dispersion of printing facilities, and to the printing of fine lithographs by artists who might otherwise have found it impossible to work in the medium. In many cases the prints produced on the project were at least the equal of those that were privately printed, either by the artist or by a collaborating printer. Indeed, as Aline Kistler concluded in 1937 after examination of prints submitted for review by *Prints* magazine:

> From the evidence at hand, one must . . . give credit to [the] government projects which have stimulated the production of distinguished graphic art. In a number of instances . . . the prints for the government are of finer quality than those done by the artist on his own. I cannot account for this . . . [but] the stimulus of a definite objective seems to me to have raised the level of accomplishment.[24]

THE AMERICAN SCENE: ART AND POLITICS

As the depression disrupted the economy at home and as the threat of war in Europe became ever more apparent, a wave of Americanist sentiment was felt in the United States. Among artists, Thomas Hart Benton came to be its spokesman:

> We [Benton, Curry, and Wood] were all in revolt against the unhappy effects which the Armory Show of 1913 had on American painting . . . and we believed that only by turning the formative processes of art back again to meaningful subject matter, in our cases specifically American subject matter, could we expect to get . . . an American art which was not empty.[25]

Benton's student Herman Cherry recalls that "the reaction against European painting was very very strong,"[26] with the consequence that even Holger Cahill, director of the Federal Art Project, adapted to its spirit. In 1934 he wrote that "American art is declaring a moratorium on its debts to Europe and returning to cultivate its garden. . . . Art for art's sake is a tattered banner which has blown down with the wind. . . . The cultivation of sensibility has become a blind alley."[27]

It was an essentially negative Americanism, a rejection of European influences, of the modernist spirit, and of internationalism in art; as such it departed radically from the position of Stuart Davis, Louis Lozowick, Charles Sheeler, and other "urban optimists," who in their work affirmed art as well as America. The new flag-waving Americanism of the depression years found its sources both in politics and aesthetics—areas of thought which became curiously (and inconsistently) intermingled in the 1930s. John Sloan found it necessary to resign as director of the Art Students League, a realist stronghold, during a controversy that surrounded the hiring of a "foreign" teacher, George Grosz, who had come to New York as a refugee from the Nazis. Benton, never noted for the moderation of his language, attacked the Stieglitz group as "an intellectually diseased lot, victims of sickly rationalizations, psychic inversions, and God-awful self-cultivations,"[28] while his friend and former roommate, the critic Thomas Craven, spoke of

130

a battle waged and won [culminating in] a decisive victory over . . . cheap internationalism. Today, save for a few feeble Marxians, and a handful of defeated purists who believe with Picasso that art is a species of vacuous dabbling . . . there is not a self-respecting artist in the country who is not eager to contribute to a movement which has gained the sympathies and support of the American public.[29]

Foremost among the artists identified with the movements to which Craven refers were the artists of the "American Scene," including both the regionalists of the Midwest and a number of urban realists, many of whom—though strongly committed to representation of the quality of human life in the American metropolis—sharply rejected Craven's bigotry and prejudice. Diverse in style as well as in attitude, these realists included some who continued the traditions of Daumier and Gavarni; some who worked in the spirit of Bellows, Sloan, and Henri; some who brought to American art a distinctly sad and tender mood, Russian or European in flavor; some who were strongly influenced by the Mexican artists Orozco, Rivera, and Siquieros; and some who conceived of art as an instrument for social and political change. A few were forthright Marxists who shared Craven's contempt for modern art, although from the perspective of the left rather than the right.

Many of these artists worked extensively in lithography; others chose the intaglio print as their primary medium. Working principally in New York, they together created a body of work which—whatever its formal or aesthetic character—accurately reflects the varied character of the period: the bawdy vitality of burlesque shows, street fairs, and Coney Island; the quiet lives of the city's people in their rooms and apartments; and the unhappy existence of lonely, unemployed men on the Bowery and in the all-night missions. Among the many artists who dealt with at least some of these themes in their prints of this period are Ida Abelman, Peggy Bacon, Will Barnet, Isabel Bishop, Paul Cadmus, Nicolai Cikovsky, Minna Citron, Glenn Coleman, Mabel Dwight, Eugene Fitsch, Don Freeman, Aline Fruhauf, Wanda Gág, Harry Gottlieb, William Gropper, Edward Hopper, Mervin Jules, Chet La More, Martin Lewis, Jack Markow, Reginald Marsh, Fletcher Martin, Kenneth Hayes Miller, Robert Riggs, Isaac Soyer, Moses Soyer, Raphael Soyer, Benton Spruance, and Harry Sternberg.

Art, like politics, makes for strange bedfellows, and by the early thirties many realist and modernist artists had made common cause to form a union (the United American Artists, C.I.O.) and the Artists' Committee of Action. "By November 1934 [the two groups] had not only pulled together a large organization with Stuart Davis at its head, but also commenced publication of *Art Front,* a news and criticism vehicle which appeared with Davis's proclamation that it was 'the crystallization of all the forces in art surging forward to combat the destructive and chauvinistic tendencies' "[30]

The art community became increasingly polarized. *Time* and *Life* magazines beat the drums loudly for a pure, American art, purged of foreign contamination; the Hearst press did likewise; and Peyton Boswell, Jr., editor of the *Art Digest,* spoke of "an American School of Painting which promises to be the most important movement in the world of art since the days of the Italian Renaissance. . . . Nationalism, robust and sometimes ruthless . . . bred of disillusion-

79
80
81
82
83
84
85
86
87
88

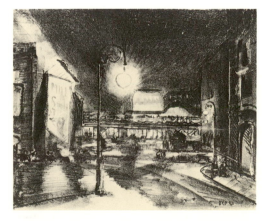

79 Eugene C. Fitsch (b. 1892), *Astor Place,* 1931. 217 x 264, printed by the artist. Collection, Tamarind Institute.

131

80 Will Barnet (b. 1911), *Conflict,* 1934. 414 x 484 [Cole 3], printed by the artist. Collection, Art, Prints and Photographs Division, New York Public Library, Astor, Lenox, and Tilden Foundations.

ment with international entanglements . . . is the prime cause behind the development of the new school of American painting—the only new development today in the world of art."[31]

Benton and Craven were even more intemperate in their remarks. Recalling Royal Cortissoz's description of the Armory Show as "Ellis Island art," Craven at one point spoke of Stieglitz as that "Hoboken Jew." Benton, who was not at heart the "fascist, jingoist, anti-Semitic, and reactionary son-of-a-bitch" that his opponents made him out to be, nonetheless earned his reputation through swinging attacks on the "coteries" of the modernist art establishment, made up of critics, college art professors, and museum boys: "a pack of precious ninnies who [walk] with a hip swing in their gaits."[32]

Davis, whose liberal credentials went back to his days on the *Masses,* used *Art Front* to reply in kind: Benton, he said, "fired off a big gun in salute to America which was loaded with a commodity not listed in the *Consumer's Weekly.*" Craven's criticism, in Davis's

132

81   Glenn O. Coleman (1887–1932), *The Bowery,* 1928. 309 x 438, printer
unknown. Collection, Philadelphia Museum of Art, anonymous gift.

view, was little more than "vicious and windy chauvinistic bally-
hoo. . . . The slight burp . . . may not indicate the stomach ulcer of
Fascism. I am not a political doctor, but I have heard the burp and
as a fellow artist I would advice those concerned to submit themselves to a qualified diagnostician, other than witch doctor Craven,
just to be on the safe side."[33]

PUBLICATIONS AND PUBLISHERS

No field of the visual arts more directly felt the effects of this political and economic climate than did lithography. Within a few short
years, the 1930s had seen the consequences of the Great Depression,
the founding of the Federal Art Project and its graphic arts division,
the formation of the artists' union and other artists' political organizations, the influence of Mexican populism, and a strong and conscious
effort to develop an entirely new market for the work of American
printmakers.

The latter was an effort that had had its beginnings soon after
the First World War, at a time when the fashion among a circle of
wealthy print buyers was for etchings of the British school—Whistler,
Muirhead Bone, D. Y. Cameron, and Seymour Haden, among
others—and as it was the deliberate practice of these artists to print
quite small editions, the market that developed was based on "a spe-
cious rarity and preciousness that at times bordered on the absurd.

82   Raphael Soyer (b. 1899), *Self Portrait,* 1933. 337 x 248 [Cole 26], printed by George C. Miller. Collection, Nicolai Cikovsky.

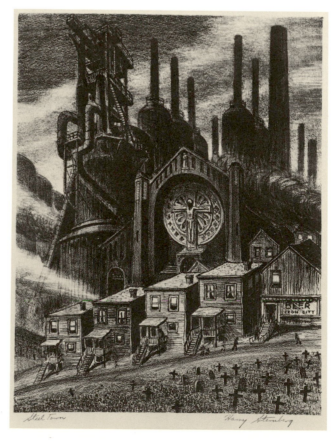

83   Harry Sternberg (b. 1904), *Steel Town,* 1937. 336 x 258 [Moore 144], printed by the artist. Collection, Tamarind Institute.

84   Raphael Soyer (b. 1899), *The Mission,* 1933. 310 x 448 [Cole 27], printed by
George C. Miller. Collection, Philadelphia Museum of Art. Purchase, Lola
Downin Peck Fund from the Carl and Laura Zigrosser Collection.

37/50

85   Don Freeman (1908–1978), *Washington Square Art Show,* n.d. 245 x 300, probably printed by George C. Miller. Collection, Tamarind Institute.

The addition of a few strokes to the plate by a popular English etcher, for instance, could produce a unique artist's proof that commanded even higher prices than his already artificially limited edition."[34]

It was this tradition of scarcity that was directly challenged by such publishing ventures as Carl Zigrosser's portfolio, *Twelve Prints by Contemporary Artists,* sold by the Weyhe Gallery for fifty dollars in 1919, and the portfolio *Six American Etchings,* issued in 1924 by *New Republic* magazine in an effort to attract new subscribers. Never had a greater value been offered: for a total price of eight dollars, purchasers acquired one print each by six artists—Peggy Bacon, Ernest Haskell, Edward Hopper, John Marin, Kenneth Hayes Miller, and John Sloan—yet even at this price, the editions were undersubscribed.

Similar efforts were made throughout the 1930s, with varying success. In February 1933 the Contemporary Print Group was formed by ten prominent printmakers: Thomas Hart Benton, George Biddle, Jacob Burck, John Steuart Curry, Adolf Dehn, Mabel Dwight, George Grosz, Charles Locke, Reginald Marsh, and José Clemente Orozco. "In addition to the question of their personal survival in difficult times, they also sought to bridge the gulf that they perceived existed between artists and public, a goal that might best be accomplished through the wide distribution of affordable prints."[35] Two portfolios were issued, *The American Scene No. 1* and *No. 2,* each consisting of six lithographs printed by George Miller and each priced at fifteen dollars.* Although the plan was to issue a series of such

*   The artists represented in the first portfolio were Biddle, Burck, Dehn, Grosz, Marsh, and Orozco; and in the second, Benton, Curry, Gropper, Russell Limbach, Charles Locke, and Raphael Soyer.

89

86 Wanda Gág (1893–1946), *Evening,* 1929. 205 x 303, printed by George C.
Miller. Collection, Tamarind Institute.

portfolios on a monthly basis in editions of 300 impressions, it was
short-lived; the public did not respond, and the group disbanded in
1934. The success of the portfolios was certainly not assisted by the
fact that, as Janet Flint observes:

> [They were] dominated by dramatic representations of
> strikes, lynch mobs, and the oppressed, as well as satirical
> judgments of establishment stereotypes. The introductions
> to the portfolios by Suzanne La Follette and Anita Brenner,
> respectively, underlined the group's fundamental belief in
> the artist as interpreter and critic of contemporary life.[36]

But even those artists whose subject matter was somewhat easier for the public to accept found it difficult to establish an audience.
By comparison with the prints of Gropper, Grosz, and Orozco,
Dehn's satirical comments on human follies were lighthearted and
good-natured, although this was of little help when it came to sales.
Much as Dehn loved lithography, he was faced with a dilemma: he
could neither bring himself to abandon the medium nor could he
make it pay. Following his sojourn in Europe, he had continued his
work in lithography with American printers—Grant Arnold, Jacob
Friedland, and George Miller—with the result that despite his growing critical reputation, a massive inventory of unsold prints had
accumulated in his studio—the inevitable result of an untiring productivity and a badly depressed art market.

87   Nicolai Cikovsky (b. 1894), *Portrait of a Girl,* c. 1930. 242 x 182, printed by Jacob Friedland. Collection of the artist.

88   Mabel Dwight (1876–1955), *Self Portrait,* 1932. 268 x 211, printed by George C. Miller. Collection, Tamarind Institute.

89 Charles W. Locke (b. 1899), *City Wharves,* 1934. 210 x 290, printed by
George C. Miller. Published by Contemporary Print Group in *The American
Scene, No. 2.* Collection, Art, Prints and Photographs Division, New York
Public Library, Astor, Lenox, and Tilden Foundations.

In 1933—the same year in which the Contemporary Print Group
published its first portfolio—Dehn formed the Adolf Dehn Print
Club in an effort to stimulate sale of his lithographs. He published a
brochure and sent it out through the mail; offered club memberships
at five dollars, for which price each member would be given the
choice of one of the four lithographs illustrated in the brochure, and,
with characteristic optimism, had the lithographs printed in editions
of one hundred impressions. While the response was not overwhelm-
ing, sufficient sales resulted so that Dehn was encouraged to continue
the club over a period of several years.

Dehn and the other artist-members of the Contemporary Print
Group were neither the first nor the last to cling to the notion that
original prints could somehow find a market, even during the Great
Depression, if they were sold at a low enough price. Many such efforts
were made, but none more successful than that of Reeves Lewenthal,
a former newspaper reporter, publicist, and artists' agent, who—not
long after Dehn began his print club—established a new print-
marketing venture which he was to call the Associated American
Artists (AAA). "There was no art business, certainly not in prints,
in those days," Sylvan Cole states, "[but] it was Reeves's idea that a
print that would sell for five dollars might find a market."[37]

ASSOCIATED AMERICAN ARTISTS

In July 1934, Lewenthal gathered together a group of artists, including Adolf Dehn, for a discussion of his proposal.* As a result of this meeting, a marketing format was determined: etchings and lithographs would be published in editions of 250 impressions; they would sell for five dollars each and would be marketed through leading department stores. Lewenthal would pay the cost of printing and the artist would receive a two-hundred-dollar fee. Nobody would get rich, but perhaps a new public could in this way be led to buy original prints. *Prints* magazine carried this report of the undertaking:

> To popularize fine art by putting prints by the best American artists on sale at five dollars each in department stores throughout the country is the aim of the Associated American Artists. The plan was launched on Monday, October 15th in fifty large cities. Reeves Lewenthal, public relations counsel to the National Academy of Design and the Society of American Etchers, is president of the organization and director of its activities. . . .
>
> "Here is the first real movement against the flood of cheap foreign prints of little artistic or other value," says one of the formal statements issued by the organization. Also, it is a part of a campaign of education to convince the public that good pictorial art can be made available at a low price, and to discourage the sales in certain department stores at "bargain prices" of $3.98, etc. of "old masters" and other prints which are being represented as what they are not. No department store will be allowed to handle the work of this group of artists without a pledge to sell no print under an even five dollars. This low price is made possible by a plan whereby each member of the organization makes 250 prints from each plate or lithographic stone or block executed for these sales.[38]

The exhibition and sale of AAA prints opened nearly simultaneously in department stores throughout the country: at B. Altman's and Wanamaker's in New York, Marshall Field in Chicago, Thalheimer's in Richmond, Bullock's in Los Angeles, and comparable stores elsewhere. Prints by some artists soon sold out, while others moved very slowly, with the result that in violation of AAA policy Thalheimer's marked some prints down to $3.98. "That made Reeves angry," Cole says. "He took an ad in *The New York Times*— it cost him $400—offering, for the first time, original art by mail. It brought in $9,000 worth of business."[39]

The prestige that etching enjoyed among the general public caused Lewenthal to emphasize etchings in a series of hard-sell advertisements which, in their language and approach, departed dramatically from the way in which art had traditionally been sold: "How would you like to possess a genuine, signed original by Grant Wood, Thomas Benton, John Steuart Curry, George Biddle, Luigi Lucioni or any one of 56 other famous artists? Now you can . . . at a price that will seem incredible . . . only $5.00!"

But though etchings were featured in Lewenthal's advertisements, many of the finest prints published by AAA were lithographs. Most of these lithographs were printed by George Miller, for whom Lewenthal's commissioned editions soon became a vital part of his

* According to published accounts, Lewenthal's meeting was attended by Thomas Hart Benton, John Steuart Curry, Doris Lee, Adolf Dehn, Gordon Grant, Boardman Robinson, and Grant Wood, among others. Sylvan Cole has expressed his doubt that all of these artists in fact attended the meeting (Cole, interview, May 1979).

business. Some were printed by Lynton Kistler, Lawrence Barrett, or by other professional printers; and a few were printed by the artists, who then received a small payment for the printing in addition to their two-hundred-dollar fee.*

As ten artist's proofs were included in each edition, a total of 260 impressions was ordered from the printer. "Frequently, editions were never fully printed, either because of a lack of interest in the work, or because something happened to the plate or stone. Often editions were ordered at the rate of 50 at a time until the full edition was completed."[40]

Burr Miller recalls that in 1947, when he joined his father at the press after World War II, they had so much printing to do for AAA that by the first of April it had become impossible to accept any further work for the remainder of the year. As the city's summer heat and humidity combine to create impossible conditions for fine printing, it was George Miller's practice to print at his home in Vermont during the summer months. "My father and I would get going about seven o'clock in the morning on an Associated American Artists stone. We could finish the two-hundred-and-sixty in one day,† without telephones, without any salesmen coming in, with no interruptions, the two of us would get it done. He'd pull about forty and I'd crank, and then I'd pull and I'd crank. I'd crank *all* the time!"[41]

Aggressive as was Lewenthal's hard-sell advertising of the AAA editions, it was not untruthful. Between 1934 and 1949 AAA published a long and diverse series of fine prints—a total of over one thousand editions—among them such notable lithographs as John Steuart Curry's *John Brown,* William Gropper's *Paul Bunyan,* Ivan Albright's *Self-Portrait, 55 Division Street,* Joseph Hirsch's *Hecklers,* and Grant Wood's *Shriners' Quartet,* each of which was originally sold at AAA's established price of five dollars.‡ Given the economic climate of the times, it is likely that had it not been for these commissions and the financial support they provided, many of the fine lithographs created during the thirties and forties might not now exist. While Miller's printing charges and the amounts Lewenthal paid to the artists now seem small, they were then substantial sums.

90
91
92
93
94

PRINTS FOR THE MASSES: POPULIST ATTITUDES

In the fall of 1936, Aline Kistler, then editor of *Prints,* the most influential print journal of the period, addressed herself to the new trend in print publishing that Lewenthal had begun, a trend that had now been given additional momentum by the American Artists Group, publishers of "unsigned, unlimited edition impressions . . . at two dollars and seventy-five cents each."[42]

The editions published by Lewenthal's Associated American Artists, though larger than ordinary, had been limited in size, and had been accompanied by "the promise of the artist that he will check on the quality of each impression by signing it to attest it as a satisfactory imprinting of his conceived design." The new, unsigned editions had no such guarantee, a practice to which Aline Kistler strongly objected:

> When the artist affixes his signature to each print before issuing it, the chances are that inferior impressions will be discarded. When the print is unsigned, the discarding of an unrepresentative impression rests entirely in the hands

* Lewenthal made the decisions as to the prints that AAA would publish. Benton comments: "[AAA] was not strictly speaking an association, at least not in the usual sense of the term. The artists involved had no hand in policy or management. Lewenthal was shrewd enough to see the disruptive possibilities of artistic pride in such practical matters as showing and selling and kept the direction of the business well in his own hands." (Thomas Hart Benton, *Artist in America,* p. 279.)

† Sylvan Cole says that orders were frequently placed for partial printing of editions: "We would order full editions on what we thought were sure sellers, such as Gordon Grant, or Benton, or any of the 'name artists'. But [with] some of the lesser known artists . . . we'd start off with 50 to 100 and see where things went. Reeves would also keep track of [the] balance of editions to be printed." (Cole to Adams, 13 July 1982.)

Burr Miller, on the other hand, recalls that on some occasions "because of the tremendous volume of work . . . we'd only run off a hundred. . . . We'd talk to someone up at AAA and say, 'How's this going? Will a hundred hold you for a month or two weeks?'. . . Eventually, we'd get back and finish up the edition a month or a few weeks later, whatever the case would be. But we always printed 260—we never really cut the edition short that I can remember." (Miller interview, 4 May 1979.)

‡ AAA published 329 editions between 1934 and 1939, and 678 between 1940 and 1949 (these figures include prints in all media). After 1949 AAA published prints at a much reduced rate; only 176 editions were published between 1950 and 1959. Many of the lithographs originally sold for $5.00 now command prices in excess of $3,000.

90 John Steuart Curry (1897–1946), *John Brown,* 1939. 378 x 275 [Cole 34],
printed by George C. Miller. Published by Associated American Artists.
Collection, Tamarind Institute.

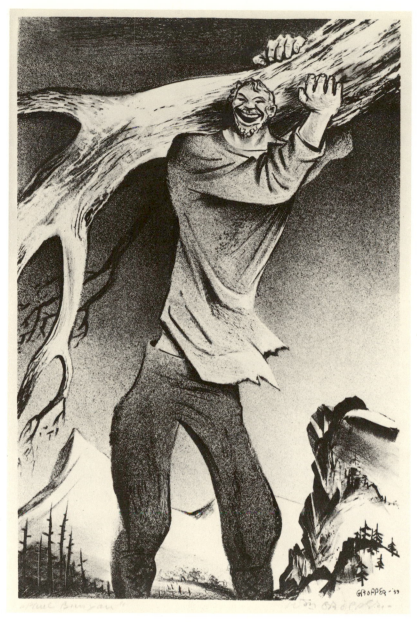

91   William Gropper (1897–1977), *Paul Bunyan*, 1939. 343 x 226, printed by
George C. Miller. Published by Associated American Artists. Collection,
Tamarind Institute.

of the printer, the publisher or the dealer and the
responsibility of choice may be passed on to the buyer
himself.[43]

The American Artists Group, a leading distributor of greeting
cards, began publication of original prints at the instigation of Carl
Zigrosser, who still in the mid-thirties served as director of Erhard
Weyhe's print gallery. Weyhe emphatically rejected participation in
the project which he believed "would not work and furthermore
would ruin the print business completely."[44] That Zigrosser persisted in spite of Weyhe's opposition was a factor in a growing es-
trangement between the two men.* Zigrosser gave serious thought
to the growing problems they were encountering. The effects of the
depression had been "catastrophic," particularly in terms of its psychological impact on Weyhe, and hence upon the gallery and himself.
He drafted a letter to Weyhe (perhaps never sent): "I don't think

*   When some time later Carl Zigrosser looked
back upon the publications of the American Artists Group, he made this appraisal of them: "We
tried to slant the subject matter of the prints for
popular appeal—pictures for the masses. . . .
We had two aims: to furnish works of art and
to be popular . . . [but] our duality of purpose
involved us in a certain amount of compromise,
and as is often the case with half-measures, produced neither art nor popularity. If a large number of the ninety prints we published now seem
trite and commonplace, a score perhaps still have
not lost their luster, and another score stood out
above the average of their time. We certainly
gave the public good value for the money."
(Carl Zigrosser, *World of Art,* pp. 56–57.)

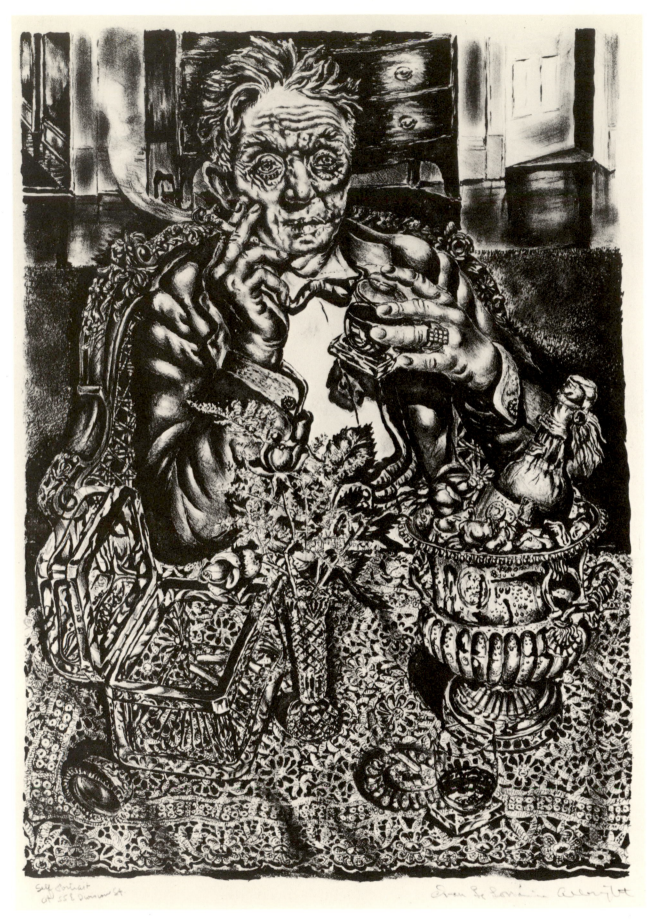

Self Portrait
at 55 E Division St.

Ivan Le Lorrain Albright

92   Ivan Albright (b. 1897), *Self Portrait, 55 Division Street,* 1947. 360 x 258
[Pollack 10], printed by George C. Miller. Published by Associated American
Artists. Collection, Tamarind Institute.

144

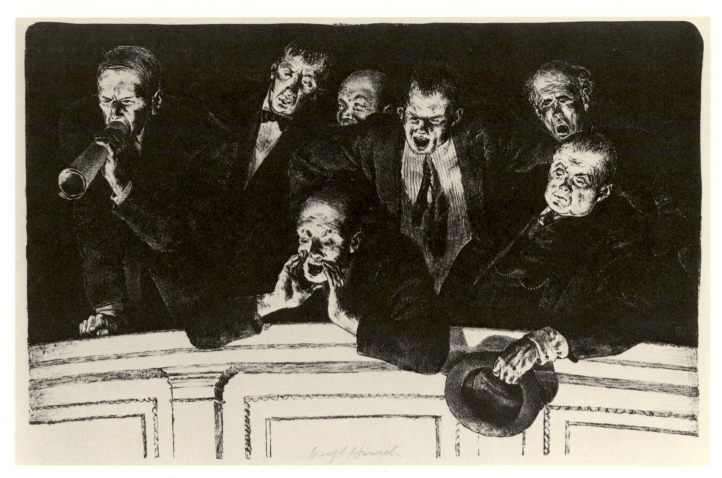

93 Joseph Hirsch (1910–1981), *The Hecklers,* 1948. 250 x 358 [Cole 7], printed
by George C. Miller. Published by Associated American Artists. Collection,
Tamarind Institute.

you realize to what an extent by your negative attitude you have
killed my interest in the gallery and stiffled initiative in its activities."[45]

In Zigrosser's mind the situation had become impossible, and
on 15 July 1940 he wrote Weyhe to tell him that he had been asked
by Fiske Kimball to become curator of prints at the Philadelphia Museum of Art.

> In view of the unsettled business prospects at the present
> time this is probably the most satisfactory solution both
> for you and for me. It relieves you of a responsibility for
> the gallery which must at times have been irritating and
> disadvantageous. And it provides me with a much more
> congenial outlet for my activities. I know that I can be of
> considerable benefit to you in my new position. The
> Museum has no print reference library and practically no
> prints. I shall be a good customer.[46]

Weyhe wished him well in the new position. "I hope you will forget the irritations which occurred from time to time between two
different temperaments like yours and mine. . . . I know my limitations. I shall never be a good art dealer."[47]

In December 1940 Zigrosser moved to Philadelphia. Martha
Dickinson subsequently directed Weyhe's print gallery, but at a less
ambitious level than before.

Aline Kistler—who was not related to Lynton Kistler—did not
share the view held by Weyhe and others that the effect of the new
print publishing ventures would be to bring about "the beginning

145

94   Grant Wood (1892–1942), *Shriner's Quartet*, 1939. 220 x 300 [Czestochowski
17], printed by George C. Miller. Published by Associated American Artists.
Collection, Tamarind Institute.

of the end of all that artists and conoisseurs hold dear,'' but she did
perceive that some new complications had been introduced into the
marketplace. Some of the artists published by American Artists
Group, she reported, "have also issued a limited number of signed
impressions of the same plates at prices ranging from four to five
times the Group publication price. . . . In some cases I have found a
Group impression that is better than an artist's proof of the same
plate. In other cases I have found unsigned impressions that are inferior to a proof pulled by the artist."[48] Kistler drew these conclu-
sions from her examination of the prints:

> Those who are sensitive to fine treatment as well as
> interesting design will seek the best prints in the finest
> obtainable impression, whether it be signed or unsigned,
> whether it be sold at two or twenty dollars, whether there
> be tens or thousands of other impressions of it.
>
> The quantity production and lower price of a few
> prints cannot radically affect the whole print market,
> except to extend its scope and draw into its fold people
> who have not before seriously considered entering it. A
> premium will always be paid for work of recognized
> value, whether that value rests upon rarity, reputation or
> artistic excellence. As long as people seek art, those who
> can will pay for it.[49]

The print publishing projects of the 1930s were based not solely

146

in economic motives—although these may have been paramount in the minds of some publishers—but also in a political philosophy which, as a matter of principle, advocated large editions and low prices. The populist concept of printmaking as a "medium for the masses" was commonly accepted among artists, and nowhere was it more clearly stated than in a brochure, *Good News for Printmakers,* jointly published in February 1939 by the Brooklyn Museum and the United American Printmakers (a division of the United American Artists, Local No. 60) as an announcement of an exhibition, "Fine Prints for Mass Production."* The fact that a representative group of printmakers chose so to organize as a division of an artists' union does much to describe their intentions:

> If [artists] are not to lose contact with the art patrons of the future [they] must, with the changing economic status of the younger generations, adopt production methods that will make extremely low prices possible. . . .
>
> Prints have always been intended as a product for the many. They were first conceived out of a need of the masses. . . . Later they were artificially made into a rare and expensive art product (to the dishonor of those artists who lent themselves and their talents to such a malicious practice). Prints must again become an art product for the many—without the slightest concession in quality: for the *best* is just good enough for the masses.[50]

JEAN CHARLOT AND ALBERT CARMAN

Jean Charlot had long been convinced that fine prints should be made for the masses. He was equally convinced that offset lithography was an ideal medium for the production of large editions at low cost, a conviction that had been strongly reinforced by the success of his *Picture Book,* and he was now determined, as he returned to New York in 1934, to explore the process further. He took a teaching position at the Florence Cane School and set out to acquire a small, Multilith press:

> The salesman at Multilith was very astonished when we said we wanted to do plates directly by hand. He said: "Well, I don't know—we've never done that." Anyway, he gave me a zinc, and I did the drawing and brought it back. They were careful not to show us how it was done. They went into another room and did mysterious things. They ended up giving us this little edition [twenty impressions], right or wrong. And we saw that it *could* be done.[51]

Within a month's time, a small press was purchased by the school, and Charlot and his colleague, the painter Albert Carman, set out to explore its potential: "We got the Multilith press to the school, but we didn't know front from back. So the salesman came. Again, I had done a drawing on a plate, and he printed it. But again he didn't tell us how to print, so we still didn't know.[52]

Early in 1935, the Mexican artist and printer Emilio Amero—with whom Charlot had collaborated in Mexico City—came to New York to teach stone lithography at the Cane School.† Throughout the winter of 1934–35, Charlot and Carman, now joined by Amero, continued to experiment and print with the Multilith press, though often with a frustrating lack of success.‡ Finally, in March of 1935,

* According to the prospectus, Eleanor Roosevelt was to be a member of the exhibition's jury, which was also to include Rockwell Kent, Lynd Ward, Monroe Wheeler, Ruth Green Harris, Max Weber, and Carl O. Schniewind, then curator of prints and drawings at the Brooklyn Museum. When the jury met on 3 May 1939, Hyman Warsager replaced Mrs. Roosevelt. Subseqently, controversy erupted and the exhibition, originally scheduled to open at the Brooklyn Museum on 19 May, was first postponed, then cancelled by the museum. The union protested the museum's "arbitrary and autocratic" action in an open letter of 16 June 1939.

† According to Ted Wahl, he set up the lithography workshop at the Cane School in advance of Amero's arrival (Interview, 8 May 1979).

‡ Without knowledge of the work done by Charlot and Carman, other artists explored use of the Multilith press in the making of original lithographs. Harry Sternberg, who first used Multilith plates in 1936, incorrectly believed that he was probably the first artist to use the process. (James C. Moore, *Harry Sternberg, A Catalogue Raisonné of His Graphic Work,* note to catalogue number 139.)

they were able for the first time to print a large edition: Charlot's *Mayan Murals,* printed from two plates in an edition of 3,000 impressions. "For the color plate we [used] a rainbow roll, a single inking roller with colors applied freely side-by-side. We did it to economize. A lot of old posters use this. Toulouse-Lautrec did it, and it also is used in printing Mexican and Spanish bullfight posters."[53]

The small Multilith press originally purchased by the school soon proved to be inadequate, and in May of 1935 it was replaced by a larger one. Charlot and Carman were convinced that the process had a high potential and they worked together to develop a refinement through which two or more pressruns might be made from a single plate. It was their plan that after printing the entire edition from the first drawing on the plate, they would remove the image—while leaving a visible ghost of it—and then, upon this same plate, make a new drawing for the second color.[54] The advantage of this procedure was that it assured perfect registration; its disadvantage, as they were soon to learn, was that the printing of a second edition from the original plates became impossible.*

Though a painter by training and inclination, Albert Carman quickly came to share Charlot's commitment to offset lithography. Intrigued by the potential he saw in the process, Carman abandoned teaching to embark on a career as a printer.† His wife Norma later wrote to Peter Morse of the "struggles and difficulties" Carman encountered when, in order to establish himself in his new vocation, he was forced to do purely commercial work:

> How he abhored such use of his time and talents—but [he had to do it in order] to make possible the continuance of the things he really wanted to do, in order to make them financially possible. I remember our being in a little loft downtown in Greenwich Village, several nights until two and three a.m. while he labored over the production. He had never been in the least mechanical, but did apply himself to learning about that press. . . . Eventually he was able to get into production, although it was a few years and many almost heart-breaking experiences before his work became well-enough known and accepted for it to pay a pressman and enable Albert to fully utilize his talents in the medium. . . . Many times the press company was going to—and sometimes did—repossess the press for months at a time until we could manage to bring payments up to date.[55]

By October 1937 Carman had printed a sufficient number of offset lithographs so as to stage an initial exhibition by "The Artists Color Proof Associates" at the Charles L. Morgan Galleries on Fifty-seventh Street. Morgan's gallery, it was stated, would be the permanent headquarters of the associates: "a cooperative movement initiated by artists, for artists, to place at the service of print makers and their patrons a complete print studio organization." The associates' brochure then went on to claim that the printing of the lithographs would be done by the

> well known painter and print maker, Albert Carman, whose vision and perseverance have made this group possible. Under old methods the cost to the artist to produce an original print in several colors was prohibitive. This cooperative plan relieves him of these

* Their first major project using the special process was a series of lithographs executed by Charlot as illustrations for *Characters of the Reformation* by Hilaire Belloc. Five thousand impressions were printed for inclusion in the book. When it quickly sold out, the publishers wished to do a second printing, and as the plates no longer existed, Charlot was forced to redraw them.

† Before leaving the Cane School, Carman participated in the printing of a portfolio of offset lithographs published by the American Abstract Artists in connection with their first exhibition at the Squibb Galleries in April 1937. Janet Flint (in *Art for All: American Print Publishing Between the Wars,* unpaged) comments that "the portfolios were sold for fifty cents apiece, as much, or perhaps more, for promotion of the exhibition as for the sale of serious works of art. Because of the abilities of the participants [the portfolio included lithographs by Werner Drewes, Ibram Lassaw, and Louis Schanker, among others] and the uncommon nature of this excursion into commercial techniques, the portfolio has, however, come to be regarded as a highly interesting document of twentieth-century American printmaking."

large expenses, yet places at his command a color medium of great brilliance . . . [and of a] quality and beauty quite unsurpassed in any of the great periods or methods of the past. But what is more significant, these proofs will retail at $5.00.[56]

Other exhibitions followed, and by 1941 Carman had managed to interest a number of artists in making prints at his press, among them Charlot, Howard Cook, Don Freeman, Albert Gallatin, Stefan Hirsch, Barbara Latham, Russell Limbach, Louis Lozowick, Carlos Mérida, George L. K. Morris, Pablo O'Higgins, and David Park. By and large, however, the lithographs published by the Color Proof Associates were a disappointing lot. Considerations of mass appeal and commercial success had caused Carman and Morgan to include in their exhibitions a number of prints that were no better than kitsch: sentimental depictions of dancers, flowers, kittens, or horses depicted by artists whose names have long been (deservedly) forgotten. Even the established artists who made color prints with Carman too often compromised their personal aesthetic to meet what they conceived to be the requirements of popular taste. Neither in Louis Lozowick's flimsy, harbor landscape nor in Howard Cook's drawing of a wide-eyed Mexican girl does one find a trace of the rigor that characterizes their best work.[57]

Despite the praise sometimes received from uncritical reviewers,* few of the lithographs that Carman printed for the Color Proof Associates have interest other than as footnotes to the history of the medium, and among these only the two abstract compositions by George L. K. Morris stand well the test of time. From a technical standpoint, few of the prints justify the claims that were made for them, nor do they serve to demonstrate either the creative potential of offset lithography or the considerable skills of their printer.

These skills soon led Carman to the project which was to be his *tour de force:* his collaboration with Marc Chagall on the thirteen, complex color lithographs for *The Tales from the Arabian Nights.* Chagall, who spent the wartime years in New York, was then resuming his work in lithography after a long interruption. "His etchings had taken on an increasingly painterly character, which fact was bound to find natural expression in lithographic technique. But what particularly interested him about lithography now, was color."[58] In Carman, Chagall found both a sensitive colorist and an accomplished printer, and the work went rapidly forward, achieving publication in 1945.†

But never, as it happened, was Carman to have an opportunity to collaborate with an American artist on a work of comparable scope and quality. After 1945 he spent much of his time in production of a series of magnificently printed, reproductive folios for the Metropolitan Museum of Art.‡ Then, in the summer of 1949, Carman died at the age of fifty.

THE PRINT CLUB OF CLEVELAND

The Contemporary Print Group, Associated American Artists, American Artists Group, and Artists Color Proof Associates were but four among a number of organizations formed as a part of an effort to stimulate publication and sale of prints by American artists. They had in common the premise that in order to find an audience

* An example of such praise is found in an unsigned review which spoke of the delicate tonal range and richly complex grain of the "prints made by the Carman offset process. . . . They have a brilliance and complexity and richness you just don't get in commercial prints." (*New York World-Telegram,* 2 August 1941).

† On 2 April 1953, while making plans for the third of the biennial exhibitions of color lithography at the Cincinnati Art Museum, Gustave von Groschwitz wrote Curt Valentin, the New York art dealer, to ask whether Marc Chagall had in fact drawn the plates for *The Tales from The Arabian Nights.* Valentin forwarded von Groschwitz's inquiry to Chagall, who responded on 6 May:

"Au sujet de la lettre du 2 avril, du Cincinnati Museum, concernant mes illustrations des "Mille et une nuit," je réponds que dans cet album même, qui est imprimé par l'Editeur Panthéon, il est indiqué que les littos ont été fabriqués chez Albert CARMAN. J'ai tout dessiné de ma propre main pour donner la personnalité, après avoir fait de grandes maquettes. J'ai choisi toutes les couleurs. J'ai corrigé et j'ai critiqué impitoyablement ces couleurs en visitant cet atelier très lointain de New-York à plusieurs reprises. Je ne peux pas dire, comme toujours, que je suis content des résultats au point de vue des couleurs. Peut-être, comme vous le savez, suis-je trop exigent?"

Von Groschwitz comments: "Chagall begs the question of originality. I believe Chagall drew the black and white areas and [that] Carman probably drew the color plates from the maquettes (gouaches) which still exist." (Von Groschwitz to Adams, 12 June 1982; Chagall's letter is in the personal files of von Groschwitz, to whom I am indebted for its use.)

‡ For a time, Carman maintained his press in a basement room at the Metropolitan Museum of Art.

149

prints should be published in large editions and be sold at very low prices.

A quite different premise motivated the print clubs of the time, many of which commissioned artists to create special editions for distribution to their members. Among the oldest and most influential of these clubs was the Print Club of Cleveland, known until 1950 simply as the Print Club.[59]

Although the club was founded in 1919, it was not until 1923 that it began to issue "an annual presentation print exclusively for its membership." The series of prints thus commissioned is important not only for its intrinsic quality, but also for the fact that, as a direct result of the invitations issued by the club, many artists were led to make lithographs who might otherwise not have done so.

Charles Burchfield offers a case in point. On 1 April 1932, Leona E. Prasse wrote to Burchfield on the Print Club's behalf, expressing a hope that he might be willing to undertake a presentation print. Burchfield responded promptly:

> I'm sorry but my "prints" are still of the future. My good intentions in that direction never seem to bear fruit. I don't know whether I'm just lazy or whether it's not my field; perhaps some of both. At any rate, I find it difficult to think in any terms but color. I still tell myself tho, that I must do some lithographs, so I hope I will get around to it.[60]

And get around to it he did, though not until eighteen years later. The Print Club, in the person of Leona Prasse, refused to go away, and eventually, in September 1950, Burchfield agreed to undertake a lithograph in collaboration with George Miller. He submitted a group of drawings to the Print Club so that a choice might be made, then went to Miller's shop: "I had two sessions with Geo. Miller yesterday," he wrote, "and expect to go in again tomorrow or Friday. I was fortunate in meeting both Feininger and Wengenroth there. The latter especially I think is among the best in the lithographic field."[61]

The lithograph Burchfield made for the Print Club, *Summer Benediction,* proved to be but one of several which Burchfield now undertook:

> I had George draw proofs of my two new lithographs (*Crows in March . . .* and *Autumn Wind*). We made corrections, one radical on the Crows, and I now have the prints in hand. Stow Wengenroth came in while we were proving them, and he was very enthusiastic about the Crows especially, which pleased me. I showed proofs to Carl Zigrosser, and he too liked them very much. . . . I have another stone on hand, and as soon as I am up to it, I want to continue the work.[62]

Like Burchfield, Lyonel Feininger was working at George Miller's shop in direct response to a commission from the Print Club,* and he too wrote to Prasse about his experience there:

> We are so pleased that this first graphic work I made since 1906 proved so successful.† Having, after spoiling two stones gotten the "hang" of the treatment, I find that I have been bitten by the "bug" and it is in my plan to do

95

96

* Feininger had first been requested by Henry Sayles Francis to make an etching or drypoint "similar in composition" to a watercolor, *Her Majesty the Barque II,* which had been acquired by the Cleveland Museum of Art. It was only after Feininger refused to do this that a lithograph was agreed upon. George Miller wrote to Prasse of the collaboration: "Mr. Feininger has made two lithos and today he has started a third which we hope to get finished by the end of the week. He is very conscientious and like all great masters, is never satisfied until he has turned everything inside out to get the utmost out of the medium. I have enjoyed working with him very much and he enjoys working down in my studio." (Miller to Prasse, 4 January 1951. Papers of the Cleveland Print Club, Archives of American Art, Smithsonian Institution, reel 809, frame 68.)

† Actually, as Prasse notes, Feininger's early lithographs were made between 1906 and about 1910 and 1912. (Leona E. Prasse. *Lyonel Feininger,* p. 103.)

95 Charles Burchfield (1893–1967), *Summer Benediction,* 1951–52. 306 x 232, printed by George C. Miller. Published by the Print Club of Cleveland. Collection, Tamarind Institute.

some work on stone again soon. Mr. Miller is very pleased at this my decision to continue on.[63]

Other artists who accepted commissions from the Print Club to create lithographs as presentation prints between 1923 and 1957 were Thomas Hart Benton, George Grosz, Leon Kroll, Louis Lozowick, Reginald Marsh, Peter Takal, Stow Wengenroth, and three Cleveland artists, William S. Gisch, Henry G. Keller, and Paul B. Travis.

But though the Print Club's commissions served to attract artists to lithography and to Miller's shop, the club was not the easiest of clients. On the club's behalf, Leona Prasse and Henry Sayles Francis quibbled with Miller about the paper he used, and, on at least one occasion, took issue with an artist about the character of his drawing. In a letter to Reginald Marsh, Prasse was obliged to report that "the Publications Committee of The Print Club met to look at

96 Lyonel Feininger (1871–1956), *Manhattan (Stone 2),* 1955. 270 x 215 [Prasse
L.19], printed by George C. Miller. Published by the Print Club of Cleveland.
Collection, Tamarind Institute.

97   Reginald Marsh (1898–1954), *Switch Engines, Erie Yards, Jersey City,* 1947.
229 x 339 [Sasowsky 30], printed by George C. Miller. Published by the Print
Club of Cleveland. Collection, Tamarind Institute.

97   your lithograph of switch engines and the drawing from which it
was made. And now it is my unhappy task to tell you that the
members of this committee felt that your lithograph is not a satisfactory translation of your wonderful drawing."[64] Somewhat surprisingly, Marsh accepted this verdict with good grace and redrew
the lithograph. Eventually, it was the third of three stones that was
printed in an edition for distribution to the Print Club's membership.

The club made a standard financial arrangement with the artists whose prints it commissioned. The offer to Benton was typical:
"For an edition of 200 signed impressions . . . the artist will be paid
the sum of $500.00. In addition to this, the Club will pay the cost of
printing the edition, which we prefer to have done under the supervision of the artist. The Club will own the entire edition, the cancelled plate, and impressions from the cancelled plate."[65] Then, the
lithograph completed—it was Benton's *Approaching Storm*—Francis
wrote to ask that he donate to the club his "preliminary sketches or
other material relating to the plate."[66]

REGIONALISM

Early in 1936 *Prints* magazine set out to assess the then current state
of American printmaking.* Questionnaires were sent "to museum
directors, print curators, collectors, critics, and artists throughout
the United States asking them to name the artists they would consider most noteworthy." The June issue was then devoted to publi-

*   During the eight-year period during which
Prints was published (1930–38) it gave important encouragement to printmakers throughout
the United States. Although conservative in
policy, particularly in the years before Aline
Kistler's appointment as editor in October 1935,
Prints filled an important void. Then as now,
the attention of the critics who wrote for the
major newspapers, journals, and art magazines
was focused primarily upon the "major arts"
of painting and sculpture, with the result that
serious critical articles seldom dealt with prints.

cation of the results of this survey, in which Rockwell Kent was most often named as "one of the ten national printmakers."[67] In her introduction Aline Kistler acclaimed what she felt to be the disappearance of "stultifying boundary lines" between prints classified as "conservative, modern, [or] radical." She also noted a lack of discrimination among media. Few of the lists that *Prints* received were limited solely to etchers: "I doubt that this would have been true of a survey made only a few years ago when . . . an almost solid front of etchers [was ranged against] the more progressive lithographers and wood engravers."[68]

In an effort to secure a broad perspective, *Prints* had divided the United States into regions and had asked its respondents to identify the "ten best" printmakers nationally and regionally.* The lists that resulted demonstrated the extent to which prints were then made in all parts of the country. No longer were printmaking and print collecting concentrated exclusively—or even primarily—in the older cities of the East and Midwest. The established print clubs and societies of New York, Philadelphia, Cleveland, Cincinnati, Chicago, and other eastern cities had now been joined by new organizations in the South and West, some of which adopted the Cleveland plan and commissioned prints for distribution to their members. The cumulative effect of the print clubs and societies, together with the increased activity of the New York print publishers—foremost among them the Associated American Artists—was greatly to stimulate printmaking in all parts of the United States.†

The Prairie Print Makers, organized in Wichita in December 1930, was typical of these new print societies. Two of its charter artist-members, Birger Sandzen and C. A. Seward, were later to be included in the *Prints* survey among the ten best printmakers of the Midwest (Sandzen was placed even ahead of Benton and Curry). Because both Sandzen and Seward were lithographers, the Prairie Print Makers was from the beginning open to all printmakers, regardless of medium, and its first invited member was William J. Dickerson, the young Wichita artist who had been a member of Bolton Brown's class at the Art Institute of Chicago.

Dickerson had attended the Art Institute at the suggestion of C. A. Seward, who was employed as supervising artist at the Western Lithographic Company in Wichita. A frequent prizewinner in regional exhibitions, Seward was the driving force behind the Prairie Print Makers and author of a book on *Metal Plate Lithography*, the first work on the subject intended specifically for artists, and illustrated by lithographs drawn not only by Wichita artists, but also by George Biddle, Rockwell Kent, Wanda Gág, and Louis Lozowick.‡

Sandzen, who had first studied lithography in Europe before coming to the United States, was commissioned to make the first of the annual "gift prints" to be distributed to the club's associate (or subscribing) members in 1931. The club's publications continued annually for more than thirty years, and—as at Cleveland—took on a less regional flavor with the passage of time. The membership also expanded to take in John Taylor Arms, John Steuart Curry, Peter Hurd, Claire Leighton, Stow Wengenroth, Ernest Watson, and other artists throughout the country. Similarly, Seward held membership not only in the Prairie Print Makers, but also in the Chicago Society of Etchers, the Rocky Mountain Print Makers, the California Print Makers, and even the Honolulu Print Makers. The net effect of such interchange of memberships among artists who belonged to print

---

* Kistler wrote: "The composite list of the *ten best national printmakers* is made up of the names of those artists who were included most often in the national lists. From this, it may be seen that, although Rockwell Kent is in first place, it does not necessarily imply that the majority of those who participated in this survey consider him the best living American printmaker. This tabulation shows only that he was included most often as one of ten national printmakers. As there were *one hundred and thirty-three* different artists named for national honor, it is evident that the final list of ten nationals does not begin to include those whom many of you consider to have made a national contribution." (Aline Kistler, "The National Survey," p. 245.)

Following Kent on the national list were John Taylor Arms, Kerr Eby, Frank W. Benson, Peggy Bacon, Arthur W. Heintzelman, Adolph (sic) Dehn, Thomas Nason, Wanda Gág, and John Sloan. Heading the regional lists were, in the East, Emil Ganso, Stow Wengenroth, Reginald Marsh, Louis Lozowick, and Ernest D. Roth; in New England, Martin Lewis, Ernest Fiene, Louis C. Rosenberg, Samuel Chamberlain, and Charles H. Woodbury; in the Midwest, Levon West, Birger Sandzen, Thomas Benton, John Steuart Curry, and Henry G. Keller; in the South, Alfred Hutty, J. J. Lankes, Anne Goldthwaite, Ellsworth Woodward, and Prentiss Taylor; in the Southwest, Howard Cook, George Elbert Burr, Gustave Baumann, Kenneth M. Adams, and Gene Kloss; and in the West, Thomas Handforth, J. W. Winkler, Paul Landacre, Armin Hansen, and Roi Partridge. (Ibid., p. 244.)

† For a brief account of the history and activities of the print clubs, see Lisa Peters, "Print Clubs in America."

‡ The lithographs illustrated in Seward's book were drawn on metal plates and were printed by a number of printers, among them Dickerson, Fred Blume, and E. W. Bullinger in Wichita; and Jacob Friedland, George Miller, and J. E. Rosenthal in New York.

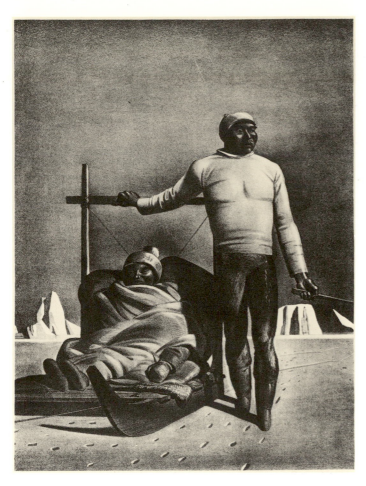

98 Rockwell Kent (1882–1971), *Sledging,* 1933. 290 x 219 [Jones 99], printed by George C. Miller. Collection, University of New Mexico Art Museum.

organizations in different parts of the country, and of participation by printmakers in exhibitions distant from their place of residence was greatly to diminish regional differences, with the result that in his assessment of western printmaking (included with the national survey in the June issue of *Prints*) Junius Cravens was able to report that

> printmaking on the Pacific Coast differs little if any in
> quality from printmaking elsewhere in the Western
> World. When one attends a Western local print annual,
> for instance, one finds little in its character as a whole,
> with the exception of subject matter of course, to
> distinguish the quality of its contents from that of local
> shows from Boston, New Orleans or Podunk. Differences
> in American standards are not regional ones.[69]

But though printmaking in some media may have differed little from city to city, the problem of access to equipment and to qualified printers placed some limitations upon the spread of lithography. Artist-lithographers continued to cluster around the relatively few professional printers who were available to them—Miller in New York, Arnold in Woodstock, Kistler in Los Angeles, Barrett in Colorado Springs, Dickerson in Wichita, Cuno in Philadelphia—or around one of the small number of art schools or universities that then offered instruction in the medium.

Some artists printed for themselves, some took their completed stones great distances to their printers, and some managed to work "by mail." Miller, Kistler, and Barrett all conducted a portion of their work in this manner, shipping grained stones to artists in specially constructed boxes, getting the stones back after the artists had completed their drawings, proofing them, sending the proofs to the artists for approval, then printing the editions. While most often such printing was done for artists who had previously worked at first-hand with the printer, this was not always the case.

When in 1938 a group of Texas artists formed the Lone Star Printmakers, Jerry Bywaters reported that "most of the local prints were done at first as metal plate or paper transfers and printed by Cuno in Philadelphia. Lately more work has been done on stone and during this year [1940] I hope we can establish a workshop and own our own equipment. . . . My latest prints were made at the Colorado Springs Fine Arts and printed by Barrett."[70]

Similarly, although the artist and printer never met, George Miller printed all of Grant Wood's nineteen lithographs. Wood drew his stones in Iowa and shipped them to Miller to be printed. Miller then proofed the stones—one proof a little on the light side, another fully inked—and sent them along to Wood for approval. It is Burr Miller's recollection that never at any time did Wood wish to make a change in a stone after sending it to New York.*

The at times cautious and carefully "knitted" look of Wood's lithographs is in part a consequence of the remote relationship between the artist and the printer. The finest lithographs come into being when an artist and a printer work closely together in circumstances which permit development of a true collaboration: a relationship in which the artist's creative grasp of the essential character of lithography is enriched by the printer's technical knowledge and experience, and in which the printer's empathic understanding of the artist's work develops in the process.

* Wood made all of his lithographs between 1937 and 1941. He had somewhat earlier installed a lithograph press at the Stone City Art Colony in Iowa, but had not then been sufficiently interested in the process to explore it personally. John Steuart Curry's *Storm over Stone City* was printed on that press when he visited Wood in July, 1933.

NOTES

1 Burr Miller, tape-recorded interview, 4 May 1979.

2 Ibid.

3 Dore Ashton, *The New York School: A Cultural Reckoning*, p. 18.

4 For further information about the series of art programs initiated by the Roosevelt administration, see Francis V. O'Connor, ed., *Federal Art Patronage, 1933 to 1943* and *The New Deal Art Projects: An Anthology of Memoirs*.

5 Olin Dows, "The New Deal's Treasury Art Program: A Memoir," in O'Connor, *New Deal Art Projects*, pp. 11–12.

6 Ibid., p. 12.

7 Audrey McMahon, "A General View of the WPA Federal Art Project in New York City and State," in O'Connor, *New Deal Art Projects*, pp. 52–53.

8 Ibid., p. 53.

9 Ibid., p. 54.

10 Ibid.

11 Jacob Kainen, "The Graphic Arts Division of the WPA Federal Art Project," in O'Connor, *New Deal Art Projects*, pp. 157–58.

12 Cincinnati Art Museum, *First International Biennial of Contemporary Color Lithography*.

13 Limbach also wrote the article on lithography for an intended national progress report on the project's accomplishments; this article, "Lithography: Stepchild of the Arts," is included in Francis V. O'Connor, ed., *Art for The Millions, Essays from the 1930s by Artists and Administrators of the WPA Federal Art Project*, pp. 145–47.

14 See C. Van Northrup, "Colour Lithographs of the Works Progress Administration Federal Art Project: New York City, 1935–1942."

15 Kainen, "Graphic Arts Division," p. 162.

16 Ibid., p. 170.

17 Ibid., p. 166.

18 Ashton, *New York School*, p. 44.

19 See *Jackson Pollock: The New-Found Works*, checklist and essay by Francis V. O'Connor.

20 Theodore Wahl, tape-recorded interview, 8 May 1979.

21 Interview with Wahl. Pollock made no further lithographs after Wahl left New York.

22 Grant Arnold, in conversation, 11 March 1982.

23 Barbara Rose, *American Art Since 1900*, p. 127.

24 Aline Kistler, "Prints of the Moment," p. 163.

25 Thomas Hart Benton, *An Artist in America*, p. 314.

26 Cherry, quoted by Ashton, *New York School*, p. 42.

27 Holger Cahill, "American Painting 1865–1934," in Holger Cahill and Alfred H. Barr, eds., *Art in America in Modern Times*, pp. 43–44.

28 Benton, *Artist in America*, p. 48.

29 Thomas Craven, *A Treasury of American Prints*, not paged.

30 Ashton, *New York School*, p. 62.

31 Peyton Boswell, *Modern American Painting*, p. 11, 14.

32 Benton, *Artist in America*, p. 281.

33 Stuart Davis, "The New York American Scene in Art," *Art Front* (1935), reprinted in Diane Kelder, ed., *Stuart Davis*, pp. 151–54.

34 Janet Flint, *Art for All: American Print Publishing between the Wars*, not paged.

35 Ibid.

36 Ibid.

37 Sylvan Cole, Jr., quoted by Fred Ferretti, "The AAA and How it Grew," p. 57.

38 "Making Fine Prints Popular," p. 17.

39 Cole, quoted by Ferretti, "The AAA," p. 57.

40 Sylvan Cole, Jr., *AAA: Fortieth Anniversary Exhibition, 1934–1974.*

41 Burr Miller, tape-recorded interview, 4 May 1979.

42 Aline Kistler, "New Market Trends," p. 32.

43 Ibid., p. 35.

44 Carl Zigrosser, *A World of Art and Museums,* p. 56.

45 Undated draft. Carl Zigrosser papers, University of Pennsylvania Library.

46 Zigrosser to Weyhe, 15 July 1940, ibid.

47 Weyhe to Zigrosser, 19 July 1940, ibid.

48 Kistler, "New Market Trends," p. 32, 36.

49 Ibid., p. 36.

50 Carl O. Schniewind, "The Market for Prints," in *Good News for Printmakers.*

51 Charlot, quoted by Peter Morse, *Jean Charlot's Prints, a Catalogue Raisonné,* p. 142.

52 Ibid., p. 143.

53 Ibid., p. 149.

54 For a full description of the process patented by Carman and Charlot, see Morse, *Charlot's Prints,* Appendix A, pp. 432–34.

55 Norma Marks to Morse, 20 February 1972. I am indebted to Peter Morse for this letter and other assistance in connection with the discussion of Albert Carman's work as a printer.

56 Charles L. Morgan, exhibition brochure, 1937.

57 The Metropolitan Museum of Art has a bound folio of prints from the Artists Color Proof Associates, selected and given to the museum by Carman.

58 Franz Meyer, *Marc Chagall, His Graphic Work* (New York: Harry N. Abrams, 1957), p. xxvi.

59 See *The Print Club of Cleveland, 1919–1969,* for a brief account of the club's history.

60 Burchfield to Prasse, 8 April 1932. Papers of the Cleveland Print Club, Archives of American Art, Smithsonian Institution, reel 809, frame 441.

61 Burchfield to Prasse, 7 March 1951. Ibid., frame 457.

62 Burchfield to Prasse, 26 March 1952. Ibid., frame 485.

63 Feininger to Prasse, 15 February 1951. Ibid., reel 810, frame 79.

64 Prasse to Marsh, 10 January 1948. Ibid., frame 1045.

65 Francis to Benton, 1 February 1939. Ibid., reel 809, frame 188.

66 Francis to Benton, 4 May 1939. Ibid., frame 197.

67 Aline Kistler, "The National Survey," pp. 240–50. Published with the survey were three supplemental articles, John Taylor Arms, "An Exhibition that Came True"; Junius Cravens, "A Western Viewpoint"; Willard Hougland, "Prints in the Middle West"; and biographical data on the seventy-three printmakers whose names were included on the national and regional lists.

68 Ibid., p. 241.

69 Cravens, "A Western Viewpoint," p. 262.

70 Bywaters to Carl Zigrosser, 20 July 1940. Carl Zigrosser papers, University of Pennsylvania Library.

5 · The 1940s and 1950s

ABSTRACT EXPRESSIONISM: LITHOGRAPHY REJECTED

In 1940, H. W. Janson, the art historian, took note of the fact that fine lithographic craftsmen were becoming increasingly rare:

> This situation spells danger for the survival of lithography. . . . Soon the artist-lithographer will no longer be able, as he has been in the past, to reinforce his own knowledge of the process with the rich professional experience of his humbler commercial colleague. Even today, many artists are content to entrust the printing of their "lithographs," whether in black and white or in color, to the offset press, and neither they nor the public seem to realize the loss in subtlety of texture and individual expression that separates these mechanical reproductions from the carefully controlled hand-made print.* This decline in lithographic craftsmanship is particularly regrettable because at present lithography as an artistic medium is much more popular in this country than it is in Europe. It is being more and more widely taught in art schools, college art departments, and WPA print shops, and seems on the point of developing into a peculiarly American tradition.[1]

Janson's remarks on the state of lithography were made in a preface to an article by Emil Ganso, who, during the year before his death in 1941, had served with Janson as professor of art at the University of Iowa.† They argued in that article that developments in the field made it essential that every teacher of lithography should develop high skills in printing so that "the student will be encouraged to explore the intricacies of lithographic technique on his own."[2]

Although access to technical information was an increasing and very real problem, it was the least of those faced by American lithographers as World War II began in Europe. The government's

* In a reply to Janson's comment, Stefan Hirsch, then an instructor at the Art Students League, took him to task for failing to distinguish between "mechanical reproductions" and "lithographs executed directly and entirely on plates by the artist and printed under his supervision on . . . an offset-type power press." Hirsch cited the work of Jean Charlot and Albert Carman, who, Hirsch said, produced "the finest color lithography" using such a process. (Stefan Hirsch, letter, *Parnassus* 13, January 1941: 2–3.)

† When Ganso went to Iowa, it was the intention of the chairman, Lester Longman, and of the faculty that he should develop a lithographic workshop in the art department. This intention was frustrated by Ganso's sudden death of a heart attack, at the age of forty-six, shortly after his appointment to a tenure professorship. Subsequently, Mauricio Lasansky was appointed to the position that Ganso might otherwise have continued to occupy, with the result that printmaking at Iowa took an entirely different turn.

Ganso's assistant at Iowa was Maxil Ballinger, later influential as instructor of lithography at Indiana University.

* Arnold moved from Woodstock to Washington in 1940, and worked during the war for the Coast and Geodetic Survey. While in Washington, Arnold completed work on his book, *Creative Lithography,* but did not do any printing. "I still had the press, but it was up in Woodstock. After the war, after I completed my degree at Syracuse [University], I was teaching [in a high school] all the time. . . . I had the press and everything else, but I just couldn't get to it. Once I left Woodstock and decided to teach, all my contacts were gone." (Arnold, quoted in Clinton Adams, "Grant Arnold, Lithographer: Woodstock and New York, 1928–1940.) When Arnold retired from teaching in 1971 he accepted an adjunct professorship at the State University of New York, Oswego.

† The painter Paul Brach speculates that printmaking was rejected in the 1950s for quasi-ethical reasons: "The unique individual painting [was seen to be a reflection of] the artist's existential crisis. . . . The object for sale was secondary—an aide-mémoire for the sharing [of the] painter's situation. To produce a series of plates, stones, or screens from which a multiple could be made would have contradicted the uniqueness of the statement and would have admitted the salability of the product." (Brach to Adams, 10 August 1982.)

‡ Intaglio printmaking is a generic term for processes that include etching, drypoint, aquatint, engraving, soft-ground, etc. It came broadly into use in the 1940s and 1950s in an effort more accurately to describe prints in which two or more of these processes were combined, but also as a means to avoid the word *etching* which in many minds was closely associated with prints of conservative or "traditional" artists.

financial support of the Federal Art Project and its graphic workshops came quickly to an end, the shops were closed, and the printers who had worked in them drifted into other occupations. Even before the United States entered the war in 1941, Lynton Kistler had closed his Los Angeles studio and had taken a defense job in the East; Grant Arnold had gone to Washington to work for the government.* Although George Miller and Theodore Cuno were exempt from military service by reason of age and Lawrence Barrett by reason of health, their work was made more difficult by wartime restrictions on materials and supplies.

Even more critical was that fact that there was little interest in lithography among the new generation of artists in New York. A number of these artists—Robert Motherwell, Jackson Pollock, and Mark Rothko among them—had made intaglio prints at Stanley William Hayter's Atelier 17, after it was relocated from Paris to New York in 1944. In so doing they had met the many distinguished émigré artists who had by then come to New York from Europe: artists who—in the European tradition—saw the making of prints as a natural part of their total work. But neither the attitudes of the Europeans nor the experience with Hayter served to overcome the American artists' prejudice against printmaking, an activity which they identified with ideas and methods completely foreign to their work. As Franz Kline later put it, "Printmaking concerns social attitudes, you know—politics and a public. . . like the Mexicans in the 1930s; printing, multiplying, educating; I can't think about it. I'm involved with the private image."[3] Will Barnet confirms that not only Kline but many New York artists of the late forties and early fifties came to hold this view: "The entire art world was turned over, overnight," and as "ivory-tower" attitudes replaced the social consciousness of the depression years "the graphic medium was considered the lowest possible way of expressing yourself."[4]

The rejection of printmaking—and of lithography in particular—stemmed in part from a rejection of the nationalist art and politics of the social realist painters, and in part from a rejection of the necessarily indirect technical methods which are intrinsic to printmaking.† For the younger artists, Barnet adds, "[art] had to be direct, it had to be on canvas, and it had to be immediate."[5] The New York painters did not perceive that in the proper circumstances (circumstances which, admittedly, did not exist in the 1940s and 1950s) lithography was capable of providing precisely the immediacy they sought.

Whatever their basis in fact, the perceptions and attitudes were real, with the result that in the postwar years printmaking and painting took widely divergent paths. Throughout the twenties and thirties, most of the finest American prints had been made by painters—as would again be the case after 1960—for many of whom lithography was the medium of choice. In the forties and fifties, however, printmaking became the province of printmakers: for the most part intaglio printmakers, strongly influenced by Hayter and his American followers, Mauricio Lasansky, Gabor Peterdi, and Karl Schrag.‡ So great was the momentum thus provided to the intaglio print that many artists and critics came to think of lithography as an old-fashioned undertaking, an inherently conservative art, strongly identified with the regionalism of Benton, Wood, and Curry.

In actuality, the lithographs of the forties and fifties were far more diverse in style than this perception suggests, particularly in

99 Herbert Bayer (b. 1900), *Convolution,* 1948, from the folio *Seven Convolutions.* Color lithograph, 343 x 447, printed by Lawrence Barrett. Collection, Tamarind Institute.

California. Artists in areas distant from New York were the first to recognize that in its autographic quality—its immediate response to the artist's touch—lithography was a medium perfectly suited to the emerging Abstract-Expressionist sensibility. As early as 1948 a group 102 of avant-garde artists in San Francisco—among them Richard Die- 100 benkorn and Frank Lobdell—created a series of original offset lithographs that effectively demonstrated the power of the medium to accommodate images parallel to those of Kline and Pollock.* A similar spirt was reflected in work of the Los Angeles painter Hans 101 Burkhardt, earlier a close friend of Arshile Gorky in New York; in the calligraphic lithographs drawn and printed by Emerson Woelffer in Colorado Springs in the early fifties; in the mythic abstractions 103 of Harold Paris, including *Caballa,* printed in 1952 by Robert Blackburn in New York; in the figurative expressionism of Nathan Oliveira, who created a series of haunting images in San Francisco during 116 the later 1950s; and, above all, in the vivid images of Sam Francis, a California painter whose first series of lithographs was made in Zurich in 1960.

Artists who worked in styles related to earlier Cubist and Bauhaus traditions also made effective use of lithography during the 99 1940s and 1950s, among them Herbert Bayer, whose *Convolution* 104 series was printed by Lawrence Barrett in 1948; Karl Fortess, who used the medium to create a number of fine Cubist cityscapes; and

* Similar in aim to the portfolio published in 1937 by the American Abstract Artists in New York (see footnote, page 148), these offset lithographs were printed from aluminum and paper plates on a Multilith press in Mill Valley, California. Printed in editions of between 100 and 150 impressions, the portfolios were sold for one dollar. "It was just an experiment—nobody took them very seriously. . . . We made enough for a case of Scotch, and had a party, as I remember it." (Frank Lobdell, interview, 11 November 1982.) Also included in the portfolio were lithographs by John Hultberg and Walter Kuhlman.

100   Frank Lobdell (b. 1921), *Untitled,* 1948. Offset lithograph, 250 x 208, printed by Eric Ledin. Collection, University of New Mexico Art Museum, gift of Walter Kuhlman.

101   Hans Burkhardt (b. 1904), *Destruction,* 1948. 250 x 363, printed by Lynton R. Kistler. Collection, Tamarind Institute.

102 Richard Diebenkorn (b. 1922), *Untitled,* 1948. Offset lithograph, 278 x 215, printed by Eric Ledin. Collection, University of New Mexico Art Museum, gift of Walter Kuhlman.

103 Harold Paris (1925–1979), *Caballa,* 1952. 293 x 396, printed by Robert Blackburn. Collection, Art, Prints and Photographs Division, New York Public Library, Astor, Lenox, and Tilden Foundations.

104 Karl Fortess (b. 1907), *Cityscape,* 1953. 340 x 215, printed by William Wetzel. Collection, Tamarind Institute.

Ralston Crawford, who produced a striking series of simple but dramatic color lithographs throughout the 1950s. 70

CONSTANCE FORSYTH AND GEORGE MILLER

Notwithstanding the impetus given to intaglio printmaking by Hayter, Lasansky, and their followers, there remained a number of artist-teachers in art schools and universities who, as a result of the personal interest or experience, sought to offer instruction in lithography.

Among these artist-teachers was Ward Lockwood, who in 1938 had become chairman of the department of art at the University of Texas. Two years later, in 1940, it became possible for Lockwood to appoint Constance Forsyth as a member of the Texas faculty (Forsyth had been among Lockwood's students in that improvised lithography class at the Broadmoor Art Academy in Colorado Springs during the summer of 1932); together they set out to start a program in printmaking, including lithography, and to fight what Forsyth describes as "the World War II battle for supplies."

At Texas, as at other schools across the United States, there were shortages of all kinds. Government restrictions affected almost everything that printmakers needed and used. The companies that supplied art materials had deleted page after page of printmaking items from their catalogues. Carborundum (essential for the graining of stones) was often unavailable, and imported French papers had all but totally disappeared from the marketplace. In desperation, Lockwood wrote to George Miller for advice. But even Miller had found it impossible after 1941 to obtain the Rives papers he preferred to use in his work. According to Forsyth, Miller wrote to Lockwood that "he had had a paper company make some [paper] for him as nearly like Rives as possible. It was called Sevir, Rives spelled backward."[6] Unfortunately, however, Sevir was no substitute for Rives: it contained no sizing and proved to be unsuitable for lithography.

But Forsyth managed to make do with what was available: "Our lithography had periods of success and periods of failure. I was determined to find out the reasons for both. With continual experimentation I had solved some problems, but not to the extent I wanted. In May 1945 I wrote to George Miller about a class. He answered saying he was not having one."[7]

Miller was seldom willing to accept students at his place in Vermont, and at the time he received Forsyth's letter he was particularly reluctant to do so. "My father didn't want her to come," Burr Miller recalls, "because he was a mile-and-a-half from the bus stop, and he [would have] to go and get her every day, and [because of wartime rationing] he didn't have the gasoline."[8]

Ultimately, however, George Miller relented, sent Forsyth his summer schedule, and invited her to come to Burlington on a Friday afternoon:

> As I remember our first conversation [it] went something like this: He said he was not teaching rivals.* Nor did he teach students. The only person he would really teach was his son [and] he was not giving away any secrets or tricks. Looking me over, I'm sure he decided I wasn't going to be a rival. I assured him I had no [such] intention. . . . What I wanted was a straight, dependable, routine process to use in class. I told him I was not interested in secrets or tricks, that I already knew too many.[9]

These introductory remarks notwithstanding, Miller openly and generously shared his knowledge of lithography with Forsyth during the week that she worked with him in Burlington:

> He printed in the mornings and took the afternoons off. He spent two weeks at a time in Vermont, bringing stones to be printed from New York. . . . Miller said he like to print in Vermont because it was cooler in the summer than New York City. . . .
>
> The great revelation to me . . . was George Miller's handling of the leather roller. The full answers to questions asked and unasked came in just watching him work. . . . [In lithography it is] not what you do but how you do it. How 'hard' is hard? How 'fast' is fast? Words mean little, one has to see the real expert in action.[10]

LITHOGRAPHY IN THE ART SCHOOLS AND UNIVERSITIES

Constance Forsyth's summer of study with George Miller was in every sense exceptional. Few of the artist-teachers of lithography during the forties and fifties had such an opportunity to learn how

* With those whom Miller viewed as possible competitors, he was much less open than with Forsyth. Will Barnet found Miller unwilling to answer technical questions while Barnet was printing at the Art Students League. When the artist-printer John Muench opened a small lithographic workshop in 1954 in the Delmonico Building, where Miller also had his workshop, Miller was quite cool to him. (Barnet and Muench, in conversation, 1979 and 1982.)

to print from an "expert in action." Francis Chapin, Dale Phillips, and William Dickerson had worked directly with Bolton Brown; Reginald Neal had served as Lawrence Barrett's assistant. Some had gained experience by working as apprentices or journeymen in commercial lithography workshops. A number had studied lithography at the Art Students League with Charles Locke or Eugene Fitsch, or at the Art Institute of Chicago with Chapin or Max Kahn. Others had learned how to print in Europe, or had worked with Mexican printers at the Taller Gráfica in Mexico City or in San Miguel de Allende. Many had found it necessary to learn how to print through trial and error. Inevitably, in these circumstances, the quality of lithographic instruction had come to vary widely from region to region and from school to school. In some areas there were a number of active workshops; in other areas, very few.

Characteristically, the art-school workshops established before World War II were small and poorly equipped. And while the rapid rise in art school and university enrollments after the war made it easier to get money for presses, rollers, and stones, it also made for congested space in basements or temporary buildings—often G.I. barracks. Even so, it was largely in these workshops that lithography survived and—in some dimensions—developed during the late 1940s and throughout the 1950s.

Among the many artist-teachers who contributed importantly to American lithography during this period—in addition to those whose names have already been mentioned—were Ture Bengtz in Massachusetts; Albert Heckman, first in New York, then in Connecticut; Will Barnet and Robert Blackburn in New York; Robert Gardner, Jerome Kaplan, Raphael Sabatini, Benton Spruance, and Roswell Weidner, all in Pennsylvania; Garo Antreasian, Maxil Ballinger, Arthur L. Helwig, Alfred Sessler, Robert von Neumann, and Emil Weddige in the Midwest; Reginald Neal, in Illinois, then in Mississippi;* Caroline Durieux, Maltby Sykes, and Richard Zoellner in the South; Emilio Amero and Alexandre Hogue in Oklahoma; Elmer Schooley in New Mexico; and Raymond Bertrand, Leon Goldin, Jules Heller, and Nathan Oliveira in California.

Garo Antreasian is convinced that despite the limitations imposed by limited knowledge and inadequate facilities, the influence of this generation of artist-teachers was of central importance to American lithography:

> Though much of their teaching methodology might be characterized as informal and somewhat casual, their individual enthusiasm for the art of the print was extraordinarily strong and infectious. Through their teaching and through their commitment to their own art, they were an inspiration to many of my generation while at the same time helping to keep printmaking alive during that bleak period of the thirties and forties.[11]

Antreasian had himself first encountered lithography in a quite remarkable technical high school in Indianapolis. The school's staff included a number of professional artist-teachers, among them one, Sara Bard, who was a friend and admirer of Stow Wengenroth; with her encouragement Antreasian began to make lithographs on an abandoned handpress at the high school. Upon graduation he received a scholarship to the John Herron Art School, only to find that regular classes in lithography (which until the previous year had been of-

105

* While serving as chairman of the Department of Art at the University of Mississippi between 1951 and 1957, Neal produced a film, "Color Lithography: An Art Medium," which was at the time of its completion the finest film to date on the art of lithography. It was winner of the Golden Reel Award at the American Film Festival in 1956.

Neal was responsible during his long academic career for establishment of instructional programs in lithography at Millikin University, the University of Mississippi, and at Douglass College, Rutgers University.

105   Nathan Oliveira (b. 1928), *The Elder,* 1957. 644 x 474 [Long Beach 31],
printed by the artist. Collection of the artist.

fered at Herron by Francis Chapin and Max Kahn) had now been
discontinued.* In a summer class taught by Maxil Ballinger, Antreasian made his first color lithograph; thereafter, in the absence of
formal instruction, he had no alternative but to continue work on
his own. When he completed his studies—after an interruption for
military service—he joined the Herron faculty as instructor in printmaking and then, in the summer of 1949, augmented his experience
through work with Will Barnet at the Art Students League and with
Stanley William Hayter at his Atelier 17 in New York.

COLORADO SPRINGS AFTER THE
SECOND WORLD WAR:
JEAN CHARLOT AND LAWRENCE BARRETT

In this way—against the grain of the times—some lithography programs survived and others came into being during the postwar years.

*   Chapin and Kahn taught primarily at the Art
Institute of Chicago but had also offered classes
in lithography at the John Herron Art School
during alternate spring semesters.

Not in all places, however, were the artist-lithographers as fortunate as Forsyth and Antreasian, both of whom received the support of sympathetic administrators. It was a different story for Lawrence Barrett.

By the end of World War II, Colorado Springs was no longer "the Newport of the Rockies": the old days were gone forever. During the war the art school had coped with by reduced enrollments, reduced budgets, and an interruption of its visiting-artist program; now it was forced to respond to the very different strains and tensions of the postwar period. The G. I. students who came to the school in large numbers were, as a group, more serious in purpose than the students the school had previously attracted, and the atmosphere was greatly changed. All over the country, the independent art schools were losing ground in competition with the professionally oriented art departments which were developing rapidly in the universities, and Colorado Springs was no exception. The artist-teachers who had been Mike Robinson's favored visitors in the years before the war—Biddle, Blanch, Lee, Dehn, and others—no longer served as drawing cards to students of the postwar generation. New faces were needed if the school was to stay afloat.

Robinson, who had not been in good health for several years, was forced to retire in 1947. To Mitchell Wilder, who had become the center's director in 1945, the need for change was apparent. The wave of G. I. students had provided the school with but a temporary reprieve. Rico Lebrun's presence as instructor in 1945 had signaled the kind of change that was needed, but Lebrun—a powerful draftsman and a dynamic teacher—had not stayed at the school. It was now imperative "to do something to bring in students. The only way to do it was to get a name—someone like Jean Charlot—and develop the summer school."[12]

Charlot and Zohmah Day had finally married in May 1939. During the 1940s they had led a nomadic life—in Georgia, New York, Massachusetts, California, and Mexico—with the result that Charlot was now quite willing to consider the possibility of settling down in Colorado. Barrett's presence as resident printer was an added attraction, and even on a brief visit to discuss the directorship of the school with Wilder and the board in August 1947, Charlot found time to draw a quick stone. Later, after Charlot accepted the position, he and Barrett formed a good relationship. Among other lithographs, Charlot found time to complete three commissions for Associated American Artists during his stay in Colorado. "[Barrett] was a rare combination of artist and artisan . . . [and] I remain grateful for the days I could work with him."[13]

It was Barrett's style to remain detached from the changes that were taking place around him. While Rico Lebrun was in Colorado Springs, he and Barrett had worked together on a series of lithographs that were Lebrun's finest work in the medium, including the direct and effective *Rabbit* (which was to be among the illustrations selected by Barrett to accompany his article on lithography in the *Encyclopedia Britannica*),* and several color prints, among them *Villon's Ballad #2.* In the same year that he had worked with Lebrun (1945), Barrett had also been actively involved in a massive project with Adolf Dehn: a series of lithographs related to the stories of Guy de Maupassant which Dehn was to execute as illustrations for a book to be published by the Book-of-the-Month Club. Later, he had

106

67

* Barrett's article on lithography replaced an earlier article by George Miller. It appeared in all printings of the fourteenth edition of the *Encyclopedia Britannica* between 1960 and 1970, and was accompanied by fifteen illustrations, seven of them lithographs printed by Barrett; one each by Randall Davey, Rico Lebrun, and Peppino Mangravite, and two each by Dehn and Barrett. Correspondence between Dehn and Walter Yust, the Britannica's editor (July and August 1957) indicates that Dehn was first invited to write this article; Dehn declined and apparently suggested that Barrett do it instead (Dehn papers, Archives of American Art, Smithsonian Institution, reel 1049, frames 462–63).

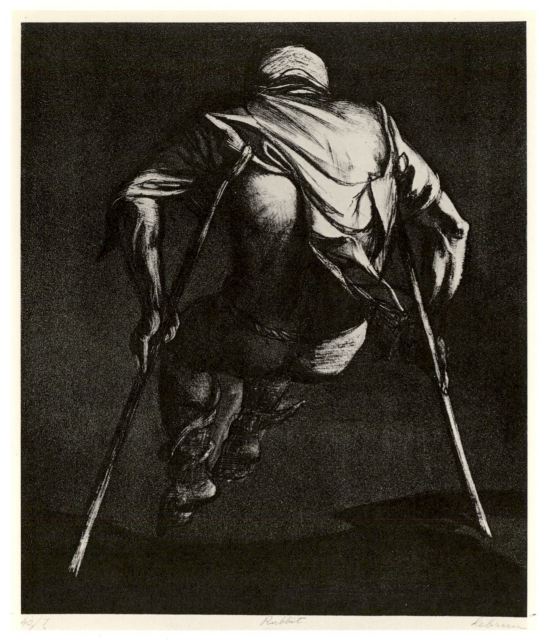

106   Rico Lebrun (1900–1964), *Rabbit,* 1945. 367 x 314, printed by Lawrence Barrett. Collection, Santa Barbara Museum of Art, Artist in Residence Fund.

worked with Howard Cook, Herbert Bayer, and with other artists who had come to the school, and all along he had actively continued to create and exhibit his own lithographs.

Charlot enjoyed his collaboration with Barrett, but in other ways his two-year stay in Colorado Springs was distinctly less pleasant. Despite the great difference in their artistic styles, Charlot's populist attitudes did not differ greatly from Robinson's, and in neither case did they sit well with the conservative members of the art center's board. Little was done to make Charlot comfortable in his position as director of the school:

> [The Board of Directors] wanted me to do a print for the
> members . . . [but] at the time they really did not like
> me, so they decided to refuse this print [*Mexican Kitchen*].
> It's a good print. I think there is something democratic
> about it, and the trustees were not especially democratic.

169

You know my feelings about "art for the people," and this is very much it.[14]

He left in 1949 and accepted a faculty appointment at the University of Hawaii. Barrett later mentioned to a friend that "he was sorry not to have fought for Charlot's retention. . . . He felt that Charlot's forced departure was the beginning of the end for the remainder of the staff."[15]

Certainly it was the beginning of the end for Barrett. As elsewhere, the pressure was on for the school to become more "progressive." In Colorado as elsewhere, Mauricio Lasansky's intaglio program at the University of Iowa was perceived to be the wave of the future insofar as printmaking was concerned, and lithography had no place in it.

So Barrett had to go. Emerson Woelffer, an Abstract-Expressionist painter from Chicago, had replaced Charlot (after a brief interim) as director of the school, and when the board failed to renew Barrett's contract, Woelffer inherited the problem. "There was a demonstration with the students. They took the old man's side." One night, as Woelffer tells the story, Barrett returned to his studio,

> after he was let go—one night or over the weekend. His press was an electric press, like a Rube Goldberg, he had put it together himself, it was an old hand press that he had motorized. It was the damndest thing! He would hit this lever and that one and it would start clanking through. We went in one morning and there it was! He had disassembled the whole thing and laid all the parts up on the table. Then he had put it back together as a hand press, just as he'd first found it.[16]

Understandably bitter, Barrett left the school exactly what it was entitled to, not a whit more. Many of the stones were his, so he carted them away. He might as well have saved his energy in reassembling the school press. It was never used again.

After leaving the Fine Arts Center, Barrett was at one point offered a faculty appointment at Oklahoma State University, but whether "afraid of the climate . . . or afraid of change," he turned it down and took a job as an illustrator at the air force base.* He sold his press, stones, and other equipment to a former student; abandoned lithography; and took up sculpture in bronze, working always with his favorite subject, horses, overcoming the trembling hand of Parkinson's disease in this way, for though he could no longer draw, he could manage to model in wax most precisely.†

LYNTON KISTLER RETURNS TO LOS ANGELES

During these same years, Lynton Kistler was again printing in Los Angeles.‡ He returned to California from the East in 1945 and gathered together his savings to purchase a house on Third Street, west of Alvarado, on the corner of Carondelet. He set up his Fuchs & Lang press in what had been the dining room of the two-story house—the kind of California house which in stucco and brown-shingled versions lined the streets of Hollywood and Pasadena, complete with palm trees and bougainvillea vines.

Kistler made use of every inch of space in a pressroom that was at once intimate and congested. Because he printed on dampened

*   Eric Bransby, who was Barrett's supervisor in a special unit at Ent Air Force Base, speculates that these were the reasons Barrett declined a position elsewhere. Barrett did little printing after leaving the school, and it is Bransby's memory that his final collaboration may have been with the Santa Fe painter Randall Davey, about 1960.

†   Barrett died on 26 May 1973 at the age of seventy-five.

‡   Kistler was in the East, principally in Providence, R. I., from 1940 to 1945. While there he met George Miller and gave a demonstration of lithography at the New York World's Fair, but did no printing for artists.

2/10   o = X   Woelffer 51

107   Emerson Woelffer (b. 1914), *O = X*, 1951. 280 x 372, printed by the artist. Collection, Tamarind Institute.

paper—as was then customary—much room was taken up by damp boxes and screw-presses in which the paper, between blotters, could be prepared for printing. He turned the front room of the house into a print gallery and set up a graining table on a porch. He and his wife Helen lived upstairs. Kistler now intended to work full time as an artist's printer, and he knew that in order to do so, he would have to interest a large number of California artists in lithography. "I would have carried a stone halfway across the desert to get it into the hands of an artist, I was so anxious to do work."[17] He relied heavily upon the word-of-mouth recommendations of artists for whom he had printed, but he also advertised, printed brochures, arranged exhibitions in his gallery, and gave talks at schools and art clubs—often dismantling his press and reassembling it elsewhere to provide demonstrations of the process. Slowly, his business grew.

Before the war, during a period of transition in the printing industry, many commercial printing houses had retained their hand presses for proofing purposes. After the war, however, they rapidly disposed of the last of their stones and handpresses, now obsolete for all commercial purposes. Throughout the United States, tons of fine stones were discarded in landfills, used as paving materials, or dumped in the nearest river or bay.

Kistler's experiences, as he endeavored to obtain the stones and

171

108   Lawrence Barrett (1897–1973), *Untitled (Horses in Winter)*, n. d. 209 x 270, printed by the artist. Collection, University of New Mexico Art Museum, gift of Verna Jean Versa.

equipment he needed, were typical. The Crocker Company, a large printing firm in San Francisco, had great quantities of stone:

> By that time I had gotten enough artists interested [in lithography] so that they were coming to me wanting stones, and I didn't have enough . . . [so] I offered to send a truck to San Francisco and buy as much stone on time as Crocker would allow me to. They said they would sell me all the stone I wanted but that I'd have to pay cash and take delivery. . . . Crocker dumped tons of stone into San Francisco Bay, which just broke my heart.[18]

Nor was this his only such experience. On another occasion he sought to buy some handpresses and received a promise from another company that he would be given first refusal if they decided to sell them. One day, when he was in San Francisco, he visited their offices:

> The manager greeted me cordially, but when I inquired about the presses he told me to my dismay that he had sold them as junk only the day before. I reminded him of his promise, but the only consolation I could get from him was the address of the junk company. I rushed down. . . . They led me out into their yard and showed me the presses. They had already broken them up with a sledgehammer. I was disconsolate for days.[19]

172

Such incidents were commonplace, not only in California, but in all parts of the country. Some stones were saved by artists and schools that had use for them; in far greater numbers they were destroyed.

Despite problems and disappointments, Kistler persisted in his work. After a ten-year interruption, he resumed his collaboration with Jean Charlot during the summer of 1947—the summer of Charlot's initial visit to Colorado Springs. They worked for most of that summer on a single, five-color print, *Sunday Dress*. "It was finished the day of the testimonial dinner at Taix Restaurant [9 September 1947; a dinner for ninety-five people, with Merle Armitage as chairman]. We hung it on the wall and it was stolen. Jean did not mind. He was tickled that anyone would think enough of his work to steal it."[20]

KISTLER AND THE ARTISTS OF LOS ANGELES

In 1946, after four years in the army and air force, I returned to Los Angeles to accept a faculty appointment at the University of California. The art department at UCLA was still small in those postwar years, and printmaking had not yet been developed as a part of its curriculum. S. Macdonald-Wright, who was then professor of art history, had made lithographs in collaboration with Lynton Kistler, and early in 1948 he arranged for Kistler to meet with us to talk about lithography.

Shortly thereafter, as a result of that meeting, William Bowne, Gordon Nunes, Jan Stussy, and I began to work with Kistler. Stussy vividly recalls his first experience in the "crowded, homemade" atmosphere of Kistler's house-studio on Third Street: "He scared me to death with his sense of mystery and magic. Do you remember how he would mix several little jars of etch and test the stone with a feather to watch it froth? I still see him in Merlin's cap today."[21] That sense of the magic of lithography, Kistler's personal warmth and friendliness, his obvious dedication to his work, and the air of good-fellowship that came into being as we all worked together, made an evening at the workshop a memorable experience. And above all, there were those wonderfully seductive grey stones. We quickly became infatuated with them, and throughout the spring and summer worked incessantly at Kistler's shop.

It is not surprising to me that most of Southern California's more prominent artists of that time came to work at Kistler's place at one time or another, principally during the late 1940s and early 1950s, among them Edward Biberman, Emil Bisttram, William Brice, Hans Burkhardt, Robert Chuey, Phil Dike, Lorser Feitelson, Michael Frary, Richard Haines, Rico Lebrun, Helen Lundeberg, Dan Lutz, Phil Paradise, Edward Reep, Sueo Serisawa, Millard Sheets, Wayne Thiebaud, June Wayne, and Howard Warshaw. Some of the artists drew only two or three stones; others adopted lithography as a medium of central importance to their work.

Kistler does not know how many editions he printed between 1945, when he opened the Third Street shop, and 1958, when he stopped printing from stone. "Unfortunately, I'm not a good record keeper and I'm not a good collector. . . . I gave away things that I should have kept, and I sold things that should have remained in my collection. . . . When I made prints I didn't want them to pile up in stacks or be put in drawers. I wanted to see them on the wall, I

*109
110*

173

109 Jan Stussy (b. 1921), *Coast Tree (Witches' Tree),* 1948. 286 x 372, printed by Lynton R. Kistler. Collection, University of New Mexico Art Museum, gift of Clinton Adams.

wanted people to use them, I wanted to see them framed so people could enjoy them."[22]

But pile up in stacks they did, which was one reason that so many of the artists who worked with Kistler made only two or three editions. By current standards, his prices for printing were still very low, ranging from thirty to fifty dollars for an edition of twenty impressions, but for an artist who had no market, such costs were not inconsequential. The Los Angeles County Museum—then a combined museum of art, science, and natural history, and located in Exposition Park—presented no regular exhibitions of contemporary prints; nor were the leading Los Angeles art dealers—Dalzell Hatfield, Felix Landau, Frank Perls, and Earl Stendahl—interested in showing prints, even by artists whose paintings they exhibited.*

This lack of interest in prints was matched by that of the Los Angeles art schools and universities which, by comparison with those in the East and Midwest, were slow to develop programs in printmaking. Kistler's activity as a printer had had no effect upon the schools, and as late as the end of World War II, instruction in lithography was unavailable in Los Angeles. The first such program was begun at the University of Southern California by Jules Heller, who

*   The very small prices that American prints commanded in the marketplace were an important factor in the dealers' attitudes. Most of the lithographs listed in Kistler's 1951 catalogue were priced at five, ten, or fifteen dollars. A few, including the Man Ray and Charlot's *Hawaiian Drummer,* were listed at twenty-five dollars. That was a high price for an American lithograph in 1951.

110   Clinton Adams (b. 1918), *Second Hand Store I,* 1953. 247 x 353, printed by
Lynton R. Kistler. Collection, University of New Mexico Art Museum, gift of
the artist.

shortly after joining the faculty in 1945–46 obtained use of a small
room on the second floor of a temporary barracks building as a printmaking studio.

Heller had studied printmaking prior to the war at Teachers
College, Columbia University, where Arthur R. Young offered general instruction in all printaking media, including lithography. The
experience was less than satisfactory, Heller recalls. The class learned
about lithography only on zinc plates and "only by the numbers."

> We all finished our crayon drawings *together* before we were
> taken to a basement shop where Young and his assistant
> had us go through all of the steps *simultaneously* as we
> passed around the etch (we never knew what was in the
> etch, how it was mixed, etc.). We were only allowed to
> assist the assistant in pulling our prints. . . . I resolved
> then and there, that if ever I was in a position to teach
> lithography . . . I would do it with stones and have each
> student do it himself or herself. . . .[23]

The experience Heller describes had much to do with the character
of the workshop he later developed in Los Angeles. He spent the
summer of 1947 at the Taller Gráfica Popular in Mexico City, working extensively in lithography, which had come to be his medium

of choice. By 1948 he had managed to expand the printmaking workshop at the university to take over the entire second floor of the barracks, and had acquired a second Fuchs & Lang press, along with an adequate stock of stones. Many of the more talented students in the art department were soon attracted to Heller's workshop, among them Dick Frankel, Joe Funk, James Jarvaise, Craig Kaufmann, Kenneth Price, and Joe Zirker. Funk, an expert in the kind of technical improvisation that was one of the G.I.'s best-learned lessons, became Heller's assistant.

Aware of Kistler's work at the Third Street studio, Heller and Funk sought him out as a source of information. According to Heller, Kistler was unwilling to provide assistance. "He was worried that we would steal his secrets and ruin his business. We didn't see it that way at all. The more artists and students became interested in lithography, the better it would be for him."* But Kistler was not unapproachable: later he took Funk on as his apprentice, to grain stones, damp paper, and serve as press assistant.

Heller quickly became an important advocate of printmaking in Los Angeles. Between 1950 and 1952 he organized a short-lived series of national exhibitions at the University of Southern California. He wrote a textbook, *Printmaking Today,* which gained national use after its publication in 1958. While completing work on the textbook, Heller also founded *Impression,* an ambitious journal, handsomely produced, and intended as a serious critical voice in the field of printmaking. It was not easy to gain support for such a project in Los Angeles, nor was the timing propitious: *Impression* survived to publish only four issues.†

* Heller, in conversation, 24 October 1977. Kistler's version differs: "I was always willing to give out information to others, but I felt it should be an equal exchange." (Kistler, quoted in Adams, "Lynton R. Kistler," p. 103.)

† *Impression* left an important legacy, which Kneeland McNulty describes as follows: "In many ways it resembled its successor, *Artist's Proof;* its demise was owing to financial circumstances. The connection between the two magazines is relevant. When *Impression* was in its last throes, Jules Heller contacted Fritz Eichenberg . . . Director of the Pratt Graphic Art Center, to see if he could help to rescue the situation. *Impression* had a list of subscribers, and some of them had paid for five-year subscriptions, but there was not enough money to continue.

"Mr. Eichenberg had long wanted to publish a magazine of this nature. Without much hope he prepared a dummy under the new name *Artist's Proof* and showed it to Harold Hugo of The Meriden Gravure Company, a long time friend, and asked for an estimate of the printing cost. After a few minutes Mr. Hugo said: 'Let's go ahead.' When Mr. Eichenberg protested that he had not been given an estimate, Mr. Hugo replied that if he was, the magazine would never appear." (Kneeland McNulty, "Introduction to *Artist's Proof,*" *Artist's Proof: A Collector's Edition of the First Eight Issues,* p. 7.)

EUGENE BERMAN AND MAN RAY

During these same years, Kistler collaborated on several occasions with Eugene Berman, Max Ernst, and Man Ray. They were but three of the many artists, musicians, intellectuals, and writers who were attracted to Southern California—particularly to Hollywood—during and after the second war.

Among the émigré artists, Kistler worked most extensively with Berman. "He was a difficult man to work with," Kistler recalls. "He never knew there was a twentieth century, he never discovered it. He was a perfectionist, and everything had to be right."[24] The result was that Kistler proofed and reproofed Berman's lithographs—particularly those in color, *Nocturnal Cathedral* and *Verona.* Berman marked up the proofs with comments. "There was one proof that I thought was a classic. He really tore it apart: 'This is too light, this is too dark, this is terrible. . . .' Everything seemed to be wrong with it."[25] But problems aside, Berman and Kistler enjoyed an active collaboration which lasted for several years.

It was through William Copley that Kistler met Man Ray and Max Ernst. They were two of six Surrealist artists—the others were Magritte, Cornell, Matta, and Tanguy—whose work was shown in a series of exhibitions at Copley's short-lived gallery in Beverly Hills. In 1948 the Copley Galleries published the first edition of Man Ray's *Alphabet for Adults,* designed by Man Ray and printed by Kistler. Kistler also collaborated with Man Ray on one original lithograph, *Le Roman Noir.* Man Ray drew with a stylus to create a white line drawing against a black ground, and at his suggestion the image was

111 Garo Antreasian (b. 1922), *Limes, Leaves and Flowers,* 1959. Color
lithograph, 610 x 838 [Lewis 7], printed by the artist. Collection, Indianapolis
Museum of Art.

printed using a roller on which four colors—black, red, blue, and
brown—had been blended together. Neither Man Ray nor Kistler
had used the method before.* "That was Man Ray's idea," Kistler
says. "He suggested to me that it might be done that way. I was
rather quick to take up with any idea an artist advanced if I thought
it might work out."[26]

Concurrently, Kistler was also working with Copley and Max
Ernst on the catalogue for a retrospective exhibition of Ernst's paintings which was to be held at Copley's gallery in January and February of 1949. Ernst designed the catalogue and Kistler printed it in an
edition of 513 numbered copies, of which numbers one through
twenty-two contained an original etching (printed by Joe Funk in
Heller's workshop at the university). Ernst also wanted to do a series of lithographs, but he expected Kistler to accept a part of each
edition as payment for his services. Kistler, whose practice was to
work with artists on a cash basis, turned Ernst down. "That was
one of the biggest mistakes I ever made. . . . I've always kicked
myself."[27]

* As Charlot had earlier used blended inking
in his work with Albert Carman, it is surprising
that he had not introduced Kistler to the process.

GUSTAVE VON GROSCHWITZ AND THE CINCINNATI BIENNIALS

In national exhibitions, lithographs fared little better than in Los Angeles. Kistler made it a practice to assist the artists with whom he worked by matting their prints and entering them in juried competitions throughout the country, but among the jurors of the fifties—particularly with those who selected the prestigious annual exhibitions at the Brooklyn Museum—lithographs were distinctly out of fashion. Awards and purchases were few and far between.*

Among the few museums to provide consistent support and encouragement to lithography during the 1950s, foremost was the Cincinnati Museum, where Gustave von Groschwitz had been appointed curator of prints in 1947. Von Groschwitz, after leaving the Federal Art Project in New York, had held a position as print curator at Wesleyan University in Connecticut, and had over the years become increasingly interested in the history and development of color lithography. Now, at Cincinnati, he proposed to the museum's director, Philip Adams, that they undertake a series of international biennial exhibitions of color lithography. Adams approved the plan and von Groschwitz went to work: "It had never been done before . . . [but] I got together a relatively small show of 235 lithographs. I remember the opening. It was a cold night, there weren't many people. But we got it off the ground."[28]

Coming at a time when lithography was otherwise given little attention or emphasis, the five Cincinnati biennials (1950–58) did much to restore the prestige of the medium. Through their international scope and well-designed catalogues the effect of the exhibitions was felt by artist-lithographers throughout the country, but with particular impact by those who came from nearby states to see the prints themselves. For Garo Antreasian, as for many artists, the exhibitions were a revelation of the medium's unsuspected dimensions, and a clear demonstration of how far behind the work of the modern European masters—Picasso, Miró, Leger, and Chagall—American lithography then lagged.

111

* The number of lithographs included in the annual exhibitions at the Brooklyn Museum declined in the mid-1950s. While lithographs received 34 percent of the purchase awards between 1947 and 1951, they were given only 7 percent of the awards between 1952 and 1956. Among 504 prints exhibited in four major exhibitions in 1954 (Brooklyn Museum, Museum of Modern Art, University of Illinois, Seattle Art Museum) only 15.6 percent were lithographs.

NOTES

1   H. W. Janson in an introductory paragraph to Emil Ganso, "The Technique of Lithographic Printing," p. 16.

2   Ibid.

3   Franz Kline, quoted in Thomas B. Hess, "Prints: Where History, Style and Money Meet," p. 29.

4   Barnet, tape-recorded interview, 22 September 1979.

5   Ibid.

6   Forsyth to Adams, 15 August 1979.

7   Ibid.

8   Burr Miller, interview, 4 May 1979.

9   Forsyth to Adams, 15 August 1979.

10   Ibid.

11   Garo Antreasian, "Education in American Printmaking since 1900."

12   Mitchell A. Wilder, in conversation, 16 May 1978.

13   Charlot to Adams, 16 July 1978.

14   Charlot, quoted by Peter Morse, *Jean Charlot's Prints, a Catalogue Raisonné,* p. 282 (print no. 518).

15   Eric Bransby to Adams, 24 June 1978.

16   Woelffer, tape-recorded interview, 1 June 1978.

17   Kistler, quoted in Clinton Adams, "Lynton R. Kistler and the Development of Lithography in Los Angeles," p. 104.

18   Ibid., p. 103.

19   Ibid.

20   Kistler, quoted in Morse, *Charlot's Prints,* p. 274.

21   Stussy to Adams, not dated (November 1977).

22   Kistler, quoted in Adams, "Lynton R. Kistler," pp. 104, 108.

23   Heller to Adams, 15 November 1977.

24   Kistler, quoted in Adams, "Lynton R. Kistler," pp. 105–06.

25   Ibid., p. 106.

26   Ibid., p. 105.

27   Ibid.

28   Von Groschwitz, quoted in Adams, "Color Lithography in the 1950s: The Cincinnati Biennials, a Conversation with Gustave von Groschwitz," p. 86.

6 · Toward the 1960s

JUNE WAYNE AND LYNTON KISTLER

By 1952, after years of almost daily work at the press, Lynton Kistler developed a painful allergy to the acids used in hand-printing. Although he tried to protect his hands by wearing rubber gloves, it was evident to him that the time during which he could continue to print from stone was coming to an end. His income from artists' printing was far from adequate. While his wife Helen was supportive of his work, she had a good sense of financial realities, and she now urged him to move back into a commercial printing business. Reluctantly, he did. He opened a shop on Temple Street, in the Echo Park district of Los Angeles, and although he kept one handpress in the back of the building, he did very little printing from stone after 1953, and only for artists who—like Jean Charlot, June Wayne, and I—had worked with him before.*

I had first met Wayne at Kistler's studio in the summer of 1948, a few months after I began to work there. She had then been making her first lithographs. During the five-year period between 1948 and 1953 we had been among the most active of the artists who worked with Kistler, with the result that we had frequently met at his studio, discussed our work, and formed a professional friendship.

Born in Chicago, June Wayne came from a background very different from my own. She had dropped out of school as early as possible "in order to pursue her education as an artist." Her first large exhibition was held at the Palacio de Bellas Artes in Mexico City when she was eighteen. At much the same time she worked on the Federal Art Project in Chicago and was active in its behalf, testifying on one occasion before a committee of Congress. She then worked for a time in New York as a designer of ornaments for the garment industry. The practical, political, and business experience gained in these early phases of her career stood her in good stead after she moved to California.

* Kistler printed his last lithograph from stone in 1958; like his first from stone, twenty-five years before, it was drawn by Jean Charlot.

181

In Los Angeles Wayne assumed a leading role in defense of modernist artists who, during the McCarthy era, were frequently under attack as "tools of the Kremlin" by the city's reactionary forces, including members of the Los Angeles City Council. She and I worked together during this difficult period as participants in a program developed by the art critic, Jules Langsner, for the Ford Foundation's Fund for Adult Education.

In 1954 I left California to assume the headship of the department of art at the University of Kentucky and did not return to Los Angeles until the summer of 1956, at which time I made my final lithographs with Kistler. It was not the same as before. Kistler did little printing from stone now, and the new circumstances in which he worked made it difficult for me to achieve the result that I wanted. When I talked with June Wayne I discovered that she had encountered similar problems in her recent work with Kistler.

In 1955 and 1956 she had made a new series of lithographs which he had printed from her hand-drawn plates on an offset press. Then in 1956 she had made two additional prints on stone. But neither in the offset lithographs nor in the new prints from stone did Wayne find what she sought from the medium. Kistler's energies were now directed primarily toward establishment of a successful commercial business, and great though might be his interest in her work, the conditions were not right. Wayne became convinced that if she wished to continue her work in lithography she must do it elsewhere.

In 1957 she went to Paris to work with Marcel Durassier, and there found it possible "to use European lithography techniques not feasible with Kistler. She began to do color lithographs. . . . She printed on fine French papers that were unavailable in the United States at that time and she incorporated tusche washes on zinc into her technical vocabulary."[1] In April 1958 Wayne wrote to Gustave von Groschwitz at the Cincinnati Art Museum: "[I] will rely largely on trips to Europe for my lithography in the future. It seems a long way to go to make a lithograph, but unless someone, somewhere realizes the straits this medium is in, it will have vanished with the present batch of printers."[2]

When I again visited California in the spring of 1958, Wayne and I talked on several occasions of her experience with Durassier and of the sorry state of lithography in the United States. We spoke, I remember, about the possibility that some means might be found to revive the art of lithography in America. Wayne then returned to Paris to undertake a "lithographic marathon" that ended only on Christmas Day, 1958, when she and Durassier completed the lithographs included in her *livre de luxe, John Donne: Songs and Sonets.*

MARGARET LOWENGRUND AND THE CONTEMPORARIES

In Woodstock, Grant Arnold's departure had left a void that was not filled until the early 1950s when, after an interim during which the press in the basement of the Artists Association building had gone untended and unused, Margaret Lowengrund set out to revive the workshop.

Lowengrund had first encountered lithography in 1923 when she moved from Philadelphia to New York to study with Joseph Pennell at the Art Students League. In Philadelphia she had studied at the Pennsylvania Academy of Fine Arts and had written a column,

112   Stuart Davis (1894–1964), *Detail Study for Cliché,* 1957. Color lithograph,
316 x 377 [AAA 23], printed by Arnold Singer. Collection, Cincinnati Art
Museum.

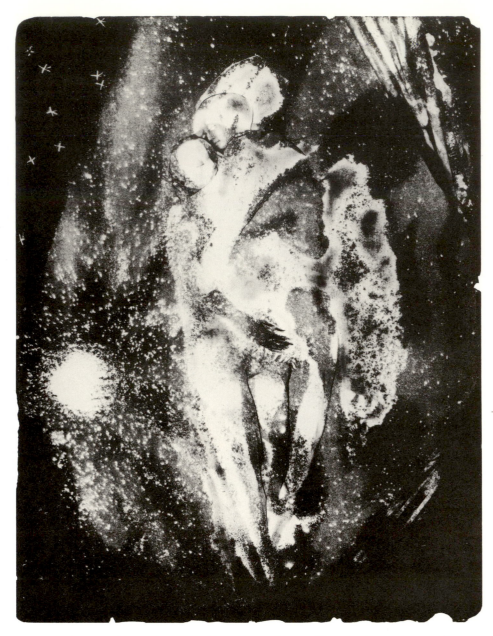

113   June Wayne (b. 1918), *Shine Here to Us and Thou Art Everywhere,* 1956. 473 x 625 [Baskett 92], printed by Lynton R. Kistler. Collection, University of New Mexico Art Museum, gift of the artist.

illustrated with her drawings, for the Philadelphia *Public Ledger;* in New York she undertook to write a similar column, "Little Sketches About Town," for the *Evening Post.* "Joseph Pennell . . . criticized my newspaper stuff as roundly as my work in his class. He saved the clippings daily and went over them with me. When visitors to the graphics room came by, he always pointed out the fact that some students also worked for a living commercially, and did it as a part of professional training, not as a separate thing."[3]

With the money saved from her newspaper work, Lowengrund then went to England, where she studied lithography with A. S. Hartrick, a friend of Pennell's and a founding member of the Senefelder Club. In addition to her work in England, she also studied painting in Paris with André Lhôte, exhibited in the Autumn Salon, and attracted the attention of Campbell Dodgson, then keeper of prints at the British Museum. Dodgson purchased one of her litho-

graphs for the museum's collection, with the result that when Lowengrund returned to New York in the fall of 1927, the *Evening Post*
headlined an article: "American Girl Artist Back with Honor Record Abroad."[4]

She had her first American exhibition at the Kleeman-Thorman
Galleries in 1928 and then, in the mid-1930s, established a home in
Woodstock. She continued active work in lithography and taught
at the New School for Social Research in New York, where in 1938
she offered a "Workshop in Color Lithography" in collaboration
with the printer Irwin Lefcourt.* She was also active as an illustrator,
radio interviewer, writer, and critic, serving for a time in the 1940s
as associate editor of *Art Digest*.

Whatever her other activities, Lowengrund remained deeply
committed to printmaking. Founding a small gallery in New York,
she called it The Contemporaries, and set out to become one of the
few dealers in the 1950s to give serious attention to the graphic work
of contemporary American artists. Aware that artists in Woodstock
no longer had access to a lithographic printer, Lowengrund also re-
established the workshop in the basement of the Artists Association
building—a workshop that had largely been inoperative since the
departure of Grant Arnold. In the summer of 1952, Michael Ponce
de León, a young artist whose work she had begun to show in her
New York gallery, became her first assistant.† She was later joined
by Reginald Neal, who, while serving as chairman of the Department of Art at the University of Mississippi, became her printer during the summer of 1954.‡

Simultaneously, she also installed a small print workshop at her
gallery in New York. The artist-printer John Muench provides this
description:

> [The gallery] was on the second floor and [had] a tiny back
> room which contained a small etching press and an
> ancient, ungeared flatbed litho press. Stones (such as they
> were) were grained on a small bathroom sink and there
> was absolutely no storage space. Very often the acid used
> for lithography was used for etching and vice versa. How
> we did as well as we did, I shall never know.
>
> I went to work for Margaret as Associate Director and
> did some teaching and printing as well as turning out
> several modest editions of my own. Michael Ponce de
> León taught intaglio classes. It seems to me, in retrospect,
> that there was never any money and everyone was always
> hungry.[5]

It was certainly a far from propitious time to start a new lithography workshop in New York.§ Even George Miller in his long-estab-
lished shop had felt the financial pressure. Miller had reconstituted
the firm as George C. Miller & Son in 1948 when, after a period of
military service, Burr Miller had joined his father in the workshop.
It was in the "middle fifties," Burr recalls, "[that] we hit a low." In
1955, they moved to a new and larger space in a building on Twenty-
second Street and, so as to be able to undertake large editions for
book publishers—among them the Heritage Press and the Limited
Editions Club—acquired their own offset press. "[The publishers]
were doing big editions in childrens' books. . . . This was an excellent income, which helped [us] get through the hard times."[6] The

* Lefcourt had assisted his friend Emil Ganso
in the printing of lithographs in Woodstock during the early 1930s.

† When Ponce de León went to Lowengrund's
Woodstock workshop he had experience only
in intaglio printing and knew nothing of lithography. He tells this anecdote: "She introduced
me to the process. . . . My first assignment was
to open up the shop next morning and to get
two stones in readiness for . . . David Smith
the sculptor. Margaret Lowengrund was to
come two hours later to do his printing. Not
knowing that my knowledge of printmaking
was based only on what Margaret had told me
the day before, he urged me to start printing
his first stone. I was too embarrassed to admit
I had never printed a litho before. Besides, had
not Margaret told me how to print a lithograph
a few hours before? With a great deal of camaraderie and beer drinking we began to print from
the first stone. We had no running water in the
workshop, so David suggested that rather than
go out and fetch and bring in water [from the
brook behind the building] we should use beer,
of which we had several packs. And so we
printed. . . . When Margaret arrived ready to
start the printing and was told that we had already printed the first stone she almost col-
lapsed, and in great desperation she rushed to
the drying pile of our first prints only to discover to her great amazement that the whole
edition was rather well printed. Without pulling any punches, Margaret gave me a blister-
ing lecture and made me aware of all the
inumerable disasters that could have taken place
in the process. 'You are either the luckiest fool
I have ever met or a born genius,' she told me.
'Time will tell,' she said." (Michael Ponce de
León, interview, 12 March 1983.)

‡ Neal managed the Woodstock workshop
for Lowengrund, receiving a portion of the income from printing in payment for his services.
He printed editions for a number of artists, including Adolf Dehn, Richard Florsheim, Doris
Lee, and Edward Millman.

§ Despite the economic problems that artists'
printers then faced, Muench also opened a small
lithography workshop after he left Lowengrund
in 1954. His shop was on Fourteenth Street, in
the Delmonico Building, where Miller was also
then located. Muench printed lithographs for
Karl Fortess, Antonio Frasconi, Jack Levine, and
Julian Levi. See also footnote, page 165.

114   Man Ray (1890–1976), *Le Roman Noir,* 1948. Color lithograph, printed by Lynton R. Kistler. Collection, Juliet Man Ray.

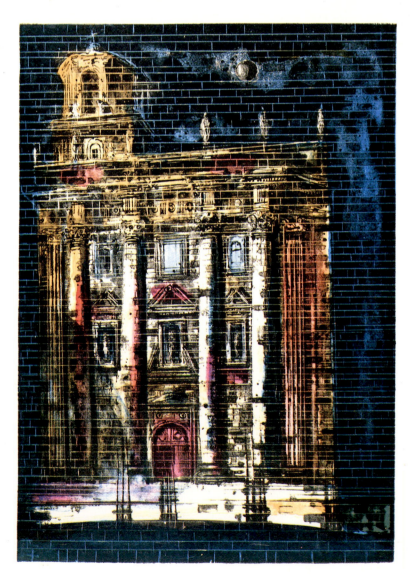

115   Eugene Berman (1899–1972), *Nocturnal Cathedral,* 1951. Color lithograph, 330 x 230, printed by Lynton R. Kistler. Collection, Tamarind Institute.

116   Sam Francis (b. 1923), *The White Line,* 1960. Color lithograph, 906 x 630, printed at the Atelier Emil Mattieu. Collection, Museum of Modern Art, New York, gift of E. W. Kornfeld.

drawings were done on stone by the artists, transferred to press-plates, then run on the offset press.*

Lowengrund, however, was not deterred by the financial problems that afflicted lithography in the mid-fifties. Spurred on by the relative success of the summer workshop in Woodstock, Lowengrund determined to open a larger workshop in the city. In 1955, she obtained space in a building at Third Avenue and Seventy-seventh Street, about three blocks from her gallery, and engaged Walter Rogalski and Arnold Singer, then the lithographic printer at the Art Students League, to equip it for her.†

Singer speaks of Lowengrund with obvious respect: "She was very ambitious [and] strong-willed. She was the kind of woman who accomplished a lot. One would just have to give her credit for what she did. She started the Contemporaries on a shoestring and just out of sheer willpower, she made the thing run."[7] The painter, Henry Pearson, who worked for Lowengrund at her gallery, shares Singer's respect for her accomplishments: "[She was] difficult to get along with [and] excessively demanding [but] she was fighting for something that seemed to be a lost cause, in attempting to reestablish printmaking in America."[8]

In November 1955, Lowengrund sent out an invitation: "We're at home, Sunday, November 6th, 1955, to celebrate the opening of The Contemporaries Graphic Art Centre." The staff would be on hand and Neal's new film on color lithography would be shown.

Lowengrund's plan for the workshop was twofold: it would engage in contract printing and it would also permit her to develop publishing projects with established artists whose prints would then be sold through her gallery. Among the projects undertaken by the workshop (then and later) were many that number among the finest of the period, including Stuart Davis's powerful color lithograph, *Detail Study for Cliché,* printed by Arnold Singer, as well as prints by Alexander Archipenko, Milton Avery, George Biddle, Adolf Dehn, Kurt Seligmann, David Smith, Graham Sutherland, and Rufino Tamayo.

But Lowengrund soon came to feel severe financial pressure. The gallery was by now located in a large, ground-floor space on Madison Avenue, and "the backers who helped her set things up deserted her. Margaret had a monthly rental of thirteen-hundred dollars—a very high rental for a print gallery."[9] And the character of the contract printing at the workshop was far less than satisfactory, as a number of the clients were wealthy dilettantes: "It was a difficult situation. . . . So many of [them] had a very over-inflated view of their capabilities; they didn't consider themselves dilettantes, they were artists. Anyway, they kept the shop going."[10]

Lowengrund sought outside support for her graphics workshop and received a favorable response from the Rockefeller Foundation, which however required that in order to become eligible for a grant she must first associate her workshop with a nonprofit institution. She met the foundation's condition by developing an association with Pratt Institute; in 1956 the workshop's name was changed to the Pratt-Contemporaries Graphic Arts Center; Fritz Eichenberg, chairman of the graphics program at Pratt Institute, became its codirector; and in November of that year the Rockefeller Foundation made the new center a $50,000 grant for operation of its workshop over a three-year period. Although it was the stated intention of the center that

* Over the years George Miller had maintained his union card against a day he might need it. But now, as he sought to use the union label on one project, he encountered a barrier. The men at the union said, " 'We have to come up and inspect your shop.' He said, 'Well, it's just my son there, we have a helper.' But they said, 'You have to have a union pressman . . . Do you have a stone-grainer?—you have to have a union stone-grainer. You have to have a union paper-handler.' Frankly, he told them to go to hell. So he got kicked out of the union for insubordination. About a year later he got a great big scroll from the union, commending him on thirty-seven years of meritorious service.' " (Burr Miller, interview, 4 May 1979.)

† Arnold Singer, who had studied with Will Barnet, was appointed printer at the Art Students League in 1952. He continued to print at the league while also printing for Margaret Lowengrund at her Contemporaries Graphic Art Center; for its successor, Pratt Graphics Center; and for Robert Blackburn. Singer continued to work as a printer in New York City until in 1966 he left to accept a faculty appointment at Cornell University.

117 Margaret Lowengrund (1902–1957), *Milkweed,* 1952. Color lithograph, 465 x 350, printed by the artist and Michael Ponce de León. Published by International Graphic Arts Society. Collection, Art, Prints and Photographs Division, New York Public Library, Astor, Lenox, and Tilden Foundations.

all of the graphic mediums would be explored, its advisory board was soon to determine that "lithography [was] the most popular process and the one with the greatest money-making potential as a service."*

Margaret Lowengrund's sudden death in 1957—long before full realization of the new center's potential—removed from the scene a passionate advocate of lithography, and although (as Eichenberg immodestly reports) "the workshop flourished under Fritz Eichenberg,"[11] the fact that his background and interests greatly differed from Lowengrund's caused substantial changes in its program. The workshop, now called the Pratt Graphics Center, moved to a new location on Broadway.

* Minutes of the Advisory Board of the Pratt-Contemporaries Graphic Art Center, 17 January 1957. Among the members of the advisory board were Khosrov Ajootian, Theo J. H. Gusten, Una Johnson, Karl Kup, William Lieberman, and Gabor Peterdi.

118   Raymond Parker (b. 1922), *Untitled*, 1961. Color lithograph, 692 x 889 [Tamarind 285], printed by Garo Antreasian. Tamarind collection, University of New Mexico Art Museum.

TATYANA GROSMAN:
UNIVERSAL LIMITED ART EDITIONS

Unlike Margaret Lowengrund, who had made lithographs for more than thirty years, Tatyana Grosman knew little about the process at the time she founded her print publishing venture, Universal Limited Art Editions (ULAE) in the late 1950s.

Grosman and her husband Maurice had come to the United States in 1943 as refugees from Europe. Escaping from Paris two days before the city fell to the Germans, they had first gone to Marseilles, then on foot to Barcelona. After securing visas to Lisbon, they had made their way to New York, where Maurice, a painter, had managed to support them by making silk-screen reproductions of modern paintings for sale in the Marboro Book Shops. When in 1955 Maurice Grosman suffered a heartattack, the Grosmans moved to a small summer cottage in West Islip:

> It was at this point that Tatyana decided to go into business
> as an independent publisher of silk-screen reproductions.
> Her editions would be small and of the highest quality,
> and, most important, in each case she would get the artist
> to collaborate actively with Maurice in the reproduction
> process—to supervise the matching of colors, the choice
> of paper, and all other details.[12]

But fine printing and the direct participation of the artists notwithstanding, Grosman's initial projects for Mary Callery, Max Weber, and Jacques Lipchitz remained reproductions, not original prints. When she showed her work to William Lieberman at the Museum of Modern Art and to Carl Zigrosser in Philadelphia, they made her realize that this distinction was crucial. "After that," Grosman says, "I knew I wanted to make originals. . . . What I really wanted was for the artist to work with his hand on a surface."[13] It was about at this time, she relates, that "by some miracle," she discovered two small lithograph stones in the front yard of her house. Through a second coincidence, she soon had an opportunity to buy a used lithograph press for fifteen dollars. Thus equipped, with these two stones and this press, she set out to become a publisher of lithographs:

> I had just read a lovely book that inspired me very much,
> a book by Monroe Wheeler . . . in which he spoke about
> artists doing graphic work to illustrate books of
> poetry. . . . He said that the ideal thing would be for an
> artist and a poet to work together on a book. The idea
> seemed very beautiful to me . . . and somehow I got the
> idea that I could use these stones to make a book of the
> kind Mr. Wheeler had described.[14]

Grosman's lack of knowledge of the technical processes of lithography did nothing to discourage her, and when she approached a friend, the painter Larry Rivers, to interest him in her project, coincidence again intruded, for on the day that Grosman went to Rivers's Southampton studio the poet Frank O'Hara was also visiting there.

It was this series of events that led to Grosman's first lithographic publication: a suite entitled *Stones,* with drawings by Rivers and poems by O'Hara. Only after Rivers had drawn the first stone, did Grosman seek out the printer Robert Blackburn in New York.

Blackburn was by 1957 one of the most experienced lithographers in the city. He had first encountered the medium almost twenty

Where are they
whose hands
turned pages in elusive
dog-ears threw it
on the floor

up from
the floor they come
in black to act
as book-worms devouring
all but the trace
of what we read

119 Larry Rivers (b. 1923) and Frank O'Hara (1926–1966), "Where are they . . . ," Plate 11 from *Stones,* 1957–60. 354 x 413, printed by Robert Blackburn. Published by Universal Limited Art Editions. Collection, Museum of Modern Art, New York, gift of Mr. & Mrs. E. Powis Jones.

* First called the Bob Blackburn Workshop, the name was later changed to the Creative Graphics Workshop, and then in 1959 to the Printmaking Workshop.

120 Robert Blackburn (b. 1920), *Strange Objects,* 1959. Color lithograph, 398 x 550, printed by the artist. Collection, Philadelphia Museum of Art, gift of the Print Club.

years earlier, in 1938, at the Harlem Community Art Center; subsequently, he had studied with Will Barnet at the Art Students League and had for a time served as Barnet's assistant in the printing of editions; then—with the financial assistance of Barnet and John von Wicht—he had established his own workshop in 1949.* He designed it not as a printing business, but rather as a counterpart of Hayter's Atelier 17: a place in which artists who sought to make lithographs might gain access to equipment and technical assistance, and he struggled to keep it alive. He saw it not as a means to make money, but rather as a means through which "younger, up-and-coming artists" might find it possible to make lithographs. "If it's money you want," Blackburn once said, "then don't run workshops. . . . The artistic spirit has to be the basis of the organization."[15]

Even so, the operation of Blackburn's workshop was a constant struggle. He spent 1953 and 1954 in France, where he worked as an artist with Desjobert—this in the vain hope that he might learn the technical secrets of the French master printers. He returned to New York in 1955, but as Miller and Lowengrund had already learned, it was not a good time for lithography. Blackburn's workshop continued to be limited both by his meager financial resources and by what he felt to be his still inadequate technical knowledge. Arnold Singer, who worked with Blackburn as well as with Lowengrund, remembers the shop at this time

120

as an absolutely heroic endeavor on Bob's part. He had no support; everything was done . . . in the most economical way. During the winter, coal would be delivered on the ground floor, and we'd have to go down and haul it up in buckets. Trash would have to be disposed of surreptitiously in city trash cans because there wasn't enough money to hire a carter.[16]

But somehow Blackburn got by. He developed a small but dedicated group of supporters who paid him by the month for use of the facilities. He printed editions for artists and taught occasional classes.

By 1957, when Grosman approached him about working on the project with Larry Rivers, he was quite open to her suggestion. He had earlier printed on occasion at the New School for Social Research, the National Academy, and Cooper Union. Now Blackburn went out to Grosman's little house on Long Island. There he quickly discovered that

> the stone on which Rivers had drawn did not have a well-grained surface, thus causing great difficulties in the printing. [Even so] he accepted the challenge and began commuting to West Islip to print. . . . In keeping with the title of the project, *Stones,* Grosman wanted the complete stone embossed on the paper, showing the edges of the stone. This presented technical difficulties which included the possibility of breaking the stone. Blackburn protested, but Grosman had her way and eventually, with painstaking care, *Stones,* became a reality.[17]

Stones was not completed until 1960, but from 1957 until 1962 Blackburn continued to commute from New York City to Grosman's small workshop and to print for the artists who worked with her, among them Fritz Glarner, Sam Francis, Grace Hartigan, and, later, Jim Dine, Jasper Johns, and Robert Rauschenberg.* At first, the printing had to be done in the living room of the Grosman house, but later, as the prints grew in scale, she purchased a larger press and installed it in the garage. Even so, Grosman had little concern for technical refinements, and her workshop remained for some years an improvised affair.

Few of the artists who came to Grosman's workshop in the late 1950s or early 1960s had made lithographs before; few had made prints of any kind; and never had the distance that separated the painter from the printmaker been so great as it was then. Grosman was thus forced to challenge and overcome strongly embedded prejudices, and it was only through a combination of charm, persuasion, and implacable persistence that she convinced the New York artists with whom she worked at ULAE during its early years to put those prejudices aside and give the stone a try.

JUNE WAYNE: A PROPOSAL TO THE FORD FOUNDATION

In Europe, while working with Marcel Durassier, June Wayne found the health of lithography to be little better than at home. Durassier's technical abilities were impressive, but in France as in the United States she had found that "the dismal separation of artist from artisan

121
122

* When in 1962 Robert Blackburn had the misfortune to break a stone in the press, "the artist, Robert Ruaschenberg, insisted on printing from the broken stone, a feat later accomplished by Zigmunds Priede in 1963. The appropriately titled result, *Accident,* won first prize at the Fifth International Biennial of Graphics in Ljublyana [Yugoslavia]. . . . Blackburn, however, was overwhelmed by the accident which later proved to be so fortuitous. This incident, coupled with his desire to work independently, caused him to return full-time to his own workshop in 1963." (Elizabeth Jones, "Robert Blackburn: An Investment in an Idea," p. 14; see also Calvin Tomkins, "Profiles: The Moods of a Stone," p. 68.)

121   Fritz Glarner (1899–1972), *Drawing for Tondo,* 1959. 363 x 350, printed by
Robert Blackburn. Published by Universal Limited Art Editions. Collection,
Museum of Modern Art, New York, gift of Celeste and Armand Bartos
Foundation.

created embarrassing aesthetic, financial, and moral questions [that
were] rarely a matter for public discussion."[18]

In the 1940s and 1950s lithographs of ever-increasing technical
complexity had been made by Picasso, Miró, Chagall, and a host of
younger, modernist artists. As a consequence, editions had taken
longer to print and the cost of printing them had begun to rise. After World War II a great demand had arisen in Paris for works by
the modern masters, and many artists had become aware that a portion of this demand might be met through the publication of lithographs. Some artists had been quite content to allow the skilled
technicians who worked in the ateliers to copy their drawings or
gouaches onto stones or plates. From this process came "original,"
signed lithographs that were actually no more than handmade reproductions of the artists' work.

122 Jasper Johns (b. 1930), *Coat Hanger I,* 1960. 648 x 533 [Field 2], printed by
Robert Blackburn. Published by Universal Limited Art Editions. Collection,
Museum of Modern Art, New York, gift of Celeste and Armand Bartos.

Inevitably, such ethically questionable but financially profitable practices led to disillusionment upon the part of the printers. Wayne observed that

> the master printers developed considerable contempt for the artists: a contempt which reflected itself in cynical disrespect, boredom, and even demoralization. Artisans left the métier or died off. New recruits failed to appear in sufficient numbers to keep the art from declining. The printers did not share in the prosperity they were creating and got no public recognition for their work.[19]

As a result of her experience in Europe, Wayne came to understand even more clearly than before that if lithography were to survive, an entirely new circumstance must be created for it. Although in the United States much was lacking, she found the American artists of the late 1950s thus far to be "free of the cynicism that contaminated the making of lithographs in Europe." And, in addition, "there was a developing groundswell of public interest in the arts in the United States in which prints were beginning to be bought and collected for their own aesthetic, not as substitutes for [works in] other media."[20]

Before leaving for Paris to undertake a second period of work with Durassier, Wayne had been in correspondence with W. McNeil Lowry, director of the Ford Foundation's Program in Humanities and the Arts. He had written to invite her to submit nominations in connection with a then current program of grants to American artists; she had responded by expressing a view that the foundation should seek better and more effective means through which to give support to American art. Intrigued by Wayne's letter, Lowry had invited her to visit him at the Ford Foundation, which she did on 20 August 1958; in the course of their conversation she had described what she felt to be the then desperate state of American lithography, and the circumstances which now forced her to go to Europe for completion of her project: Kistler had stopped printing from stone, and in the whole of the country there was now but few printers—all of them in New York—who continued to print for artists. This, she said, was the kind of problem to which the foundation should address itself.

Lowry had come to the Ford Foundation after an early career that had combined a strong commitment to the arts and extensive experience as a writer and journalist. He had taught creative writing at the University of Illinois; after a wartime stint with the Office of War Information he had headed a Washington news bureau; then, in 1957, after having first served the Ford Foundation as director of its education program, he had gained approval of its trustees to initiate an exploratory, five-year program to assess the state of the arts in America. He had brought to the new program a conviction that the foundation should concentrate its efforts upon support of *professional* activity in the arts. "Philanthropy, in the arts," he believed, ". . . is professionally motivated only when it accepts the artist and the arts on their own terms, and learns from the artist himself."[21]

Directed by this belief, Lowry and his staff had traveled throughout the United States, visiting 165 cities and smaller communities in 18 months; they had talked with artists in all fields, as well as with other persons professionally involved in the arts. It was in the course

123 June Wayne (b. 1918), "Twicknam Garden," 1958, from *John Donne: Songs and Sonets*. 378 x 283 [Baskett 117], printed by Marcel Durassier. Collection, University of New Mexico Art Museum, gift of Allan Sindler.

of this study that Lowry had first become aware of the problems that faced the American printmaker.

What Wayne had told him about the conditions that then existed in the field of lithography thus fit well with what he had already learned. Impressed by Wayne's ability and the force of her statements, Lowry asked that she visit him again after her stay in Paris, and it was when they met for the second time on 3 February 1959, after Wayne returned to New York—her lithographs for *John Donne: Songs and Sonets* now completed—that Lowry invited her to make a concrete proposal: What, he asked, could the Ford Foundation do to assist in the revival of artists' lithography in the United States, and how might this best be accomplished?

Back in Los Angeles, Wayne gave the matter much thought and on 21 April 1959 wrote a long letter to Lowry in which she set forth what she felt to be the essential conditions under which a project might be undertaken:

123

197

This is approximately what I would do. I would bring my French artisan over for a year or two to work with artists and to train a couple of likely apprentices to carry on the art. I would get the artists *working* in the medium. I would seek out an economically feasible base for such printers, once they were trained. . . . Once I had successfully got a shop going, I would adopt it to other locales, with your support if necessary, preferably with some other more permanent community basis.[22]

Lowry responded that the foundation was prepared "to consider tangible help." In encouraging terms, he invited Wayne to give him a plan, "simply and directly. There is no program too straightforward and simple for my consideration."[23]

Not long after her February conversation with Lowry, Wayne had written to tell me of it. Now she wrote again to tell me that she had decided to accept his invitation and to submit to the Ford Foundation a proposal for a grant to support the founding of a new American workshop: "In a month or two, I hope to be able to make definite proposals and have everything on a practical basis. . . . It's a pleasure to know that you would be available, as I can think of no one I would rather have. . . . [I] would not want to run the thing on a day-to-day basis."[24]

The months of June and July 1959 were a period of intensive work. Wayne went again to New York to "scout the available printing talent." She and I exchanged frequent letters discussing the structure of the new workshop, its physical requirements, and possible procedures for the making of grants to artists. Given the shape of lithography as it then existed, we knew that the workshop must have multiple goals: above all, it was essential to create a new generation of master printers, but beyond this—if artists and master printers were to work together successfully in intimate collaboration—it was imperative to overcome the real but artificial separation of the American painter, sculptor, and printmaker. Only in this way, we felt, could an environment be created in which the immense expressive potential of lithography could at last be realized in the United States.

On 17 July 1959, Wayne sent Lowry her proposal for establishment of a new, independent, not-for-profit corporation. She had by this time purchased a building on Tamarind Avenue in Los Angeles, a building which she planned to use as her personal studio; if the proposal were approved, sufficient space could be made available at the rear of her studio for construction of a workshop. Both because the name was neutral and unspecific and because it served to identify the address, she proposed that it be be called Tamarind Lithography Workshop.

Wayne set forth her intentions and goals in the proposal to the Ford Foundation:*

> A handful of creative people is all that is needed for a renaissance in the art, if that handful comes together at the right time, in the right place. Half a dozen master-printers, scattered around the United States, with a cluster of artists revolving around each, could cause a resurgence and a blossoming-forth of the art of the lithograph that would attract the interest of the world. Such a renaissance is the purpose of this project.
>
> If the artisans disappear, lithography will die without reaching fulfillment. Why try to save this art form when

* Wayne listed six specific goals in her proposal: (1) to create a pool of master-printers in the United States; (2) to develop American artists, working in diverse styles, into masters of the medium; (3) to accustom artists and printers to intimate collaboration so that each becomes responsive to the other, to encourage both to experiment widely and extend the expressive potential of the medium; (4) to stimulate new markets for the lithograph; (5) to guide the printer to earn a living outside of subsidy or dependence directly upon the artist as a source of income; and (6) to restore the prestige of lithography by creating a collection of extraordinary lithographs.

so many are in difficulty? Perhaps because the stone's unique sensitivity reveals the artist's hand in an expressive intimacy unlike any other print medium. Its beauty and power speak for it. . . . This project may buy only a couple of decades of time, but that is about all one can be sure of in any of the arts. It is possible that the time so bought may be enough for one of those high creative periods to take place that enrich and refresh mankind for centuries. And there is always the chance that lithography will take hold and live.[25]

Following submission of Wayne's proposal, Lowry circulated it for comment to a large number of curators, critics, artists, and other persons prominent in the world of American printmaking. Within weeks he received a number of widely divergent replies, some of which—on one or more grounds—opposed approval of the project. Wayne quickly wrote to tell me of the response that Lowry had received: "The vested interests are out in full force but . . . most of the objections confirm our reasons for wanting the project, i.e., that lithography is dead and no good; that printers are commercial and corrupt; and so on into the night."[26]

While Wayne was greatly concerned by what she felt to be "a hornet's nest of disapproval," Lowry took it in stride. It was his experience that ambitious proposals characteristically elicit a variety of responses, and that the Tamarind proposal was no exception to this rule. He summarized the opposition to the project in a formal program docket submitted to the Ford Foundation's Board of Trustees on 24 September 1959:

> There are some who do not want the Foundation to do anything in lithography without launching programs in other media of printmaking. Others advocate launching not one workshop but six in various parts of the country. Others endorse parts of the program proposed for Tamarind but would like to see them grafted onto existing schools or museums. Along with defense of vested interests, sincere doubts as to the gamble the Foundation would be making are reflected in many responses. There are also, of course, strong supporters for the proposal in its detailed forms.[27]

Indeed, although many of the respondents had reservations on one point or another—most frequently with respect to location of the workshop in Los Angeles, so far distant from New York—seventeen of the twenty-seven persons who wrote in answer to Lowry's inquiries supported the Tamarind proposal.* Most of those who failed to support it were closely identified with "vested interests" of which Lowry spoke in his docket.

At Lowry's suggestion, the distinguished print collector Lessing J. Rosenwald visited Wayne in Los Angeles in late August to hear of her plans firsthand. Rosenwald, who was also the guiding force behind the Print Council of America, an organization of print curators, told Wayne that he thought there would be advantages in associating the new workshop with "some existing university or art school such as Cranbrook. . . . His next consideration was that a program for the benefit of lithography would discriminate against the other media."[28] The following week, Wayne reported to Lowry, Rosenwald wrote her

* Those who wrote Lowry in support of the Tamarind project, either as a whole or with one or more reservations, were Garo Antreasian, Will Barnet, Vernon L. Bobbitt, Lamar Dodd, Ebria Feinblatt, Alfred Frankenstein, Arthur Heintzelman, Harold Joachim, Karl Kup, Jules Langsner, Doris Meltzer, Henry Seldis, Ben Shahn, William Smith, Gustave von Groschwitz, Bertha von Moschzisker, and Frederick S. Wight.

a most honest and kindly letter [which] could be read both as an endorsement and as a non-endorsement. . . . He wanted something rather special to happen without his coming right out and saying it. I felt he was sorry to see the money go to Tamarind rather than to the Print Council, and had the impression that he would like a compromise in which the Print Council would be in charge of Tamarind if indeed the grant went through."[29]

Sensitive to the response of the Print Council—some of whose members were also on the board of the Pratt-Contemporaries Graphic Art Center—Lowry wrote to Wayne on 22 September:

I am considering recommending that a part of our appropriation for lithography, if approved, be used in small amounts to assist Fritz Eichenberg to keep a foreign lithographer at the Contemporaries each year for three years until we know more about any complementary activities to Tamarind. Eichenberg knows that I am going to try to get consideration of that and of the Tamarind establishment at the coming Board meeting.[30]

Two days later, on 24 September 1959, Lowry presented a recommendation to the trustees of the Ford Foundation that they approve "an appropriation of $186,000 to permit the establishment of Tamarind Lithography Workshop, Inc., to support its program for a three-year period, and to support a cooperating program at Pratt Institute." Grants were subsequently made in amounts of $165,000 and $21,000 to Tamarind and Pratt, respectively.*

TAMARIND LITHOGRAPHY WORKSHOP

On 28 September 1959, I received the good news from June Wayne. The Ford Foundation had approved the grant to Tamarind:

Apparently [it] went through with little difficulty. I am unfortunately however in a bind now with my Frenchman [Marcel Durassier] who really does not want to come here. Maeght has made him such a good offer that I find myself bidding higher and higher and do not know whether I can resolve this particular problem at all. . . . Lowry is coming October 28th to discuss this with me. . . .

Isn't it remarkable that in spite of the opposition I was able to get the grant? Will wonders never cease![31]

Throughout October and November, Wayne continued to correspond with Durassier. Finally, late in November, after an exploratory trip to New York, Wayne wrote to tell me that she had "just received another letter from the Frenchman increasing his demands again. . . . I have decided not to go any further with him."[32] But in anticipation of such an outcome, Wayne had explored other possibilities. Foremost among these was Garo Antreasian.

Late in September, just after approval of the Ford Foundation grant, Wayne had read an article by Antreasian in the Print Council's newsletter and had been impressed by the degree to which his ideas paralleled her own:

In the United States there are too few first-class litho workshops. . . . It is essential for several large shops to be

---

* Emiliano Sorini, who had worked professionally as a printer in Europe, was the first to be appointed at Pratt Graphics Center under the grant from the Ford Foundation. Sorini later became a printer-fellow at Tamarind Lithography Workshop (1961).

set up in key geographical locations to serve as focal centers for this activity in the U.S. To shops such as these would fall the responsibility of servicing their immediate area as well as to disperse trained personnel throughout their region.

Fewer still are lithographic printers with sufficient knowledge or subsidy to produce work on the level of quality as high as that of their counterparts in Europe. The training necessary is a lifetime and often several generations of experience; and yet we must have men of such calibre if lithography is to flourish.[33]

Wayne promptly wrote Antreasian (whom she had not yet met) to congratulate him upon the article, and in subsequent correspondence she explored his possible interest in the Tamarind project: "Perhaps as we go along," she wrote, "an occasion for cooperation may present itself."[34]

In the meantime, Wayne moved into her new studio on Tamarind Avenue, held a "studio warming," and made concrete plans for the opening of the new workshop in the summer of 1960. At her suggestion, I made preliminary arrangements for a year's leave of absence from my position as head of the Department of Art at the University of Florida, and throughout October and November we worked together on drafts of policies to govern artists' fellowships, the printing of editions, and other workshop practices. In mid-November Wayne made a trip to Philadelphia, New York, and Chicago to talk with possible members of the national board of directors which was to be formed; while in Chicago she arranged to meet Antreasian.

Their meeting went well, and Wayne now for the first time seriously considered the possibility of an "all-American" program with Antreasian as master printer.* She wrote to tell me of her talk with him: "His command of the medium is far greater than anyone else I have run into and his color prints are as fine as anything I have seen in France. . . . I am arranging to see some of his work and will perhaps fly to Indianapolis to watch him in his own production."[35]

But even before Wayne visited Indianapolis she became convinced that we should go forward with Antreasian. She wrote a long letter to Lowry explaining why this alternative—a substantial departure from her original proposal to the foundation—now appeared advisable. In early January 1960, Lowry gave his assent. The decision was made: now the three of us must work concretely to prepare for the opening of the Tamarind workshop on the first of July, less than six months away.

Not the least of the problems which made difficult the revival of American lithography—not only at Tamarind but at Pratt and ULAE as well—was the lack of availability of many materials and supplies. Fine lithograph stones, once a surplus commodity, were no longer easy to find. With the decline of artists' lithography in the 1950s, the demand for crayons, inks, rollers, and other materials and equipment had been sharply reduced, with the result that a number of specialized products were no longer to be had. Few of the fine papers routinely used in France and Germany were imported into the United States. All of these obstacles must be overcome, the workshop building must be completed and equipped, a staff must be assembled, and the first artists must be selected and invited.†

* When it became apparent that Durassier might decide to remain in France, Wayne also explored the possibility of inviting another printer from France or Germany. She did not pursue this further after meeting Antreasian.

Aware of Antreasian's experience in printing lithographs from stone, Wayne used the time in Indianapolis to explore his ability to work successfully with tusche washes on zinc plates. As a result of their work together, Wayne made a firm decision to proceed with his appointment as Tamarind's master printer.

† After consideration of many alternatives, it had been decided that artists should work at Tamarind only by invitation, and that these invitations should be for two-month periods: a sufficient time, it was thought, for them to explore the potential of the medium and create fine lithographs.

124   Romas Viesulas (b. 1918), *Paso Doble (Toro Desconocido V),* 1960. Color lithograph, 705 x 527 [Tamarind 102A], printed by Garo Antreasian. Tamarind collection, University of New Mexico Art Museum.

* It was intended that Tamarind should work not only to achieve high technical quality, but also—with knowledge of the questionable practices then encountered in some European workshops—to establish high ethical standards in the printing of fine lithographs. From the first, details of all editions printed at Tamarind were fully recorded, and all proofs and impressions were marked with the chops or blindstamps of both the workshop and the individual printer.

† The panel of selection then included Wayne and Adams, E. Maurice Bloch, Kenneth Callahan, John Entenza, Ebria Feinblatt, Alfred Frankenstein, Gustave von Groschwitz, Harold Joachim, Douglas MacAgy, Peter Selz, Benton Spruance, James Johnson Sweeney, and Carl Zigrosser.

Antreasian made recommendations regarding the design of the workshop. Wayne sought out and employed Joe Funk, whom she and I had earlier known as Kistler's apprentice; supplies were ordered, stone racks were built, and pressroom equipment was purchased—including some from Kistler. Our earlier drafts of workshop policies were revised and revised again, then put in final form, spelling out the terms of the fellowships that would be granted to artists and establishing policies for the printing and documentation of their lithographs.* Wayne formed a national "Panel of Selection" consisting of prominent artists, curators, and museum directors, and correspondence was begun to select the first artist fellows.†

I still most vividly recall my astonishment when in late June 1960 I arrived in Los Angeles and saw what Wayne had accomplished. By contrast with the American workshops that had preceded it, the new Tamarind workshop signaled a new dimension in lithography. Here, it seemed to me, in this open, white, skylighted room, all manner of things could be accomplished: things which until now had been no more than dreams. Wayne introduced me to Garo Antreasian, whom I had not met before, and I was instantly impressed by his ability.

It was with a great sense of expectation and discovery—and considerable nervousness—that Antreasian, June Wayne, and I made final preparation for the arrival of the first of Tamarind's artist-fellows,

125 Adja Yunkers (b. 1900), *Skies of Venice VIII,* 1960. 561 x 790 [Tamarind 195], printed by Garo Antreasian. Tamarind collection, University of New Mexico Art Museum.

124
125 Romas Viesulas of Philadelphia, who was scheduled to begin a two-
126 month stay on the first of July 1960.*

We knew that many others before us had worked tirelessly in support of a medium they had loved; we knew that despite their valiant endeavors artists' lithography remained in peril of extinction in the United States. If the Tamarind project were to fail—despite its scale, its careful planning, and its substantial funding—it was unlikely that another effort would soon be made. But if it were to succeed, even partially, it might create a climate in which American lithography could at last take hold and live. At best, in the words of Wayne's proposal, it might "cause a resurgence and a blossoming-forth of the art of the lithograph that would attract the attention of the world." These, we knew, were the stakes at risk.

* Between July 1960 and June 1961, fellowships were awarded to eight artists: Glen Alps, Louis Bunce, Jules Engel, Reuben Kadish, Tetsuo Ochikubo, Aubrey Schwartz, Romas Viesulas, and Adja Yunkers. Lithographs were also made by a number of guest artists—Harold Altman, Franois Arnal, William Brown, Connor Everts, Matsumi Kanemitsu, Frederick O'Hara, Raymond Parker, Bernard Rosenthal, Antonio Scordia, Esteban Vicente, and Emerson Woelffer—as well as by Clinton Adams, Garo Antreasian, and June Wayne. A total of 204 editions was completed at Tamarind Lithography Workshop during its initial year.

NOTES

1 Mary W. Baskett, *The Art of June Wayne,* p. 57–60.

2 Wayne to von Groschwitz, 2 April 1958. Tamarind archives, University of New Mexico Libraries.

3 Margaret Lowengrund, "Fine Art and Commercial Art." In *The Art of the Artist,* p. 151.

4 New York *Evening Post,* 26 November 1927.

5 Muench to Adams, 6 December 1981.

6 Burr Miller, interview, 4 May 1979.

7 Singer, tape-recorded interview, 21 September 1979, later edited by Singer.

8 Pearson, interview, 5 May 1979.

9 Ibid.

10 Singer interview.

11 Fritz Eichenberg, *The Art of the Print,* p. 555.

12 Calvin Tomkins, "Profiles: The Moods of a Stone," p. 54.

13 Ibid., p. 59.

14 Ibid., p. 45. Grosman refers to Monroe Wheeler, *Modern Painters and Sculptors as Illustrators* (New York: Museum of Modern Art, 1936).

15 Blackburn, interview with Elizabeth Jones, 13 July 1978.

16 Singer interview.

17 Elizabeth Jones-Popescu, "American Lithography and Tamarind Lithography Workshop/Tamarind Institute, 1900–1980," pp. 94–95.

18 June Wayne, tape-recorded comment on the development of the Tamarind project, Tamarind archives, tape 107.

19 Ibid.

20 Ibid.

21 W. McNeil Lowry, *The Arts and Philanthropy,* not paged.

22 Wayne to Lowry, 21 April 1959. Tamarind archives.

23 Lowry to Wayne, 30 April 1959. Ibid.

24 Wayne to Adams, 8 June 1959. Ibid.

25 June Wayne, "To Restore the Art of the Lithograph in the United States."

26 Wayne to Adams, 14 August 1959. Tamarind archives.

27 Program docket, "Development of the Lithographic Art in the United States," 24 September 1959. Ford Foundation, Humanities and Arts Program.

28 Wayne to Lowry, 28 August 1959. Tamarind archives.

29 Wayne to Lowry, 6 September 1959. Ibid.

30 Lowry to Wayne, 22 September 1959. Ibid.

31 Wayne to Adams, 28 September 1959. Ibid.

32 Wayne to Adams, 30 November 1959. Ibid.

33 Garo Antreasian, "Special Problems Relative to Artistic Lithography," p. 11.

34 Wayne to Antreasian, 7 October 1959. Tamarind archives.

35 Wayne to Adams, 30 November 1959. Ibid.

Epilogue

Within an astonishingly short time after we began work at Tamarind in 1960 it became evident that American lithography had indeed entered a new era. Many distinguished artists came to Los Angeles and made fine lithographs; other workshops were established by printers trained at Tamarind; together, throughout the 1960s, these new workshops, Tamarind, and ULAE published a continuing series of lithographs by prominent painters, sculptors, and printmakers; and the art magazines detected what they quickly came to call a "renaissance" of lithography. For once, that overused word was not inappropriate.

The new condition of American lithography is perfectly symbolized in a story told by Thomas B. Hess, to whom a painter once remarked: "In the 1950s when you saw a friend on the Long Island Railroad on an early Wednesday morning, you knew he was going to town to see his shrink. Nowadays, you know he's on his way to work with his lithographer."[*]

It was true. Through a combination of events, lithography had arrived. Artists who ten years earlier had scorned the medium now actively sought to work in it; a new market developed for their work; and printmaking gained a prestige previously unknown in the United States. The rise of interest in lithography brought with it new opportunities for printers, and by the end of the decade lithographic workshops were prospering in Boston, Chicago, Los Angeles, New York, San Francisco, and other cities across the country. Most were staffed by printers trained at Tamarind.

As originally planned, Tamarind Lithography Workshop was to have had a short and finite existence. As time passed, however, it became clear to us that if the new health of American lithography were to be maintained, it would be necessary to establish a permanent center for the training of master printers, as well as for continuing research into the methods and materials of lithography. That

[*] Thomas B. Hess. "Prints: Where History, Style and Money Meet," p. 29.

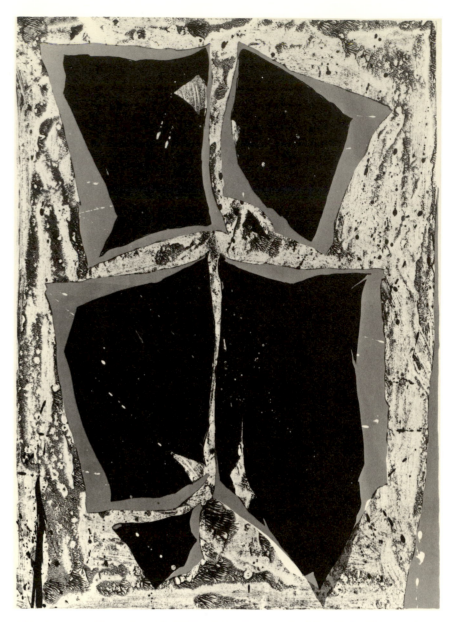

126 Matsumi Kanemitsu (b. 1922), *Color Formation I,* 1961. Color lithograph, 712 x 508 [Tamarind 223B], printed by Bohuslav Horak. Tamarind collection, University of New Mexico Art Museum.

center was established in 1970 when Tamarind Institute was founded at the University of New Mexico.

The medium itself underwent rapid change. Most of the lithographs produced in the collaborative workshops were printed in color and were of a complexity and size unheard of in the 1930s and 1940s. New presses, rollers, inks, and papers were manufactured in response to new demands, and a new generation of printers developed remarkable new techniques to serve the artists of the seventies and eighties.

It is too soon to write a full account of the work of American lithographers during the past twenty years: the distance is not yet sufficient. In any event, when that story is told, it will be quite different from the one I have related. The struggles of the American lithographers who contributed so much to the history of their art between 1900 and 1960 came about during a period in which American printmaking was far from center stage: a period too long underestimated and unknown.

Technical Appendix

Alois Senefelder, the inventor of lithography, preferred to call his new process *chemical printing*. Although his term did not gain acceptance, it was more accurate than *lithography,* for, as Senefelder recognized, the process rests upon the principle that grease and water will not mix. Lithography (derived from the Greek words for "stone" and "writing") has nevertheless been adopted as the standard term to describe all printing which makes use of this principle, whether from stone or metal plates.

By fortunate coincidence, Senefelder lived near the village of Solnhofen in Bavaria, where Kellheim stone was quarried. This exceedingly fine limestone proved to be ideally suited to lithography; its equal has been found nowhere else in the world. When grained to a smooth, even surface with sand or carborundum, it provides such a sensuous and enticing surface upon which to draw that artists who have once worked on it return again and again. Metal plates—both zinc and aluminum—have their own characteristics and hold an important place in contemporary lithography, particularly in view of the increasing scarcity of fine stones. Most of the world's finest stones were destroyed in the early twentieth century—dumped into landfills and harbors—when stones were abandoned by commercial printing plants as they switched over to offset printing.

Unlike the relief and intaglio printmaking media, lithography is planographic: the print is made from the flat surface of a stone or plate. In relief printing, the artist cuts away parts of a block of wood, linoleum, or other material; ink is applied to the remaining, untouched surface; and the print is made. In intaglio printing, a metal plate is engraved or etched through one or more of a variety of processes (including dry point, etching, aquatint, and burin engraving); ink is applied to the plate, then wiped cleanly from its surface, so as to remain only in the grooves, pits, or other roughened areas; and the print is made.

To make a lithograph, the artist first draws with greasy materials—usually with lithographic crayon or a greasy ink called tusche—to create an image on the stone or plate; the surface is then chemically treated so that only the image will accept ink. Although the solution used for this purpose is called an *etch,* it does not bite into the stone, but serves only to separate chemically the image and nonimage areas.

After etching the stone or plate, the printer uses a solvent to wash its surface clean, at which point the greasy areas remain visible as ghosts of the artist's drawing. The image reappears when the printer then inks the surface, using a hand roller; this process is repeated as proofs are pulled at the press. If required, the stone or plate may be counteretched (i.e., again made receptive to the drawing materials) so as to permit changes in the image. At some point, the artist and printer agree that a definitive impression has been achieved: one in which the artist's aesthetic intentions have been fully realized. This *bon à tirer* impression then serves as the standard against which each impression in the edition will be judged. The printer must control the chemistry of the printing element and apply the ink with great care in order to achieve fine and consistent impressions.

A *transfer lithograph* is a lithograph first drawn on one surface, usually a specially prepared sheet of paper, then transferred to another for printing. The prints are made by placing this drawing against the surface of a freshly grained stone or plate, and running it through the press, thus transferring the greasy content of the drawing materials to the receptive surface of the printing element. It is relatively easy for an experienced observer to differentiate between transferred and directly drawn lithographs upon the basis of their visual character.

To make a *color lithograph,* the artist must draw a separate stone or plate for each color that is to be used. Although the principle of color lithography is identical to that of lithography in black and white, the process is far more complex in execution. The artist draws always with black materials; these materials are then washed away with solvents and replaced by color inks. Each stone or plate must be drawn and printed in perfect registration with those that precede or follow it.

An *offset lithograph,* although based upon the same chemical principles as a lithograph printed by hand, is made through a separate and different process. In the offset process, ink is transferred not directly from the plate to the paper—as is the case in hand lithography—but rather from the plate to a rubberized printing blanket, from which it is then transferred to the paper. In consequence, offset lithographs have qualities different from those of lithographs printed by direct impression.

Bibliography

A comprehensive history of artists' lithography in the United States during the first half of the twentieth century has yet to be written.

Readers of general histories of American art might reasonably conclude that American prints were rarely made before 1960, for in such histories the etchings, lithographs, and woodcuts made by American artists between 1900 and 1960 are seldom illustrated or discussed. While excellent scholarly monographs have described the prints of some artists, other major figures in the history of American printmaking have not yet been the subject of satisfactory catalogues raisonnés, and the work of the principal lithographic printers has received even less attention than that of the artists with whom they collaborated. There is also a lack of serious critical writing about American prints of this period.

The most useful and informative accounts of American printmaking have been written principally by print curators. The earliest account to touch upon American lithography of the twentieth century is Frank Weitenkampf, *American Graphic Arts* (1912, revised 1924). Carl Zigrosser provided a series of individual portraits—but made no effort to construct a historical synthesis—in *The Artist in America: Twenty-four Close-ups of Contemporary Printmakers* (1942). Francis V. O'Connor wrote or edited a number of valuable studies of art during the 1930s and 1940s, among them *The New Deal Art Projects: An Anthology of Memoirs* (1972). To date, however, there is no full account of the work of the graphic arts division of the Federal Art Project during the Roosevelt administration.

General histories of printmaking and of lithography, particularly those written by European authors, have tended to ignore American art. Despite titles that indicated a broad scope, Jean Adhemar, *Twentieth Century Graphics* (1971);

Felix H. Man, *Artists' Lithographs: A World History from Senefelder to the Present Day* (1970); and Wilhelm Weber, *A History of Lithography* (1966), gave little or no attention to American printmaking prior to 1960. Riva Castleman, *Prints of the Twentieth Century: A History* (1976), devoted a long chapter to recent American prints but only briefly mentioned the work of American printmakers before the 1950s; and the accounts of the development of American printmaking provided by Fritz Eichenberg, *The Art of the Print: Masterpieces, History, and Techniques* (1976), and Una E. Johnson, *American Prints and Printmakers* (1980), were in each case essentially personal memoirs, related to their work at the Pratt Graphics Center and the Brooklyn Museum, respectively. James Watrous, *A Century of American Printmaking: 1880–1980* (forthcoming), gives promise of filling an important void.

Over the years, the prints made by American artists have received only limited attention in the general art magazines, and specialized print publications have been few in number. Among past publications, the most significant were *Print Collector's Quarterly,* published in the United States and England (with interruptions) from 1911 to 1950; *The Print Conoisseur,* published (with an interruption) from 1920 to 1932; *Prints,* published from 1930 until 1938; *Impression,* published in Los Angeles in 1957 and 1958; and *Artist's Proof,* published by the Pratt Graphic Art Center from 1961 to 1971. Current publications include *The Print Collector's Newsletter* (1970–   ), *Print Review,* successor to *Artist's Proof* (1972–   ), and *The Tamarind Papers,* first published as *Tamarind Technical Papers* (1974–   ).

The list below includes all books and articles on American lithography cited in the notes, and others of general interest and availability. Works that primarily concern lithography before 1900 or after 1960 are omitted.

Adams, Clinton. "Bolton Brown, Artist-Lithographer." In *Prints and Printmakers of New York State, 1820–1940*. David Tatham, ed. Syracuse: Syracuse University Press (forthcoming).

———. "Color Lithography in the 1950s: The Cincinnati Biennials, a Conversation with Gustave von Groschwitz." *Tamarind Technical Papers* 1 (1977): 86.

———. "Grant Arnold, Lithographer: New York and Woodstock, 1928 to 1940." *Tamarind Papers* 3 (1980): 38–43.

———. "Howard Norton Cook: The Graphic Work," *New Mexico Studies in the Fine Arts* 4 (1979): 11–15.

———. "Lawrence Barrett: Colorado's Prophet of Stone," *Artspace*, Fall 1978, pp. 38–43.

———. "Lynton R. Kistler and the Development of Lithography in Los Angeles," *Tamarind Technical Papers* 1 (1977–78): 100–109.

———. "The Personality of Lithography: A Conversation with Nathan Oliveira." *Tamarind Papers* 6 (Winter 1982–83): 4–9.

———. "Rubbed Stones, Middle Tones and Hot Etches: Lawrence Barrett of Colorado." *Tamarind Papers* 2 (1979): 36–41.

———. *The Woodstock Ambience, 1917–1939* [exhibition catalogue]. Albuquerque: Tamarind Institute and the University of New Mexico Art Museum, 1981.

Adhémar, Jean. *Twentieth Century Graphics*. New York: Praeger, 1971.

American Printmaking Today, A Book of 100 Prints. New York: American Artists Congress, 1936. Reprint, New York: DaCapo Press, 1977.

American Prints Today [exhibition catalogue]. New York: Print Council of America, 1959.

American Prints in the Library of Congress: A Catalogue of the Collection. Comp. by Karen F. Beall, et al. Baltimore: Johns Hopkins Press, 1970.

Antreasian, Garo. "Education in American Printmaking since 1900," *Journal of the Print World*, Summer 1981, pp. 12–13.

———. "Special Problems Relative to Artistic Lithography," *News of "Prints"*, 4 (1959): 10–12.

Antreasian, Garo, with Clinton Adams. *The Tamarind Book of Lithography: Art & Techniques*. New York: Harry N. Abrams, 1971.

Armitage, Merle. *The Lithographs of Richard Day*. New York: E. Weyhe, 1932.

Arms, Dorothy Noyes. "Annual Print Exhibition, 1948." *Print Collector's Quarterly* 29 (February 1949): 5–13.

Arms, John Taylor. *Handbook of Print Making and Print Makers* (1934) New York: Macmillan, 1934.

Arnold, Grant. "Woodstock: The Everlasting Hills." Unpublished manuscript.

Artist's Proof: A Collector's Edition of the First Eight Issues. New York: Pratt Graphics Center and the New York Graphic Society, 1971.

Ashton, Dore. *The New York School: A Cultural Reckoning*. New York: Viking, 1973.

Baro, Gene. *Thirty Years of American Printmaking* [exhibition catalogue]. Brooklyn: Brooklyn Museum, 1977.

Barrett, Lawrence, and Adolf Dehn. *How to Draw and Print Lithographs*. New York: American Artists Group, 1950.

Baskett, Mary W. *The Art of June Wayne*. New York: Harry N. Abrams, 1969.

Bassham, Ben. "The Lithographs of Robert Riggs: A Catalogue Raisonné." Unpublished manuscript.

Bellows, Emma S., comp. *George Bellows: His Lithographs*. Introduction by Thomas Beer. New York: Alfred Knopf, 1927.

Benton, Thomas Hart. *An American in Art: A Professional and Technical Autobiography*. Lawrence: University Press of Kansas, 1969.

———. *An Artist in America*. 3rd rev. ed. Columbia: University of Missouri Press, 1968.

Biddle, George. *An American Artist's Story*. Boston: Little Brown, 1939.

Birnbaum, Martin. "Albert Sterner's Prints," *Print Collector's Quarterly* 6 (1916): 213–24.

Bolton Brown, Lithographer [exhibition catalogue]. Introduction by David Tatham. Syracuse: Lowe Art Gallery, Syracuse University, 1981.

Boorsch, Suzanne. "The Lithographs of George Bellows," *Art News*, March 1976, pp. 60–62.

Boswell, Peyton, Jr. *Modern American Painting*. New York: Dodd, Mead & Co., 1940.

Broadd, Harry A. "Albert Sterner: Printmaker with Ideas," *Print Review* 14 (1981): 27–40.

Brown, Bolton. "Early Days at Woodstock." *Publications of the Woodstock Historical Society* 13 (August–September 1937): 3–14.

———. *Exhibition of Lithographs by Bolton Brown* [exhibition catalogue]. Introduction and notes on the prints exhibited by the artist. New York: FitzRoy Carrington, 1924.

———. "Lithograph Drawing as Distinguished from Lithograph Printing." *Print Connoisseur* 2 (December 1921): 138–53.

———. *Lithography*. New York: FitzRoy Carrington, 1923.

———. *Lithography for Artists*. Chicago: University of Chicago Press, 1930.

———. "Lithography since Whistler." Unpublished manuscript, Bryn Mawr College Library.

———. "My Ten Years in Lithography." *Tamarind Papers* 5 (1981–82): 8–25, 36–54.

———. "Prints and Their Makers." *Prints* 1 (November 1930): 13–24.

Cahill, Holger, and Alfred H. Barr, eds. *Art in America in Modern Times*. New York: Reynal and Hitchcock, 1934.

Cahill, Holger. *George O. "Pop" Hart* [exhibition catalogue]. New York: Downtown Gallery, 1928.

Carey, Frances, and Anthony Griffith. *American Prints, 1879–1979* [exhibition catalogue]. London: British Museum, 1980.

Castleman, Riva. *Modern Prints Since 1942*. London: Barrie & Jenkins, 1973.

Castleman, Riva. *Prints of the Twentieth Century*. New York: Museum of Modern Art, 1976.

Catalogue of Lithographs by Bolton Brown [exhibition catalogue]. New York: Kleeman Galleries, 1938.

Charlot, Jean. *American Printmaking, 1913–1947* [exhibition catalogue] New York: American Institute of Graphic Arts, 1947.

Christ-Janer, Albert. *Boardman Robinson*. Chicago: University of Chicago, 1946.

Cincinnati Art Museum. *First (through Fifth) International Biennial of Contemporary Color Lithography* [exhibition catalogues]. Gustave von Groschwitz, ed. Cincinnati, 1950–58.

Coke, Van Deren. *Clinton Adams* [exhibition catalogue]. Albuquerque: University of New Mexico, 1973.

Cole, Sylvan, Jr. *AAA: Fortieth Anniversary Exhibition, 1934–1974* [exhibition checklist]. New York: Associated American Artists, 1974.

———. *Childe Hassam: Etchings, Lithographs*. New York: Associated American Artists, 1973.

———., ed. *The Graphic Work of Joseph Hirsch* [exhibition catalogue]. New York: Associated American Artists, 1970.

———., ed. *The Lithographs of John Steuart Curry: A Catalogue Raisonné*. New York: Associated American Artists, 1976.

———., ed. *Raphael Soyer, Fifty Years of Printmaking, 1917–1967*. New York: Da Capo Press, 1967.

———., ed. *Will Barnet: Etchings, Lithographs, Woodcuts, Serigraphs, 1932–1972*. New York: Associated American Artists, 1972.

Copley, John. "Some Lithographs of the Past and Future." *Print Collector's Quarterly* 12 (February 1925): 41–66.

Corbusier, Le (pseud., C. E. Jeanneret-Gris). *Towards a New Architecture*. London: J. Rodker, 1931.

Cox, Richard. "Adolf Dehn: Satirist of the Jazz Age," *Journal of the Archives of American Art* 18 (1978): 11–18.

Cox, Richard. *Caroline Durieux's Lithographs of the Thirties and Forties*. Baton Rouge: Louisiana State University Press, 1977.

Craven, Thomas, ed. *A Treasury of American Prints*. New York: Simon & Schuster, 1939.

Cravens, Junius. "A Western Viewpoint," *Prints* 6 (1936): 262–65.

Croydon, Michael. *Ivan Albright*. New York: Abbeville Press, 1978.

Czestochowski, Joseph S. "The Graphic Work of Arthur B. Davies," *American Art Review* 3 (July–August 1976): 102–13.

———. *John Steuart Curry and Grant Wood: A Portrait of Rural America*. Columbia: University of Missouri Press, 1981.

———. "The Published Prints of Charles E. Burchfield," *American Art Journal* 8 (November 1976): 99–110.

Davis, Richard A. "The Graphic Work of Yasuo Kuniyoshi, 1893–1953," *Journal of the Archives of American Art* 5 (1965): 1–19.

Dehn, Adolf. "Revolution in Printmaking." *College Art Journal* 9 (1949): 201–3.

Dehn, Adolf, and Lawrence Barrett. *How to Draw and Print Lithographs*. New York: American Artists Group, 1950.

Donson, Theodore. *Prints and the Print Market*. New York: Crowell, 1977.

Drogseth, Dennis. *Rosella Hartman Lithographs* [exhibition catalogue]. Woodstock, N.Y.: Phantom Press, 1980.

Eggers, George W. *George Bellows* [exhibition catalogue]. New York: Whitney Museum of American Art, 1931.

Eichenberg, Fritz. *The Art of the Print: Masterpieces, History, Techniques*. New York: Abrams, 1976.

Eldredge, Charles C. "Marsden Hartley, Lithographer," *American Art Journal* 5 (May 1973): 46–53.

———. *Marsden Hartley: Lithographs and Related Works* [exhibition catalogue]. Lawrence: University of Kansas Museum of Art, 1972.

———. *Ward Lockwood, 1894–1963* [exhibition catalogue]. Lawrence: University of Kansas Museum of Art, 1974.

Emerson Woelffer [exhibition catalogue]. Introduction by Gerald Nordland. Fullerton: Visual Arts Center, California State University, 1982.

Farmer, Jane M. *The Image of Urban Optimism*. Washington: Smithsonian Institution, 1977.

Fath, Creekmore. *The Lithographs of Thomas Hart Benton*. 2d rev. ed. Austin: University of Texas Press, 1979.

Feinblatt, Ebria, and Bruce Davis. *Los Angeles Prints, 1883–1980*. Los Angeles: Los Angeles County Museum of Art, 1980.

Fern, Alan. "A Half-Century of American Printmaking, 1875–1925." *Artist's Proof* 6 (Fall–Winter 1963–64): 14–25.

Ferretti, Fred. "The AAA and How it Grew." *Art News*, February 1974, pp. 57–59.

Fine, Ruth E. The Prints of Benton Murdoch Spruance: A Catalogue Raisonné. Philadelphia: University of Pennsylvania Press (forthcoming).

Flint, Janet A. *Art for All: American Print Publishing Between the Wars*. Washingon: Smithsonian Institution, 1980.

———. *George Miller and American Lithography* [exhibition catalogue]. Washington: Smithsonian Institution, 1976.

———. *Louis Lozowick, Drawings and Lithographs* [exhibition catalogue]. Washington: Smithsonian Institution, 1975.

———. *J. Alden Weir, An American Printmaker* [exhibition catalogue] Provo, Utah: Brigham Young University Press, 1972.

———. "Matulka as Printmaker: A Checklist of Known Prints." In Carroll S. Clark and Louise Heskett, eds. *Jan Matulka, 1890–1972*. Washington: Smithsonian Institution, 1980.

———. *The Prints of Louis Lozowick*. New York: Hudson Hills Press, 1982.

Flint, Ralph. *Albert Sterner, His Life and His Art*. New York: Payson & Clarke, 1927.

Francis Chapin [exhibition catalogue]. Chicago: Fairweather-Hardin Gallery, 1973.

Francis, Henry S. "The Lithographs of George Wesley Bellows," *Print Collector's Quarterly* 27 (1940): 139–65.

Freeman, Richard B. *The Lithographs of Ralston Crawford*. Lexington: University of Kentucky, 1962.

Freundlich, August L. *Federico Castellon, His Graphic Works, 1936–1971*. Syracuse: College of Visual and Performing Arts, Syracuse University, 1978.

———. *Karl Schrag: A Catalogue Raisonné*. Syracuse: School of Art, Syracuse University, 1972.

———. *William Gropper: Retrospective*. Los Angeles: Ward Ritchie Press, 1968.

Frontiers of American Art [exhibition catalogue]. San Francisco: M. H. De Young Museum, 1939.

Fuchs & Lang. *Catalogue of Lithographic Prints in the Gallery of the Fuchs & Lang Manufacturing Co.* (1912).

Gaehde, Christa, and Carl Zigrosser. *A Guide to the Collecting and Care of Original Prints.* New York: Crown Publishers, 1965.

Ganso, Emil. "The Technique of Lithographic Printing," *Parnassus* 12, No. 7 (November 1940): 16–21.

Getlein, Frank and Dorothy. *The Bite of the Print: Satire and Irony in Woodcuts, Engravings, Etchings, Lithographs and Serigraphs.* New York: Clarkson N. Potter, 1963.

Goldman, Judith. *American Prints: Process & Proof* [exhibition catalogue]. New York: Whitney Museum of American Art, 1981.

Good News for Printmakers [exhibition brochure]. Brooklyn: Brooklyn Museum, 1939.

Goodrich, Lloyd. "Glenn Coleman's Lithographs of New York," *The Arts,* November 1928, pp. 261–66.

Grafly, Dorothy. *A History of the Philadelphia Print Club.* Philadelphia: Philadelphia Print Club, 1929.

Graphic Works of the American Thirties: A Book of 100 Prints. New York: American Artists' Congress, 1936. Reprinted, New York: Da Capo Press, 1977.

Griffith, Fuller. *The Lithographs of Childe Hassam: A Catalogue.* Washington: Smithsonian Institution, 1962. Reprinted, New York: Martin Gordon, 1980.

Harley, Ralph Leroy, Jr. "Four Twentieth Century American Printmakers [Bellows, Coleman, Hopper, and Sloan] and Their Trends Toward Formalism." Master's thesis, University of Wisconsin, 1964.

Heller, Jules. *Printmaking Today: A Studio Handbook.* 2d rev. ed. New York: Holt, Rinehart and Winston, 1972.

Hess, Thomas B. "Prints: Where History, Style and Money Meet," *Art News,* January 1972, p. 29.

Inman, Pauline W. "A History of the Society of American Graphic Artists," *Artist's Proof* 3, No. 2 (Fall–Winter 1963–64): 40–44.

Jackson Pollock: The New-Found Works [exhibition catalogue]. Checklist and essay by Francis V. O'Connor. New Haven: Yale University Art Gallery, 1978.

Jackson, F. Ernest. "Modern Lithography." *Print Collector's Quarterly* 11 (April 1924): 205–26.

Jacob Kainen: Prints, A Retrospective [exhibition catalogue]. Text by Janet A. Flint. Washington: Smithsonian Institution, 1976.

Jacobowitz, Ellen, and George H. Marcus. *American Graphics, 1860–1940* [exhibition catalogue]. Philadelphia: Philadelphia Museum of Art, 1982.

Jerome Kaplan Prints [exhibition catalogue]. Philadelphia: Print Club, 1973.

Jewell, Edward A. "Albert Sterner's Prints," *Print Collector's Quarterly* 19 (1932): 253–66.

Johnson, Robert F., ed. *American Prints, 1870–1950* [exhibition catalogue, Baltimore Museum of Art] Chicago: University of Chicago, 1976.

Johnson, Una E. *American Prints and Printmakers.* Garden City, N.Y.: Doubleday, 1980.

———. *Ten Years of American Prints, 1947–1956* [exhibition catalogue]. Brooklyn: Brooklyn Museum, 1956.

Johnson, Una E., and Jo Miller. *Will Barnet Prints, 1932–1964* [exhibition catalogue]. Brooklyn: Brooklyn Museum, 1965.

———. *Paul Cadmus Prints and Drawings, 1922–1967* [exhibition catalogue]. Brooklyn: Brooklyn Museum, 1968.

Jones, Dan Burne. *The Prints of Rockwell Kent: A Catalogue Raisonné.* Chicago: University of Chicago Press, 1975.

Jones, Elizabeth. "Robert Blackburn: An Investment in an Idea," *Tamarind Papers* 6 (Winter 1982–83): 10–14.

Jones-Popescu, Elizabeth. "American Lithography and Tamarind Lithography Workshop / Tamarind Institute, 1900–1980." Ph.D. dissertation, University of New Mexico, 1980.

June Wayne [exhibition catalogue]. Los Angeles: Municipal Art Gallery, 1973.

Kainen, Jacob. "Prints of the Thirties: Reflections on the Federal Art Project." *Artist's Proof* 11 (1971): 34–41.

———. "The Graphic Arts Division of the WPA Federal Art Project." In *The New Deal Art Projects: An Anthology of Memoirs,* edited by Francis V. O'Connor. Washington: Smithsonian Institution, 1972.

Karl Fortess Retrospective, 1921–1971 [exhibition catalogue]. New York: Associated American Artists, 1973.

Karshan, Donald H. "American Printmaking 1670–1968," *Art in America,* July 1968, pp. 22–55.

———. *Archipenko: The Sculpture and Graphic Art.* Tubingen: Wasmuth, 1974.

Kelder, Diane "Tradition and Craftsmanship in Modern Prints," *Art News,* January 1972, pp. 56–59.

Kelder, Diane, ed. *Stuart Davis.* Documentary Monographs in Modern Art. New York: Praeger, 1971.

Kistler, Aline. "New Market Trends." *Prints* 7 (1936): 31–36.

———. "The National Survey." *Prints* 6 (1936): 240–50.

———. "Western Lithographers," *Prints* 5 (1935): 16–25.

Kyra Markham, American Fantasist, 1891–1967 [exhibition catalogue]. New York: Witkin Gallery, 1981.

LaFollette, Suzanne. *Art in America, from Colonial Times to the Present Day.* New York: W. W. Norton, 1929.

Lane, John R. *Stuart Davis, Art and Art Theory.* Brooklyn: Brooklyn Museum, 1978.

Lehrer, Ruth Fine. "The Print Club of Philadelphia," *Print Review* 6 (1976): 73–75.

Lewis, Louise M. *Garo Antreasian* [exhibition catalogue]. Albuquerque: University of New Mexico, 1973.

Lippard, Lucy. *The Graphic Work of Phillip Evergood.* New York: Crown Publishers, 1966.

The Lithographs of Max Weber [exhibition catalogue]. Foreword by Una Johnson, introduction by Sylvan Cole, Jr. New York: Associated American Artists, 1970.

The Lithographs of Ture Bengtz. Text by Will Barnet, Richard C. Bartlett, and others. Duxbury, Mass.: The Art Complex Museum, 1978.

Lowry, W. McNeil. *The Arts and Philanthropy.* Waltham, Mass.: Poses Institute of Fine Arts, 1962.

Lowengrund, Margaret. "Fine Art and Commercial Art," in Arthur Zaidenberg, ed., *The Art of the Artist.* New York: Crown Publishers, 1951.

Lozowick, Louis. "The Americanization of Art," in *Machine Age Exposition* [exhibition catalogue]. New

York: Steinway Hall, 1927.

Lumsdaine, Joycelyn Pang. "The Prints of Adolf Dehn: A Catalogue Raisonné." Master's thesis, University of California, Los Angeles, 1974.

Lunn, Harry H. *Milton Avery Prints, 1933–63*. Washington: Graphics International, 1973.

Man, Felix H. *150 Years of Artists' Lithographs, 1803–1953*. London: William Heinemann, 1953.

———. *Artists' Lithographs: A World History from Senefelder to the Present Day*. New York: G. P. Putnam's Sons, 1970.

Marling, Karal Ann. *Woodstock: An American Art Colony* [exhibition catalogue]. Poughkeepsie, N.Y.: Vassar College Art Gallery, 1977.

Mason, Lauris, comp., assisted by Joan Ludman. *Print Reference Sources: A Select Bibliography, 18th–20th Centuries*. 2d rev. ed. Millwood, N.Y.: Kraus-Thomson, 1979.

Mason, Lauris, with Joan Ludman. *The Lithographs of George Bellows: A Catalogue Raisonné*. Millwood, N.Y.: KTO Press, 1977.

Maurice, Alfred P. "George C. Miller and Son, Lithographic Printers to Artists Since 1917," *American Art Review* 3 (March–April 1976): 133–44.

McCarron, Paul. *Martin Lewis, The Graphic Work* [exhibition catalogue]. New York: Kennedy Galleries, 1973.

McCausland, Elizabeth. "Color Lithography." *Prints* 8 (December 1937): 71–80.

———. "Lithographs to the Fore." *Prints* 6 (October 1936): 16–29.

———. "The Lithographs of Marsden Hartley," *Artist's Proof* 2, No. 1 (Spring 1962): 30–32.

McKinzie, Richard D. *The New Deal for Artists*. Princeton: Princeton University Press, 1973.

McNulty, Kneeland. *The Collected Prints of Ben Shahn*. Philadelphia: Philadelphia Museum of Art, 1967.

Mechlin, Leila. "Albert W. Barker's Lithographs," *Prints* 5 (1934): 44–52.

Meigs, John, ed. *Peter Hurd: The Lithographs*. Lubbock, Tex.: Baker Gallery Press, 1968.

Memorial Exhibition of the Works of Bolton Brown [exhibition catalogue]. Essay by George William Eggers. Woodstock, N.Y.: Woodstock Art Gallery, 1937.

Mendelowitz, Daniel A. *A History of American Art*. New York: Holt, Rinehart & Winston, 1961.

Miller, George C. "Craft of Lithography." *American Artist*, Summer 1943, pp. 21–23.

Miller, Jo. "The Prints of Arshile Gorky," *Brooklyn Museum Annual* 6 (1964–65): 57–61.

Moore, James C. *Harry Sternberg, A Catalogue Raisonné of His Graphic Work* [exhibition catalogue]. Wichita, Kan.: Ulrich Museum of Art, Wichita State University, 1975.

Morse, Peter. "Jean Charlot's Color Lithograph Technique," *Print Review* 7 (1977): 28–43.

———. "Lynton Kistler, The Happy Printer," *Art News*, March 1978, pp. 90–93.

———. *Jean Charlot's Prints: A Catalogue Raisonné*. Honolulu: University Press of Hawaii, 1976.

———. *John Sloan's Prints: A Catalogue Raisonné of the Etchings, Lithographs and Posters*. New Haven: Yale University Press, 1969.

Moser, Joann. *The Graphic Art of Emil Ganso* [exhibition catalogue]. Iowa City: University of Iowa Museum of Art, 1979.

Munson-Williams-Proctor Institute. *1913 Armory Show: 50th Anniversary Exhibition, 1963*. Utica, N.Y.: 1963.

Musick, Archie. *Musick Medley: Intimate Memories of a Rocky Mountain Art Colony*. Privately printed, Colorado Springs, 1971.

Myers, Jerome. *Artist in Manhattan*. New York: American Artists Group, 1940.

Nathan Oliveira, Print Retrospective: 1949–1980 [exhibition catalogue] Long Beach: The Art Museum and Galleries, California State University, 1980.

Netsky, Ronald. "Albert Winslow Barker: Graphite Crayons and Sea Salt," *Tamarind Papers* 6 (Winter 1982–83): 18–21.

New Deal for Art: The Government Art Projects of the 1930s with Examples from New York City & State. Organized and written by Marlene Park and Gerald E. Markowitz. Hamilton, N.Y.: Gallery Association of New York State, Inc., 1977.

Newton, Charles. *Photography in Printmaking* [exhibition catalogue]. London: Victoria and Albert Museum, 1979.

Norman, Dorothy. *Alfred Stieglitz: An American Seer*. New York: Random House, 1973.

Northrup, C. Van. "Colour Lithographs of the Works Progress Administration Federal Art Project: New York City, 1935–1942." Unpublished manuscript, 1981.

O'Connor, Francis V. *Federal Art Patronage, 1933 to 1943*. College Park: University of Maryland, 1966.

———. *Jackson Pollock*. New York: Museum of Modern Art, 1967.

———. *WPA/FAP Graphics*. Washington: Smithsonian Institution, 1976.

———, ed. *Art for the Millions: Essays from the 1930s by Artists and Administrators of the WPA Federal Art Project*. New York: New York Graphic Society, 1973.

O'Connor, Francis V. and Eugene V. Thaw. *Jackson Pollock: A Catalogue Raisonné of Paintings, Drawings, and Other Works*. 4 vols. New Haven: Yale University Press, 1978.

O'Neill, Barbara Thompson, and George C. Foreman, with Howard W. Ellington. *The Prairie Print Makers*. Topeka: Kansas Arts Commission, 1981.

One Hundred Prints by 100 Artists of the Art Students League of New York, 1875–1975. Foreword by Judith Goldman. New York: Art Students League of New York, 1975.

Orozco, José Clemente. *The Artist in New York: Letters to Jean Charlot and Unpublished Writings, 1925–1929*. Austin: University of Texas Press, 1974.

Peggy Bacon, Personalities and Places. Text by Robert K. Tarbell; checklist of prints by Janet A. Flint. Washington: Smithsonian Institution, 1975.

Pennell, Elizabeth Robins. *The Life and Letters of Joseph Pennell*. 2 vols. Boston: Little, Brown & Co., 1929.

Pennell, Joseph. *Artistic Lithography*. London: W. Clowes, 1914.

———. *Lithography*. New York: F. Keppel, 1912.

———. *The Graphic Arts, Modern Men and Modern Methods*. Chicago: University of Chicago, 1921.

Pennell, Joseph, and Pennell, E. R. "The Centenary of Lithography." *Fortnightly Review* 70 (December 1898): 968–83.

———. *Lithography and Lithographers, Some Chapters in the History of the Art*. London: T. Fisher Unwin, 1898. Rewritten, with the order of the authors' names inverted on the title page, New York: Macmillan, 1915.

Peters, Lisa. "Print Clubs in America." *Print Collector's Newsletter* 8 (1982): 88–91.

Phillips, S. Dale: "Bolton Brown: A Reminiscence." *Tamarind Papers* 2 (1979): 34–35.

Pindell, H. D. "California Prints." *Arts,* May 1972, pp. 32–33.

Pollack, Peter. "The Lithographs of Ivan Albright," *American Art Journal* 8, No. 1 (May 1976): 99–104.

Prasse, Leona E. *Lyonel Feininger, A Definitive Catalogue of his Graphic Work: Etchings, Lithographs, Woodcuts*. Cleveland: Cleveland Museum of Art, 1972.

Prescott, Kenneth W. *The Complete Graphic Works of Ben Shahn*. New York: Quadrangle Books, 1973.

Price, Frederic N. *The Etchings and Lithographs of Arthur B. Davies*. New York: Mitchell Kennerley, 1929.

The Print Club of Cleveland, 1919–1969. Cleveland: Print Club of Cleveland, 1969.

Printmaking: A New Tradition [exhibition catalogue]. Foreword by Carl Zigrosser, "Explanation" by Gustave von Groschwitz, and description of color lithography by Russell Limbach. New York: Federal Art Project, 1938.

Reese, Albert. *American Prize Prints of the Twentieth Century*. New York: American Artists Group, 1949.

———. *Walt Kuhn as Printmaker*. New York: Kennedy Galleries, 1967.

Reich, Sheldon. "Abraham Walkowitz: Pioneer of American Modernism," *American Art Journal* 3 (Spring 1971): 72–82.

Romano, Rosemarie, comp. "Bolton Brown: A Preliminary Bibliography." Mimeographed. Syracuse: Department of Fine Arts, Syracuse University, 1981.

Rose, Barbara. *American Art Since 1900: A Critical History*. New York: Praeger, 1967.

Rose, Barbara, ed. *Readings in American Art Since 1900: A Documentary Survey*. New York: Praeger, 1968.

Rubenstein, Daryl F. *Max Weber: A Catalogue Raisonné of His Graphic Work*. Chicago: University of Chicago Press, 1980.

Rueppel, Merrill C. "The Graphic Art of Arthur Bowen Davies and John Sloan." Ph.D. dissertation, University of Wisconsin, 1955. Reprint, Ann Arbor: University Microfilms International, 1978.

Saft, Carol. "The Growth of Print Workshops and Collaborative Printmaking Since 1956," *Print Review* 13 (1981): 55–68.

San Francisco Museum of Modern Art. *Lorser Feitelson and Helen Lundeberg: A Retrospective Exhibition* [exhibition catalogue]. San Francisco: 1980.

Sasowsky, Norman. *The Prints of Reginald Marsh*. New York: Clarkson N. Potter, 1976.

Seward, C. A. *Metalplate Lithography for Artists and Draftsmen*. New York: Pencil Points Press, 1931.

Shikes, Ralph. *The Indignant Eye*. Boston: Beacon Press, 1969.

Siblik, Jiri. *Twentieth Century Prints*. London: Hamlyn, 1970.

Sickler, D. "Will Barnet Makes a Lithograph," *Art News,* April 1952, p. 38.

Slaton, Amy. "Pratt Graphics Center, 1956–81," *Print Review* 13 (1981): 15–23.

Solomon, Elke M. *Louis Lozowick, Lithographs* [exhibition catalogue]. New York: Whitney Museum of American Art, 1972.

Sperling, Louise, and Richard S. Field. *Offset Lithography* [exhibition catalogue]. Middletown, Ct.: Davison Art Center, Wesleyan University, 1973.

Sprague, Marshall. *Newport in the Rockies: The Life and Good Times of Colorado Springs*. Chicago: Sage Books, 1961.

Spruance, Benton. "Place of the Printmaker." *Magazine of Art* 30 (1937): 614–18.

Stanton Macdonald-Wright: A Retrospective Exhibition 1911–1970 [exhibition catalogue]. Los Angeles: University of California, 1970.

Stuart Davis [exhibition checklist]. New York: Associated American Artists, 1976.

Stubbe, Wolf. *Graphic Arts in the 20th Century*. New York: Praeger, 1963.

Stuckey, Ronald and Joan. *The Lithographs of Stow Wengenroth*. Boston: Boston Public Library, 1974.

———. *Stow Wengenroth's Lithographs: A Supplement*. Huntington, N.Y.: Black Oak Publishers, 1982.

Sykes, Maltby. "Recollections of a Lithographile." *Tamarind Papers* 6 (1983) (forthcoming).

Tamarind: Homage to Lithography [exhibition catalogue]. Introduction by Virginia Allen. New York: Museum of Modern Art, 1969.

Tamarind: A Renaissance of Lithography [exhibition catalogue] Introduction by E. Maurice Bloch. Washington: International Exhibitions Foundation, 1971.

Tanis, Norman; Dennis Bakewell; and Don Read. *Lynton R. Kistler, Printer-Lithographer*. Northridge: California State University Libraries, 1976.

Teller, Susan Pirpris. "The Prints of Ivan Albright," *Print Review* 10 (1979): 21–35.

Tomkins, Calvin. "Profiles [Tatyana Grosman]: The Moods of a Stone," *The New Yorker,* 7 June 1976, pp. 62–76.

———. "Tatyana Grosman" [obituary], *The New Yorker,* 9 August 1982, pp. 82–86.

Tyrell, Henry. "Arthur B. Davies, a Muralist in Prints," *International Studio* 72 (1921): cxxvii–cxxx.

Von Groschwitz, Gustave. "American Colour Lithography, 1952 to 1954." *Studio* 148 (July 1954): 1–9.

———. "Making Prints for the U.S. Government." *Prints* 6 (1936): 135–42

———. "Color Lithography." *Design,* June 1950, pp. 17–18.

Watrous, James. *A Century of American Printmaking: 1880–1980*. Madison: University of Wisconsin Press, forthcoming.

Watson, Ernest W. "George Miller, Godfather to Lithography," *American Artist,* June 1943, pp. 13–15.

Way, Thomas R. *Mr. Whistler's Lithographs: The Catalogue*. 2d rev. ed. London: G. Bell and Sons, 1905.

Wayne, June. "To Restore the Art of the Lithograph in

the United States." Proposal submitted to the Ford Foundation, 1959. Tamarind archives, University of New Mexico.

Weber, Wilhelm. *A History of Lithography*. New York: McGraw-Hill, 1966.

Weddige, Emil. *Lithography*. Scranton, Pa.: International Textbook Co., 1966.

Weitenkampf, Frank. "American Lithographs of Today." *Scribners Magazine,* January 1923, pp. 123–28.

————. "American Lithography of the Present Day." *International Studio* 97 (December 1930): 39–42.

————. *American Graphic Arts.* 2d rev. ed. New York: Macmillan, 1924. Reprinted, New York: Johnson Reprint Corp., 1970.

Wengenroth, Stow. "Lithography as a Fine Art." *Print* 4 (1946): 33–45.

————. "Lithography vs. Lithography, Confusion in the Public Mind between Artistic and Commercial Lithography." *Print Collector's Quarterly* 24 (1937): 80–91.

Wengenroth, Stow, and Lynd Ward. "George C. Miller, Master-printer: Tribute to a Lithographic Craftsman," *American Artist,* May 1966, pp. 12–13.

Whitmore, Elizabeth. "Albert W. Barker, Poet and Lithographer," *Print Collector's Quarterly* 27 (1940): 275–99.

Wilmerding, John. *American Art.* Pelican History of Art. New York: Penguin, 1974.

Worthen, Amy. *Benton, Curry, Wood, Selected Lithographs* [exhibition catalogue]. Des Moines: Iowa Arts Council, 1978.

Wuerth, Louis A. *Catalogue of the Lithographs of Joseph Pennell.* Introduction by Elizabeth Robins Pennell. Boston: Little Brown & Co., 1931.

Zabel, Barbara. "Louis Lozowick and Urban Optimism of the 1920s," *Journal of the Archives of American Art* 14, No. 2 (1974): 17–21.

Zigrosser, Carl. *The Artist in America: Twenty-four Close-ups of Contemporary Printmakers.* New York: Alfred A. Knopf, 1942. Reprinted, New York: Hacker Art Books, 1978.

————. *Benton Spruance, Lithographs, 1932–67* [exhibition catalogue]. Philadelphia: Philadelphia College of Art, 1967.

————. *Between the Wars: Prints by American Artists, 1914–41.* New York: Whitney Museum of American Art, 1942.

————. "The Lithographs of Vincent Canadé," *Artist's Proof* 5 (1963): 32–33.

————. "Mabel Dwight," *American Artist,* June 1949, pp. 42–45.

————. *Prints and Their Creators: A World History.* 2d rev. ed. New York: Crown Publishers, 1974.

————. *A World of Art and Museums.* Philadelphia: The Art Alliance Press, 1975.

————, ed. *Prints: Thirteen Illustrated Essays on the Art of the Print.* New York: Holt, Rinehart and Winston, 1962.

Zimmermann, Agnes. *An Essay Towards a Catalogue Raisonné of the Etchings, Dry-Points, and Lithographs of Julian Alden Weir.* New York: Metropolitan Museum of Art (Papers, vol. 1, part 2), 1923.

Index to Monographs

Following is an index to books, museum catalogues, and articles on individual artists or printers. Not included are titles written by the artist or printer, or titles in which an author is not identified; as examples, a book written by Thomas Hart Benton will be found in the bibliography under *Benton, Thomas Hart;* a exhibition catalogue not identified by author will be found under *Thomas Hart Benton.*

Index

All references are to page numbers; those in italics refer to illustrations.